THE BEDFORD SERIES IN HISTORY AND CULTURE

The Enlightenment

A Brief History with Documents

Related Titles in
THE BEDFORD SERIES IN HISTORY AND CULTURE
Advisory Editors: Natalie Zemon Davis, *Princeton University*
Ernest R. May, *Harvard University*
Lynn Hunt, *University of California
at Los Angeles*
David W. Blight, *Amherst College*

Louis XIV and Absolutism: A Brief Study with Documents
William Beik, *Emory University*

CANDIDE *by Voltaire*
Edited with an Introduction by Daniel Gordon, *University of Massachusetts at Amherst*

The Enlightenment Debate on Equality: Wollstonecraft versus Rousseau
Edited with an Introduction by Olwen Hufton, *The European Institute*
(forthcoming)

The French Revolution and Human Rights: A Brief Documentary History
Lynn Hunt, *University of California at Los Angeles*

THE BEDFORD SERIES IN HISTORY AND CULTURE

The Enlightenment
A Brief History with Documents

Margaret C. Jacob

University of California at Los Angeles

BEDFORD/ST. MARTIN'S   Boston ◆ New York

In memory of John Cunningham

For Bedford/St. Martin's

Executive Editor for History: Katherine E. Kurzman
Developmental Editor: Louise Townsend
Editorial Assistant: Jamie Farrell
Senior Production Supervisor: Dennis J. Conroy
Project Management: Books By Design, Inc.
Text Design: Claire Seng-Niemoeller
Indexer: Books By Design, Inc.
Cover Design: Richard Emery
Cover Photo: Pietro Longhi (1702–1785). *The Geography Lesson.* Galleria Querini
   Stampalia, Venice, Italy. Cameraphoto/Art Resource, NY.
Composition: Stratford Publishing Services
Printing and Binding: Haddon Craftsmen, an R. R. Donnelley & Sons Company

President: Charles H. Christensen
Editorial Director: Joan E. Feinberg
Director of Marketing: Karen R. Melton
Director of Editing, Design, and Production: Marcia Cohen
Manager, Publishing Services: Emily Berleth

Library of Congress Control Number: 00-104757

For information, write: Bedford/St. Martin's, 75 Arlington Street, Boston, MA 02116
(617-399-4000)

ISBN: 0-312-17997-9 (paperback)
      0-312-23701-4 (hardcover)

Foreword

The Bedford Series in History and Culture is designed so that readers can study the past as historians do.

The historian's first task is finding the evidence. Documents, letters, memoirs, interviews, pictures, movies, novels, or poems can provide facts and clues. Then the historian questions and compares the sources. There is more to do than in a courtroom, for hearsay evidence is welcome, and the historian is usually looking for answers beyond act and motive. Different views of an event may be as important as a single verdict. How a story is told may yield as much information as what it says.

Along the way the historian seeks help from other historians and perhaps from specialists in other disciplines. Finally, it is time to write, to decide on an interpretation and how to arrange the evidence for readers.

Each book in this series contains an important historical document or group of documents, each document a witness from the past and open to interpretation in different ways. The documents are combined with some element of historical narrative—an introduction or a biographical essay, for example—that provides students with an analysis of the primary source material and important background information about the world in which it was produced.

Each book in the series focuses on a specific topic within a specific historical period. Each provides a basis for lively thought and discussion about several aspects of the topic and the historian's role. Each is short enough (and inexpensive enough) to be a reasonable one-week assignment in a college course. Whether as classroom or personal reading, each book in the series provides firsthand experience of the challenge—and fun—of discovering, re-creating, and interpreting the past.

Natalie Zemon Davis
Ernest R. May
Lynn Hunt
David W. Blight

Preface

Every generation and every century needs to rediscover the Enlightenment. Students have often heard the term used in reference to the eighteenth century, but they may not realize what it meant at that time. Saying that someone is "enlightened" today often means that the person is open-minded, fair, or without prejudice, accepting of people of all ethnicities, colors, and sexual orientations. But few students realize that this positive connotation is a result of the battles waged by a group of eighteenth-century writers, publicists, political reformers, and sometimes just angry young men and women. They saw prejudice and superstition everywhere around them, and armed with their own biases, particularly against the clergy, they entered into a war of words with the upholders of tradition, authority, and the status quo. The stakes were high. Challenging clerical authority could land a person in jail in many parts of Europe and America. Students may be even further confused by the frequently negative connotation put on the Enlightenment by the postmodernists who reacted against it late in the twentieth century.

Many new and radical ideas were published roughly between 1690 and 1790. The challenge for today's readers is to see how radical and innovative those ideas were at the time. This book seeks to place the audacious words of the enlightened in the context of the eighteenth century and then to provide a sampling of the range of opinions found in such circles. We start with John Locke because he was part of the first stirring of enlightened thought and a major contributor to its success. Locke the educator said remarkable things: for instance, it is a good idea *not* to beat children in the course of trying to teach them. Realizing that what he said in the 1690s was innovative requires that we think historically, back to a time when the hand of authority could be heavy and personally felt.

The Enlightenment began with Locke and the scientist Isaac Newton—both somber, religiously devout, and responsible critics—but within a decade, more outrageous critics appeared. This book presents perhaps the most extreme set of words written in the eighteenth century: a portion of *Treatise of the Three Impostors*. It was an anonymous work, produced in the Netherlands by a group of journalists, and it boldly proclaimed Jesus, Moses, and Muhammad to be the three great impostors. Saying such things attracted a lot of attention and necessitated secrecy and anonymity. By 1710, the apostles of the Enlightenment had gravitated toward the outrageous, and anything became possible. By 1760, people even began to argue for a political system similar to what we call democracy. All this was happening in an age dominated by kings, aristocrats, and churches established by law.

In this book, you'll meet other great philosophers such as Voltaire, Denis Diderot, and Jean-Jacques Rousseau, who made Paris the capital of the Enlightenment by 1750. The German branch of the Enlightenment is represented by Immanuel Kant and the great Jewish philosopher Moses Mendelssohn. Lady Mary Wortley Montagu stands here for the dozens of women writers who were not as well known. Many of these women used their talents as novelists or playwrights, or they simply read voraciously and educated their children to be fair-minded, well disposed toward science, and eager for learning.

Given the limitations of space, this book is merely a map to the high points, but there is no substitute for walking the terrain yourself. Treat it like a travel guide to primary sources; then search out more sources in the library or on the Internet. Dare to know, as Kant said, because in encountering those who made it possible for people to be "enlightened," we are reminded that the values of tolerance, fair-mindedness, and worldliness came at a cost. People like Locke, Rousseau, Lady Montagu, and even the iconoclastic authors of *Treatise of the Three Impostors* led the fight to make these values accepted, even commonplace, norms that have been incorporated into codes of conduct in many parts of the world. The goal of being enlightened now challenges people in every cultural setting. The Enlightenment created the modern environment wherein open-minded people are asked to shape their own identity and destiny distinct from whatever religious or ethnic affiliation they may possess. The West may have started the Enlightenment, but all the peoples of the world are now challenged to complete it.

ACKNOWLEDGMENTS

An early draft of this book was done at the Center for Advanced Study in the Behavioral Sciences at Palo Alto, California, truly one of the great places in this country to write and think. I am immensely grateful to its staff. The project was then delayed for happy reasons—a move to the University of California at Los Angeles (UCLA) and its splendid resources for the study of the eighteenth century. I am grateful to the kindness shown by UCLA's history department and the staffs of the Young Research Library at UCLA (with its superb Marteau collection), the Clark Library at UCLA, and the Huntington Library in Los Angeles. As always, Lynn Hunt read and exhorted, earning my lasting gratitude. Thanks to my research assistant, Rachel Jagoda, for her help. Gary Kates, John Marshall, and Joanne Schneider offered helpful comments. I am also grateful for the encouragement of Natalie Zemon Davis and Katherine E. Kurzman. Louise Townsend became an inspirational editor. Thanks are also due to Jamie Farrell for her hard work on text and art permissions. In the confusion of the move, my dog Reilly, then a pup, ate the corners of one volume of *Cérémonies et coutumes religieuses de tous les peuples du monde* (Amsterdam, 1723). I am sure he meant no disrespect to either the Enlightenment or the religious ceremonies of all the peoples of the world.

This book is dedicated to my late cousin John Cunningham, who died in 1996 as the result of a fall in the water tunnel then under construction in New York City. The company in charge had failed to provide the required safety tether. John was born in Northern Ireland, where he learned the meaning of religious fanaticism. An avid reader, he grew to think for himself, to become a tolerant and enlightened man. He would have loved reading the documents presented here. They helped make people like him possible.

Margaret C. Jacob

Contents

PART TWO

The Documents 73

Illustrations

THE BEDFORD SERIES IN HISTORY AND CULTURE

The Enlightenment

A Brief History with Documents

PART ONE

Introduction:
The Struggle to Create
a New Culture

In the eighteenth century, a daring and dramatically new intellectual and cultural movement arose in western Europe. Of its many characteristics—audacity, wit, an interest in the practical and the applied—none was more important than its critical, biting edge. This opinionated movement called for "enlightenment"—for new thinking about once unquestioned truths and eventually for new actions. Best characterized by the metaphor of light, the Enlightenment has retained the name it acquired early in the eighteenth century. In various European languages around 1700, the fashion arose of praising some people for being "enlightened": in French, *éclairé;* in German, *aufgeklärt;* in Dutch, *verlichte*. As praise, it meant that the person was no timid follower of the clergy or believer in magic. Rather, enlightened people read books and journals and frequented the coffeehouses, salons, Masonic lodges, and reading clubs that sprang up all over Europe and in the European colonies. Sometimes they did not even go to church or believe in God. Worldliness demanded literacy and some affluence. The well-off had the leisure time required to be inquisitive about new ideas, to go to scientific demonstrations or lectures, to travel, or just to invest in books about people in other parts of the world. In the Western world, the mental universe of the literate and reasonably well educated expanded as never before. The expansion both made the Enlightenment possible and was promoted by it.

1

No single source or person invented the metaphor of light and applied it to the new cultural style of open-mindedness, investigation, and satire. If pressed, those who praised enlightenment would probably have traced the metaphor to Newtonian science. In his *Principia* (1687) and *Opticks* (1704), the English scientist Isaac Newton described an infinite universe, a vast continuum governed by mathematically expressed laws, a sublime space without end. In addition, by putting white light through a prism, Newton revealed its multicolored nature and the mathematical precision that characterized the angle of each of its bent rays. Poets seized on the metaphor of light. Nature and its brilliant explicator became the stuff of rapture. The Scottish poet James Thomson wrote about Newton and spring light in *The Seasons* (1726–30), one of the most popular poems of the mid-century:

> Here, awful NEWTON, the dissolving Clouds
> Form, fronting on the Sun, thy showery Prism;
> And to the sage-instructed Eye unfold
> The various Twine of Light, by thee disclos'd
> From the white mingling Maze.
>
> "SPRING," LL. 208–12

To paraphrase Thomson, Newton's optical experiments with the prism revealed a "maze" of white light composed of separate beams, or "twines," of atomic particles, which split apart into a mathematically precise spectrum of discrete colors. Painters sought to capture these twines of light, while Newton was proclaimed as the very model of a pathbreaking, enlightened thinker.

Most people never saw the effects of ordinary light cast through a prism, but they had become aware of new optical effects nonetheless. Nearly a century of work in glass cutting had produced significant improvements in mass-produced eyeglasses, telescopes, and microscopes. In the seventeenth century, Europeans literally saw sights never before seen, from the rings of Saturn to the valves in the human lymphatic system. By the beginning of the eighteenth century, simple microscopes were being sold door-to-door in the Dutch republic, and the publication of microscopic discoveries had become a subject of public discussion.[1] The light that filled the universe could be channeled,

---

[1] Edward G. Ruestow, *The Microscope in the Dutch Republic* (New York: Cambridge University Press, 1996), 10, 46.

dissected, magnified, and measured by human ingenuity. The question arose, Could the light not also be trained inward to banish the darkness from human minds long trapped by conventions, superstitions, and prejudices? With that question began the struggle to dare to know, to invent an alternative to the pieties about churches and kings to which most people still subscribed.

Early in the eighteenth century definitions of the Enlightenment began to appear in daily newspapers and scholarly journals, but the most famous ones came later. Many decades after James Thomson wrote, the great philosopher Immanuel Kant, one of the leading German intellectuals of the 1780s, responded to the challenge of defining the Enlightenment. His definition, reprinted here as Document 8, is about "daring to know," about the effort to illuminate the dark corners of the human mind. The ever-cautious Kant said that the process of enlightenment should occur in the privacy of one's home. It should pose no threat to existing institutions, neither to kings nor to clergy.

Before Kant, bolder instigators of enlightened thought had thrown caution to the wind. The leaders of the Enlightenment from London to Berlin—dubbed *philosophes* (the French word for "philosophers")—had battled for three generations with the traditional clergy, both Protestant and Catholic. By the 1780s, they and their enlightened followers had moved beyond the battle of words and turned their attention to concrete social and governmental reform. Inspiration came from the American Revolution, which began in 1776. In its wake, people started to question all forms of authority, and the political barrier that Kant had said should not be breeched was mounted. What had begun in the 1680s as a movement against religious intolerance and arbitrary rule had become by the 1780s an agenda for reform, threatening courts, princes, and lay and clerical oligarchies.

The movement toward the light contributed in complex ways to the late-eighteenth-century revolutions. The American patriots Thomas Jefferson, Benjamin Franklin, and John Adams also should be seen as philosophes. Their ideas led to independence from Britain and the creation of the American republic. More fundamental changes would be necessary in Europe. In Amsterdam in 1787, Brussels in 1788, and Paris in the summer of 1789, the very structure of society and government was attacked, and violence erupted. Leading eventually to the French occupation of the Low Countries and the Napoleonic wars, the French Revolution altered the political landscape of the West forever. The Enlightenment was one factor in the birth of modern democratic and representative politics.

POLITICAL ORIGINS

The political roots of the European Enlightenment grew out of a profound revulsion against new political abuses that arose in the 1680s on both sides of the English Channel. Two nearly simultaneous events precipitated the crisis: In 1685, the English Catholic James II came to the throne, and in France Louis XIV revoked the limited toleration that French Protestants, known as Huguenots, had enjoyed for nearly a hundred years. The "Sun King" tore up the Edict of Nantes, which since the 1590s had brought a degree of religious tranquillity to the French kingdom. Suddenly, thousands of French Protestants were faced with a devastating set of choices: convert against their will to Catholicism (or pretend to do so), go to prison, or flee the country. The new laws against Protestants even urged children to report on the religion of their parents. A few chose to convert; many were sent to prison. Well over 200,000 Huguenots sought exile in Geneva, Berlin, the Dutch republic, and England. Some migrated to the American colonies.

Wherever the refugees went, the educated among them gravitated to presses and engravers' studios. In the 1690s, they began an unprecedented propaganda battle against French absolutism (see Figure 1). Louis XIV became a tyrant; his Catholic clergy were portrayed as persecutors, and the exiles were heralded as martyrs for the cause of religious toleration. After the 1680s, English Protestants, unhappy with their own Catholic king, made a political alliance with French Huguenot refugees to defeat absolutism, which they associated with Catholicism. This international alliance of Protestants remained a political force into the 1720s. The ensuing decades of crisis revealed the need for a radical break with the traditions that justified absolute monarchies and established churches. A consensus emerged in enlightened circles: The generally Catholic clergy had, for far too long, enjoyed the power to incite their monarchs to persecute at will. Soon all clerical privileges were scorned.

The crisis of the 1680s—the threat of a return to Catholicism and absolutism in England and the worsening of civil liberties in France—led to the appearance of opposition movements in both countries. But opposition in France had to be largely covert; the state had too many spies and too much power. By contrast, the English had established a revolutionary tradition that would prove decisive, leading in 1688–89 to another revolution, which exiled James II and defeated absolutism as a system of government. James had tried to rewrite the charters of local government to exclude his opponents, and he had brought

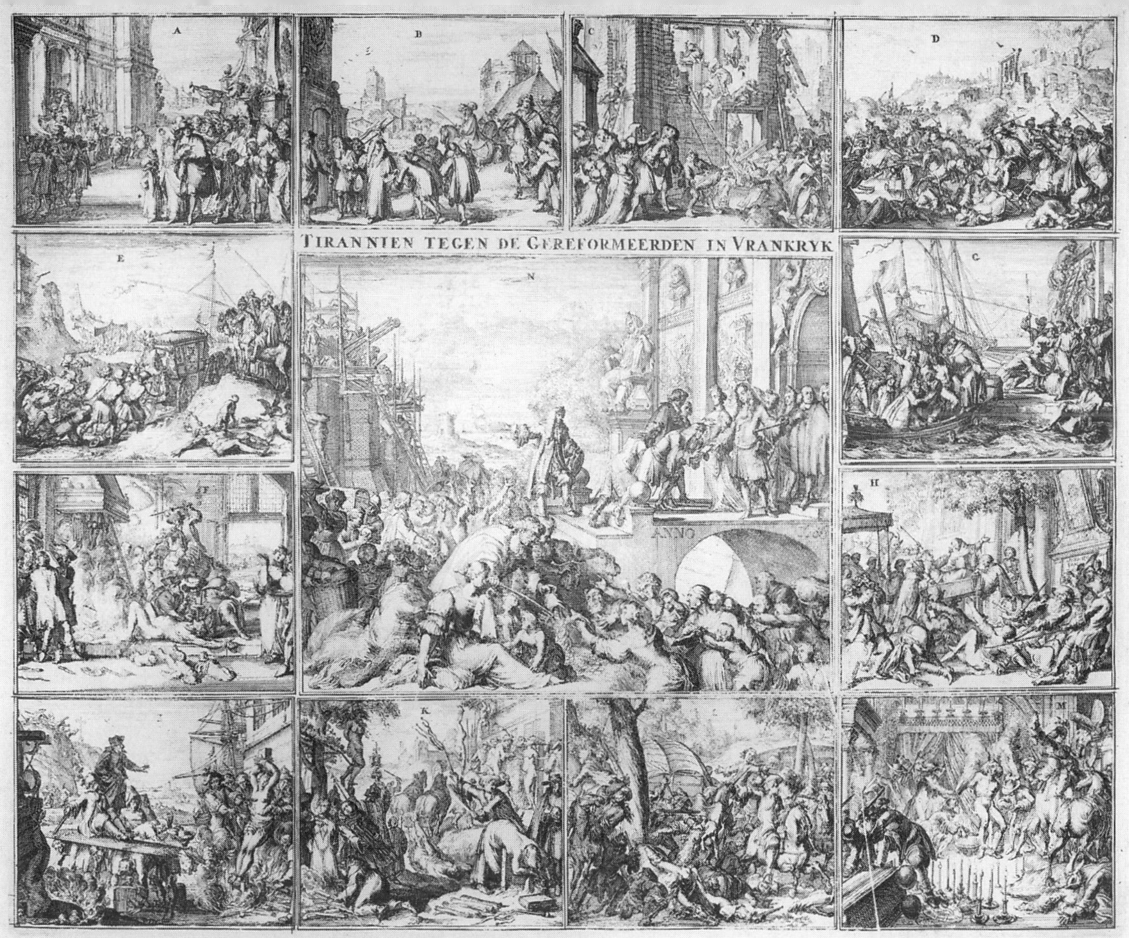

TIRANNIEN TEGEN DE GEREFORMEERDEN IN VRANKRYK

**Figure 1.
Tyranny
against French
Protestants**

Anti–Louis XIV
propaganda
originating in the
Dutch republic
shows Protestants
being murdered
(B, D), their
houses being torn
down (C), being
drawn and quar-
tered (E), forced
into exile (G),
burned alive (F, I),
raped (H), and
tortured (M). In
the central frame
their children are
being executed
before their eyes.
In that frame
Louis XIV stands
looking down
with approval.
The year is 1685
when he revoked
the Edict of
Nantes.

The Rijksmuseum,
Amsterdam

5

Catholics into high offices in the universities and the army. The Revolution of 1688–89, sometimes called the Glorious Revolution, united the Dutch and the English in a struggle to contain French absolutism (see Figure 4 on page 14). Urged on by liberal Protestant clerics and lords, a Dutch army forced James II out of England (see Figure 2). The revolution was led by William III, James's son-in-law and the head of the Dutch nation, and William's wife, Mary, James's estranged daughter. In the spring of 1689, they became king and queen of England by an act of Parliament.

The settlement of 1689 ended absolutism in England; ensured trial by jury, habeas corpus,* and toleration for all Trinitarian Protestants (those who believe in God the Father, the Son, and the Holy Ghost); and guaranteed the independence of Parliament. The revolution had enormous repercussions for civil liberties in Britain and established principles that inspired the American Revolution, among others. It also initiated a new era of cultural and intellectual ferment. During the 1690s, England and the Dutch republic, both at war with France, provided the settings for a new militance among reformers and the discontented. A new English political party, the Whigs, laid claim to the revolution as their singular achievement. Well into the eighteenth century, however, supporters of both king and church offered annual Sunday services in memory of the old-style monarchy.[2]

These pious supporters believed that much of what had happened politically in the seventeenth century had been disastrous for the Church of England. They traced the decay of religion to the 1650s and the Puritan Oliver Cromwell (see Figure 3). He and his followers had executed King Charles I in 1649 after two bloody civil wars during the 1640s. In the 1650s, England had become a republic, and the Anglican Church had been disestablished. But in 1660, monarchy and church were restored, and non-Anglican ministers were jailed. After the Revolution of 1688–89, the Church of England tried to stem the tide that had washed over it as the result of two seventeenth-century revolutions. In general, the eighteenth century would be a challenging time for all the institutions intended to uphold religious orthodoxy.

---

*Habeas corpus refers to a legal order or document requiring authorities to bring an imprisoned person before a judge or court and to show the cause of the imprisonment. It was and is especially important in cases where there is a strong possibility that the prisoner is being unlawfully detained.

[2]One such set of services, possibly recorded by a youthful parishioner, can be seen in Green Library, Stanford University. Special Collections, Misc. MS 450, on "Charles the Martyr." According to this source, King Charles I of England was executed by "cruel and bloody men."

Figure 2. Cruelty of James II to Irish Protestants

During the Revolution of 1688–89, propaganda originating in the Dutch republic depicted James II as hanging Protestants in Ireland. In fact, persecution of both Irish Catholics (by followers of William III) and Protestants was closer to the truth, but the Protestant press was far more effective at letting the world know about the injustices.

The Rijksmuseum, Amsterdam

Every revolution, real or longed for, needs theorists. One of England's most important was John Locke (1632–1704), a doctor schooled in the liberal Protestantism of the seventeenth century. As a young man, he witnessed the upheavals in England during the 1640s and 1650s, and he grew to distrust the ambitions of kings and courts — and the conservative clergy who supported them. As a believer in the rights of the propertied and the educated, he insisted that the individual must become a "rational creature." His essentially Christian understanding of human beings saw virtue and rationality as inseparably linked. Although depravity lurks in the human heart, he said, virtue can be learned and practiced, taught by parents and tutors who must be neither too familiar nor too harsh. Locke became one of the foremost educators of his time, and *Some Thoughts concerning Education* (see Document 1) bears witness to his intellectual vitality.

Figure 3. Order and Disorder in Church and State Depicted

This Church of England propaganda was aimed at political and religious radicals. It argues for linkages among Cromwell and the English Revolution, irreligion, and rebellion. It imagines a straight line from the revolution to the profanity associated with the Enlightenment. Only the established Church with Christ at its head will save England.

The Pierpont Morgan Library, New York. Peel Collection, vol. 1, p. 27, #37, 38.

Although Locke wrote for a landed and mercantile elite, readers of all social classes took his message about guiding but not bullying children to heart. His views on education would validate the search for enlightenment.

Locke's understanding of the authority of parents over children related directly to his understanding of citizenship. His experience as an educator reinforced his belief that kings could not rule arbitrarily over citizens. The presence of rationality and the possibility of education laid the foundation for Locke's theoretical dismissal of absolute monarchy. Human beings possess free will, and they should be prepared for freedom—for obedience out of conviction, not as a result of fear. It is important to remember that Locke was writing for the elite politicians—men, many of them Whigs, who possessed the property qualifications to vote or hold office and who passed those inherited privileges on to their sons. Such men could afford the kind of high-quality private schooling that Locke advocated as appropriate preparation for citizenship. He also possessed a deeply political agenda.

With Locke as a member of their inner circle, the Whigs of the 1680s had a mission: to stop the advance of monarchical absolutism in England, to prevent their country's return to the Catholic Church, and to offer theories about the nature of government that would justify their stance of dogged opposition. At first they failed, and the Whig leaders were forced to flee abroad. Locke and his friends took up exile in the Dutch republic. There they maintained close ties with the enemies of James II, both in England and in the American colony of New York.[3] The exile did not last long, but it did set up international ties across the Atlantic Ocean and the English Channel—a grid of connections that would nurture the early Enlightenment.

The Revolution of 1688–89 brought the Whigs, among them Locke, home in triumph. In a famous publication of 1690, *Two Treatises of Government,* Locke came to be seen as the champion of government by Parliament. As he saw it, contractual governments with strong legislators should represent the propertied class, and their parliamentary seats are the result of elections. Legislators owe their power to a contract with the people. Contestation lay at the heart of the process of governance. Neither kings nor wealth are divinely ordained.

Locke believed deeply in God and the natural rights endowed by divine will. In no sense should he be imagined as antireligious. But he also thought the doctrine of the divine right of kings to be nonsense. Throughout the eighteenth century, his *Two Treatises* was avidly read in the American colonies and France. As the late-eighteenth-century revolutions in America, the Low Countries, and France demonstrate, Locke's ideas about the superiority of representative government, along with those of other important theorists such as Jean-Jacques

---

[3] See MS ONA/1397 from the Rotterdam Gemeentearchief, kindly supplied by David William Voorhees, head of the Jacob Leisler Project at New York University.

Rousseau (see Document 7), had unhappy consequences for monarchs and oligarchs alike. The international influence of Locke's writings on education and government knits the Enlightenment to the late-eighteenth-century revolutions.

Having been seen to legitimate revolution, *Two Treatises* (only the second one appeared in French) spoke to generations of reformers. In 1788–89, at the hundredth anniversary of the revolution that brought William and Mary to the throne, a new generation of British reformers, inspired by the revolutionary events in Paris, hailed Locke as having popularized the principles of liberty of conscience and the right of resistance.[4] Yet even in 1788, people did not realize how subversive Locke had been. Only in the twentieth century did we learn that Locke had actually written his first draft of *Two Treatises* back in the 1680s, *before* the Glorious Revolution and at the moment when the Whigs were conspiring to undo the Stuart monarchs. *Two Treatises* did not simply legitimate; it advocated, if need arose, a magistrate-led revolution. Before such a revolution, Locke wanted to lay the philosophical foundations for a nonabsolutist, representative system of government. His ideas about education were intended to prepare gentlemen to become magistrates, to govern wisely and firmly. Locke the educator and Locke the political theorist resided comfortably within the same insightful mind.

In 1701, two French Protestant refugees translated the second treatise into French and in the process made it sound more republican than Locke had intended. He seemed to favor the republic as the best form of government. Numerous editions of the French translation circulated in Europe right up to 1789 and the outbreak of the French Revolution. Influenced by such writing and other enlightened writings, France became a republic. Together with his works on the nature of how human beings know (primarily through their senses and not as the result of a set of innate ideas), Locke's works on government, education, and epistemology (the study of cognition) became bibles in the movement toward light.[5]

---

[4]Dale Hoak and Mordechai Feingold, eds., *The World of William and Mary: Anglo-Dutch Perspectives on the Revolution of 1688–89* (Stanford, Calif.: Stanford University Press, 1996), 54; from the essay by Lois G. Schwoerer, "The Bill of Rights, 1689, Revisited."

[5]See the extremely useful essay by Katharine M. Morsberger, "John Locke's *An Essay concerning Human Understanding:* The 'Bible' of the Enlightenment," in *Studies in Eighteenth-Century Culture,* ed. Syndy M. Conger and Julie C. Hayes (East Lansing, Mich.: Colleagues Press, 1996), 25:1–19.

In England, the Whigs appeared to be the new secularists of their age. Not surprisingly, freethinkers—those who veered off into deism, anticlericalism, or even atheism—were readily found on the radical fringe of the party. Bishops loyal to the Whigs complained bitterly that "Whigs have behaved, and still do behave, . . . [with] such an open dislike of the church Establishment . . . [that] I and other bishops labored for many years to bring the body of the clergy to a liking of a Whig administration."[6] The more conservative, or Tory, clergy kept up an assault against the lay and clerical Whigs. They even said that the Whig-inclined clergy were republicans in disguise, men who would do away with kings and rule through local and national representative bodies.[7] With the English clergy quarreling among themselves, their deistic opponents could take center stage.

In the period after the Revolution of 1688–89, the Dutch republic vied with England as the center of the new liberalism and toleration. The French Protestant refugees were important, but so too were native Dutch intellectuals. Biweekly Dutch journals even told readers about English books that the authorities were trying to suppress. When the Parliament in Dublin sought to censure freethinker John Toland's *Christianity not Mysterious* (1696), the Dutch-language *Mercury* in The Hague argued that the book just tried to make people understand mysteries better, but "each sect likes to hold the opinion of its own infallibility." That was hardly a ringing endorsement for orthodoxy.[8]

In the 1690s, Protestants everywhere in northern Europe had more to worry about than the skepticism and anticlericalism expressed in Dutch and English periodicals. They watched France fight against England, Austria, and the Dutch republic to extend its borders in Europe and its territories in the Americas. Louis XIV used guns and diplomacy to further his influence in Spain, Poland, and the Low Countries. The intellectuals among his detractors could fight back only with sarcasm, wit, obscenity, and much hand-wringing. The military action fell to soldiers who fought against France in Ireland and the Low Countries. By 1697, Louis XIV had been contained, only to rise again in 1701 when he sought to bring the Spanish monarchy

---

[6]MS 11, Gibson Collection, Huntington Library, Los Angeles; 1730s.

[7]Jeffrey S. Chamberlain, *Accommodating High Churchmen: The Clergy of Sussex, 1700–1745* (Urbana: University of Illinois Press, 1997), 44–47.

[8]*Haegse Mercur,* 23 Oct. 1697, in Hendrik Doedijns, *De Haegse Mercurius 7 agugustus* [sic] *1697–1 februari 1698,* ed. Rietje van Vliet (Leiden: Astraea, 1996), 175.

under French control. The ensuing War of Spanish Succession (1701–13; see Figure 4) put the Low Countries once more on the defensive and churned up the religious and sectarian passions first released by the revocation of the Edict of Nantes in 1685.

Here is how two Protestant friends living amid the refugees, deists, and pantheists described the new atmosphere of the 1690s in England and the Dutch republic. Writing in 1706, Anthony Ashley Cooper, the third earl of Shaftesbury and a young pupil of John Locke, said to a journalist friend in the Dutch republic that "a new light spreads itself from our respective countries." The metaphor allowed him to suggest that despite war, a new tolerance was dawning. With it came a growing opposition to tyranny, and both Shaftesbury and Jean Le Clerc, to whom he wrote, were ardent supporters of the war against Louis XIV. Le Clerc, a Protestant pastor with a large refugee congregation in Rotterdam, edited in French a popular journal that disseminated science and politics to a wide international audience. Yet there was also some apprehension in Shaftesbury's letter, as he wrote that "liberty of Thought and Writing" could be threatened by "blasphemous enthusiasts and real fanatics."[9] By "enthusiasts" he meant religious fundamentalists who showed no respect for legitimate authority, and "fanatics" were those who sided with the persecutors.

Despite the presence of religious extremists, both Shaftesbury and Le Clerc were optimistic. They believed that the future lay with the lovers of liberty and letters, not with kings who persecuted their subjects because of their religion.[10] These early intellectuals at the heart of the Enlightenment were willing to take risks and to accept the discord that came with relative freedom of the press, religious toleration, and political liberty. They believed that the alternative—repression and prejudice—had to be avoided at all costs. By 1710, their optimism paid off, and Louis XIV was near defeat, his treasury empty as famine stalked the French countryside.[11]

The international group of Protestant journalists, theorists, scientists, liberal clerics, publishers, and booksellers created the context wherein the new, enlightened ideas flourished: representative government, the

---

[9]Shaftesbury to Le Clerc, March 1705/06, *Anthony Ashley Cooper Earl of Shaftesbury (1671–1713) and "le refuge français": Correspondence,* ed. Rex A. Barrell, vol. 15 of *Studies in British History* (Lewiston, N.Y.: Edwin Mellen Press, 1989), 92.

[10]Shaftesbury to Le Clerc, 1709, *Correspondence,* 95.

[11]Daniel Roche, *France in the Enlightenment,* trans. Arthur Goldhammer (Cambridge: Harvard University Press, 1998), 80.

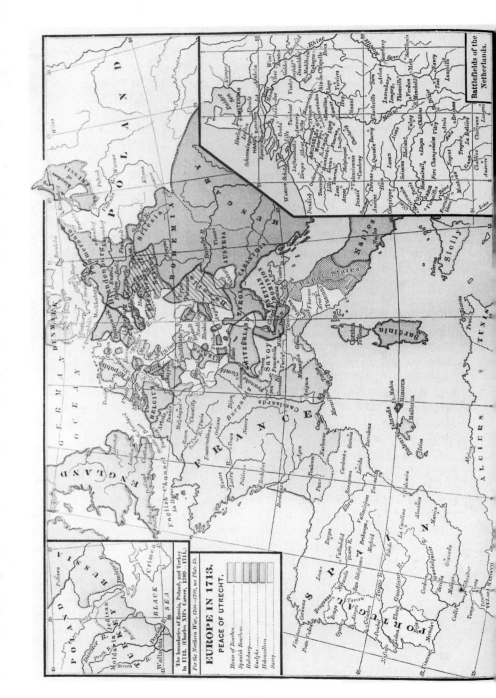

Battlefields of the Netherlands.

EUROPE IN 1713.
PEACE OF UTRECHT.

House of Bourbon..........
Spanish Bourbon..........
Habsburg..........
Guelphs..........
Hohenzollern..........
Savoy..........

The boundaries of Russia, Poland, and Turkey in 1713. (Charles XII's Career, 1709–1711.

For the Northern War, 1700–1709, see Plate 15.

need to abolish the privileges of the clergy, and a more accepting approach toward human nature, virtue and vice, sexuality and gender. Vital to the Enlightenment's momentum, French-language presses thrived in the Dutch republic; the French censors were powerless there. Equally important, the exiles and their allies had new heroes. One was the Dutch leader, William of Orange. Made king of England by Parliament, he went to war against Louis XIV not to save the French Protestants, but to save the Low Countries from French occupation and to secure his new English throne against the attempt by James II (with backing from Louis XIV) to win back his kingdom by invading Ireland (see Figure 2). The Protestant presses lionized William,[12] but other heroes were needed as well. The *Journal Litteraire* in The Hague, largely the work of Huguenot refugees, turned to Isaac Newton. Indeed, the first continental exposure to Newtonian science occurred through periodicals published by refugees or their sympathizers.[13]

SCIENTIFIC AND RELIGIOUS ORIGINS

In the midst of an international political crisis that Protestants defined as a struggle against arbitrary authority, science presented new standards for arriving at the truth. Newton's science relied on experiment, trial and error, and the belief that mathematical regularity and laws ruled the universe. Science stood for philosophical elegance—the elimination of any abstract notion for which no physical reality seemed to exist. In the 1630s, the French natural philosopher René Descartes argued that the planets were carried about in their orbits by swirling vortices—a fine aether that permitted constant pressure to effect motion and order. A generation later, Newton could find no mathematical basis for the

---

[12]For examples, see V.S. 353 413 #359; V.S. 369, Prentenkabinet, Rijksmuseum, Amsterdam, where William of Orange is presented in the style of Louis XIV; Barent Beeck with Jan Luyken as engraver, *De Koningklycke Triumphe: Vertoonende allen de eerpoorten . . . Willem de III* (The Hague, 1691); N. Chevalier, *Histoire de Guillaume III* (Amsterdam, 1692).

[13]See John Christian Laursen, ed., *New Essays on the Political Thought of the Huguenots of the "Refuge"* (New York: Brill, 1995).

Figure 4. Map of Europe during the War of Spanish Succession
Louis XIV's aggression sent the whole of Europe into a war that especially threatened the Low Countries. It provoked a crisis that fed revulsion against imperial aggression and religious persecution.
The William Andrews Clark Memorial Library–UCLA.

aether, and he dismissed this theory as "hypothesis." Newton's system became synonymous with the empirical and the practical, and with a refusal to fashion inelegant philosophical systems that never offered experimental proof. He was seen as the detractor of airy systems, the slayer of the arbitrary and the fanciful. Most important, he discovered that the movements of the planets could be expressed as a universal mathematical formula.

Science allowed alternatives to be imagined in everything from politics to religion. Lawlike behavior in the heavens suggested that human inventions such as governments also could be run by laws and procedures. The moment was propitious. As a result of the Revolution of 1688–89, laws were radically altered in the human realm. Locke offered a new set of principles for the construction of a human, not a divinely ordained, government. Scientists like his friend Newton proved by mathematical calculation that the universe is governed by laws knowable through human inquiry. Their followers reasoned that if humans could discover the law of universal gravitation, surely they could govern themselves by the light of reason and by constitutional government, in effect by a Newtonian system of government.

Although neither Locke nor Newton believed in the Trinity, each man was, in his own way, a devout Christian. By contrast, other intrepid, cantankerous spirits took up the new science and argued in favor of a "rational" religion, one that was free from the mysteries and miracles originally contained in the Bible to bring simple people into the Christian fold. The clergy, these people argued, should explicate with awe the workings of the law-bound heavens and stop scheming with absolutist princes to enhance their aura. Even the pious began to subscribe to what was called *physico-theology,* an attempt inspired by science to explain God's providence by reference to his work in nature and not primarily through his biblical Word. By 1700, physico-theology was tame in comparison to *deism,* a rational religion stripped down to a belief only in God. Then came *pantheism,* a term invented in 1705 by the freethinker and radical Whig John Toland to describe the belief that God and nature are one and the same.

The new cultural movement toward the light also changed the nature of Christian belief and worship. New, more cerebral and liberal forms of Protestantism emerged. Unitarianism is perhaps the most famous example, and it continues to attract adherents in England and the United States. The ceremonial life of Unitarian churches is kept to a minimum, and simplified doctrines center on the belief in one God, not the Trinity, and on the right of each individual to fashion his or her own understanding of the spiritual life. Many English Protestants left the Anglican or Presbyterian fold to form Unitarian churches.

The Church of England itself split into two camps: one liberal, or Low Church, and more interested in preaching and social ethics; the other conservative, or High Church, and steeped in ceremony and tradition. Each camp possessed a political analogue: Whigs tended to be Low Church, and Tories tended to be High Church.

Similar fissures opened among Dutch and German Protestants, with liberals in both places seen to favor magistrates over princes. Groups such as the Quakers in England, who had always spurned traditional religious authority, and the Mennonites in the Netherlands continued to attract adherents. They became prominent as advocates for science and a moderate form of the Enlightenment. Earlier than most other organized confessional groups, the Quakers started a campaign against slavery. Soon most of the leaders of the Enlightenment joined them in promoting that cause.

None of these more socially focused or rationally constructed forms of Protestant worship went uncontested. At first Unitarians were persecuted, as toleration in England did not apply to any Protestant who did not believe in the Trinity. Both Newton and Locke kept their anti-Trinitarianism to themselves. The Anglican clergyman Samuel Clarke also took the safe course and remained a private Unitarian. As a result, he found himself no longer fit for high clerical office, in his case a handsome bishopric that the queen sought to give him and that his conscience forced him to refuse.[14] In both England and the Netherlands, orthodox Protestants regarded Quakers, Unitarians, and Mennonites with suspicion. In England, they could not receive degrees from the established universities, Oxford and Cambridge. At the German University at Halle, the liberal Protestant and Newtonian Christian Wolff was hounded out of his professorship because his orthodoxy was suspect. Asked to leave his position in two days, he took the safer route and left in one.

Throughout western Europe, many other Protestants and their clergy opted to stay in their original churches but quietly retired concepts

---

[14]Anecdotes and remembrances in the hand of Horace Walpole, f. 16, Walpole Misc. MS 1789, Lewis Walpole Library, Framingham, Conn: "The Queen had a great mind to make Dr. Sam Clarke a Bishop but he would not subscribe the 39 articles again. Sr. R. W. To please the queen endeavoured to persuade him. . . . The Doctor pleaded that he had believed them when he subscribed tho he did not now. Sr. Robert said, then he ought to resign the living to somebody who did believe." I owe the next point about Wolff to Peter Reill.

such as mortal sin, purgatory, hell, and angels. Even in the birthplace of Calvinism, Geneva, a less doctrinal, more worldly version of Protestant worship emerged after 1700. Belief in original sin and predestination came to be seen as paralyzing. A new breed of clergymen depicted human beings as capable of self-reform and inherently good.[15] The young Jean-Jacques Rousseau, author of *The Social Contract* (see Document 7), grew up in Geneva hearing such liberal sermonizing.

Not all the changes occurred in Protestant Europe. In Catholic France, for example, as the clergy became more zealous, the laity grew detached from ceremonies, men refused to become priests, and births out of wedlock increased.[16]

Gradually, highly educated Protestants and Catholics thought more about God's work as revealed by science than about his biblical Word. As never before, science captured the imagination, particularly in Protestant Europe. Possessing natural knowledge could be interpreted as an expression of piety. The religiosity of the educated began to seem distant from the public displays, processions, and bell ringing of an earlier age and from the ornate Catholicism practiced at the time in southern Europe and transmitted to Latin America by the Spanish and the Portuguese. Religion in general was becoming more private than public, more individual than collective, and thoughts rather than ornate ceremonies began to define the believer. New forms of social interaction offered alternatives to the social life of the church and may have appealed particularly to the less pious. One indication of this lessening of public piety was that by the second half of the eighteenth century, fewer families in both Catholic and Protestant Europe left money to the church in their last wills and testaments.

The deists were among the more outrageous antagonists against religion. They repudiated the churches and their devotion to the divinely inspired Bible. Why take religious sentiments from men, they asked, "who as far as we have any account of things have—even from the earliest times—not scrupled to forge, not only whole Passages, but whole Books?"[17] Instead, they looked only to the scientific light shed on nature to explain beauty, order, and design. The deists saw God as infinite but remote, the being who had made the world and

---

[15]See Helena Rosenblatt, *Rousseau and Geneva: From the* First Discourse *to the* Social Contract, *1749–1762* (Cambridge: Cambridge University Press, 1997), 12–14.

[16]Roche, *France in the Enlightenment,* 585–87.

[17]Matthew Tindal, *Christianity as Old as the Creation* (London, 1730), 163.

then absentmindedly left it to shift for itself.[18] A French dictionary published in 1690 defined a deist as a person who saw no point in any particular religion; he recognized only a God.[19] In the decades after the publication of Newton's *Principia,* deists took up his scientific laws and used them to proclaim nature's ability to govern itself. An outrageous work like *Treatise of the Three Impostors* (see Document 2) grew out of such thinking. It held that Jesus, Moses, and Muhammad had been mere impostors and that nature alone should be worshiped.

The authors of this treatise may have started their religious odyssey from orthodoxy, slipped over into deism, and then quickly made their way to pantheism, or what most people would have called atheism. Manuscripts long buried at the university library in Leiden reveal that a French Huguenot refugee named Jean Rousset de Missy and a bookseller named Charles Levier were involved in creating *Treatise of the Three Impostors.* The actual author or compiler was probably Jan Vroese, a lawyer in the service of the Dutch government, about whom very little is known.[20] One thing is clear: These obscure men hated organized religion, did not believe in God, and thought that Jesus, Moses, and Muhammad were the greatest charlatans of all time.

Skepticism was just as dangerous to revealed religion as deism and pantheism. Ironically, persecution bred skepticism. Some French Protestant refugees, such as Pierre Bayle, endorsed skepticism as the antidote to the fanaticism that had driven him from his homeland. He invented one of the first encyclopedias, which included an entry on the ancient Greek skeptic Pyrrho. Cautiously praising his doctrines, Bayle wrote, "Society has no reason to be afraid of skepticism; for skeptics do not deny that one should conform to the customs of one's country, practice one's moral duties. . . . It is therefore only religion that has anything to fear from Pyrrhonism."[21] The pious did not know whom to distrust more—skeptics, deists, or pantheists.

---

[18]This is the first kind of deist, according to the Anglican churchman and friend of Newton Samuel Clarke, *A Discourse concerning the Unchangeable Obligations of Natural Religion, and the Truth and Certainty of the Christian Religion . . . Sermons Preached at the Cathedral-Church of St. Paul . . . 1705* (London, 1706), 19–20.

[19]Antoine Furetière, *Dictionnaire universel* (Paris, 1690).

[20]See Silvia Berti, "The First Edition of the *Traité des trois imposteurs,* and Its Debt to Spinoza's Ethics," in *Atheism from the Reformation to the Enlightenment,* ed. M. Hunter and D. Wootton (Oxford: Clarendon Press, 1992), 183–220.

[21]Pierre Bayle, *Historical and Critical Dictionary* (1697; reprint, New York: Bobbs-Merrill, 1965), 195.

For their part, deists and pantheists like Rousset de Missy seldom darkened the door of any church. In his adopted homeland, Rousset learned Dutch, became a leader among Amsterdam Freemasons, and eventually became a political activist. Men like Rousset looked for gatherings where their views would be accepted, or at least not seen to be shocking. Opposition to absolutism and a growing disaffection with the church set the stage for the emergence of a vibrant civil society. In some households, politeness allowed for the devout and the irreligious to mix amicably. William Whiston, a dedicated Newtonian, told of dinners with an English lady who "being a believer, loved to have christians of good reputation come and dine with her," while her common-law husband, "being an unbeliever, loved to have persons like himself. . . . We used to meet and to have frequent, but friendly debates, about the truth of the bible and christian religion."[22] In general throughout the eighteenth century, such debates were seldom friendly, hence best conducted in the safety of public spaces and the written word.

THE PUBLIC SPHERE

After 1700, the cities of Europe grew, with London encompassing well over a half million people, eventually surpassing Paris in size. Naples and Amsterdam had more than 100,000 people, and cities of more than 30,000, such as Bristol, The Hague, and Berlin, became more numerous. If a man could afford books and find a coffeehouse where like-minded men gathered in relative anonymity, he might begin to think new and unorthodox thoughts. The cities permitted such public spaces to flourish. Soon it became fashionable for authors writing in almost every European language to address "the public."

Ironically, the public could also be found in new and exotic private places. In London and Paris by 1710, cabarets and clubs sprang up where men may have had sex, but where they also made marriages together. The authorities called them by the derogatory term "sodomites." In Amsterdam during the same period, hundreds of free

---

[22]William Whiston, *Memoirs of the Life and Writings of Mr William Whiston,* 2nd ed. (London, 1753), 1:158; cited in Stephen Snobelen, "The Argument over Prophecy: An Eighteenth-Century Debate between William Whiston and Anthony Collins," *Lumen* 15 (1996): 195–213.

blacks, mostly men originally from Africa, congregated.[23] The cities acted as magnets; they were simply more interesting than the countryside, and they were the centers of commercial life. Young people flocked to them to seek their fame and fortune, to work as apprentices or servants, or, if prosperous, just to enjoy a season of theater and partying. Early in the century, most public spaces were dominated by men. Gradually, women appeared in the clubs, the Masonic lodges, and especially the immensely popular salons (rooms in private houses that were open in the evenings to selected guests). In Paris, salon life dominated the social universe of the enlightened. One rule prevailed: In the context of enforced politeness, people could freely speak their minds.

Of the many ways men, and eventually women, could meet "in public," the new Masonic lodges were by far the most exotic. The Freemasons set up small, secret, private societies, called lodges, which were quickly exported from England to continental Europe and the European colonies. The lodges evolved out of what had once been social clubs for working stonemasons. Largely intended as social centers, they nonetheless sought to inculcate civic virtue. They placed great emphasis on living by laws and constitutions, on voting and oratory, and on charitable works. Most Freemasons were Christians, but in 1738 the papacy condemned a Catholic for membership in a lodge. The Catholic Church was concerned that Freemasonry, with its rituals and appeals to "brotherhood," might satisfy impulses traditionally expressed in the church and thus become an alternative form of religion. The church also disliked the fact that the lodges held frequent elections, a practice that went against the ethos of absolutism. Still, plenty of Catholics, even priests, continued to belong.

Masonic lodges bred religious toleration. In the 1760s in Berlin, the Jewish philosophe Moses Mendelssohn (see Document 9) became a Freemason, as did his close friend the Lutheran Gotthold Lessing. The founders of Dutch Freemasonry included at least one Jew. Such places where Jews and Christians mixed socially were few and far between.

The monthly or bimonthly meetings of lodges all over Europe were occasions when science or simply new ideas were freely discussed in a formal atmosphere of fraternal toleration. In 1785, a lodge in the French city of Lille offered lectures on "mechanical movement," "the

---

[23]Allison Blakely, *Blacks in the Dutch World: The Evolution of Racial Imagery in a Modern Society* (Bloomington: Indiana University Press, 1993), 225–27.

duties of man in private life," *"la liaison des idées,"* and "the porosity of liquids." The program for the entire year mixed the science of man with the natural sciences.[24] In Provence, in the south of France, the social energy that once went into religious societies in the parish was transferred to the Masonic lodges, which by the 1780s proliferated. Freemasonry may seem exotic to us today, but in the eighteenth century lodges attracted worldly men and some women bent on self-improvement undertaken amid conviviality and good food and drink.

The lodges provided members with an opportunity to orate, to vote, to pay dues, and to abide by rules and constitutions. In France, where lodges for men and women became commonplace, women invented rituals by which they sought to proclaim an imagined equality. Amid all their curious rituals and oaths, the Freemasons believed that they had found the path to enlightened rationalism. By the 1790s, however, when monarchs and oligarchies all over Europe feared for their survival, the Freemasons were an obvious object of blame (see Figure 5). They were accused of having caused the French Revolution, a charge that grew out of a deep conviction that the enlarged public sphere had done irretrievable damage to the absolutist political order firmly established a century earlier by Louis XIV and his many princely imitators.

ENLIGHTENED FEMINISM

In the century of light, women became more involved in public life through travel, conversation, reading, and writing. Indeed, the Enlightenment put women's rights and their general education on the intellectual agenda as never before. Particularly as writers, but also as organizers of salon life, a few women became, in effect, public intellectuals. Yet everywhere in the Western world, women were still excluded from formal higher education in any institutional setting.

The career of Lady Mary Wortley Montagu (1689–1762; see Figure 6) nicely illustrates the distinctive opportunities that cities and books offered women. In England before her famous journey to Turkey (see Document 4), but especially after her return, she traveled in urbane, literary, and Whig circles. In them, she learned something about science and experimentation — enough, for example, to allow her to take

---

[24] "Correspondence between Lodges, 1767–1915," Fond 113, opis' 2, delo 471, p. 109, Center for the Preservation of Historico-Documentary Collections (TsKhIDK), Moscow. I am grateful to Russian colleagues who consulted the files and made photocopies to give me a sense of what is there.

Figure 5. The Freemasons Crushed

One of the earliest continental attacks on Freemasons was published in Amsterdam in 1747. The attack is contemporary with the Dutch revolution of the same year, in which the Freemasons were active. Here, their lodge is literally being destroyed as they try to build it.

The Van Pelt Library, University of Pennsylvania.

up the cause of the advanced Turkish method of smallpox inoculation and fearlessly use it on her own children. Amid much controversy, some of it fueled by hostility to a woman taking such a public stance, Montagu then introduced inoculation into England decades before it became commonplace in continental Europe. Born into the English

Figure 6. Lady Mary Wortley Montagu, 1720
The fashion of the day for ladies required them to be displayed almost bare-breasted. We may find the depiction to be sexist, ignoring the great intellect Montagu possessed. But she probably liked the portrait, just as she endorsed sensual pleasure, especially when combined with intellectual rigor, elegant writing, and the joy of encountering and appreciating things that were foreign to her.
The Van Pelt Library, University of Pennsylvania.

aristocracy, she turned herself into a crusader and an intellectual, and in the process suffered the animosity reserved for bold women.

Everything and everyone interested Montagu. When she went to Holland, she identified with its Protestant tidiness, the grandness of The Hague, and the orderliness of its gardens. In Germany, she went from city to city and decried the power of the absolutist princes over their subjects. In Vienna, she sampled the social life and praised the status accorded to older women. Most spectacularly, she came to respect Turks and Muslims, and visited incognito a bathhouse for naked Turkish women. Rather than being shocked, she praised the institution as being like "a Woman's Coffee House."[25] All these views were recorded in a remarkable set of private letters published after Montagu's death.

Through self-education and travel, Montagu became an enlightened cosmopolitan who embraced outrageous and daring places and ideas. She was a great traveler, opening her mind to foreign customs. When she returned to England, its cities, in comparison to what she had seen in the Islamic world, seemed somewhat provincial. Yet even she could not imagine how deeply the Enlightenment had penetrated the semi-urban provinces once thought to be safe havens by censors and clergy alike. By the mid-eighteenth century, journals such as *The Female Spectator* and *The Ladies' Diary,* which focused on science, flourished, reaching small towns as well as aristocratic manor houses. As a young woman, Montagu longed for women to have the right to be educated and to debate in public. Her advocacy made her many enemies. Eventually, she left England for a self-imposed exile in Italy.

Literate English women often learned of the emerging Enlightenment through novels and journals. Early on, the movement, with its Whig and secularist associations, drew feminist detractors such as the Anglican Mary Astell, who objected to the irreligious tone of enlightened circles. Yet Locke and other contemporaries stimulated Astell to think new thoughts and to champion the cause of women's education as the key to all progress. Although Montagu's Whig politics were markedly different from Astell's, Montagu may have read Astell's writings on the subject of women's education and been influenced accordingly.

The necessity for female education appeared in almost every tract written to advance women's status, from what the Newtonian Madame du Châtelet said in France at mid-century to what the radical English republican Mary Wollstonecraft argued at its end. The challenge to absolute monarchy as a theory of government also affected masculine notions of authority. By late in the century, fathers were being sentimentalized as teachers and protectors, no longer simply as masters. Yet in a world where fathers still ruled, the French philosophes the marquis de Condorcet and his wife, Madame Condorcet, made the

---

[25]See the superb biography of Montagu by Isobel Grundy, *Lady Mary Wortley Montagu* (Oxford: Oxford University Press, 1999), 138.

Figure 7. Margaret Bryan and Her Two Daughters
Bryan taught in an elite school for girls in Chelsea, a district of London. She wrote textbooks in general science and astronomy.
The Metropolitan Museum of Art, Harris Brisbane Dick Fund, 1917. (17.3.1170)

issue of women's status and education a major part of their life's work. The Enlightenment consistently raised the issue of women's education (hence status), and it remained part of public discussion for much of the eighteenth century. (See Figure 7.)

Within the context provided by the Enlightenment, we find the first scientific society for women, founded in 1785 in Middleburg, a city in Zeeland, the southernmost province of the Dutch republic. Local elites made up its clientele. The scientific lecturer of the society, Daniel Radermaker, was also an avid Freemason, a follower of Voltaire, and a friend of the leading Dutch novelist, Aagje Deken, who was also a feminist. The society lasted for more than one hundred years, its concern for female education resonating throughout enlightened circles.

While imprisoned during the French Revolution, the marquis de Condorcet, soon to commit suicide during the Terror of 1794 rather than be executed for crimes he did not commit, could dream about a time when for women "the degree of equality in education that we can reasonably hope to attain . . . is that which excludes all dependence, either forced or voluntary."[26] After his death, Madame Condorcet continued the struggle and sought to influence the education systems put in place as a result of the Revolution.

REWORKING SEVENTEENTH-CENTURY FORMAL PHILOSOPHY

It may be said that the seventeenth-century development of philosophy and science, or what was called *natural philosophy* at the time, laid the intellectual foundation on which the Enlightenment was built. The Enlightenment was based not only on *what* the seventeenth-century philosophers said—that is, the complexity and richness of their thought—but also on *how* readers interpreted them. The seventeenth century spawned such innovative philosophers as Francis Bacon, René Descartes, Thomas Hobbes, Baruch Spinoza, Gottfried Leibniz, and, of course, John Locke. More purely scientific in their writings were Galileo, Robert Boyle, and Isaac Newton. During this century, the classics of Western philosophy remained staples of higher education: Plato, Aristotle, Lucretius, the Stoics, the skeptic Sextus Empiricus, and the medieval priest Thomas Aquinas, among others. Indeed,

---

[26]Marie Jean Antoine-Nicolas, Marquis de Condorcet, *Sketch for a Historical Picture of the Progress of the Human Mind,* trans. June Barraclough (London: Weidenfeld and Nicolson, 1955), "the tenth stage."

Lady Mary Wortley Montagu used to spend her time as a girl translating the works of the Stoics from Latin to English.

By 1700, however, reformers, called moderns, were dethroning the ancients. They praised the seventeenth-century thinkers as greater than the Greeks and Romans and certainly more profound than Thomas Aquinas, a hero to the traditional Catholic clergy, who taught his philosophy in every school they controlled. All of these thinkers, to one degree or another, rejected Thomas Aquinas and his philosophy, which came to be known as Scholasticism. Briefly, Thomas Aquinas and his followers argued that immaterial "forms" give life and shape to all of nature, in effect imitating in nature the role of the soul in human beings as decreed by Christianity. The problem with this doctrine of forms lay in its unprovability, or the inability to demonstrate the existence of these forms. As frustration with Scholasticism and the clergy who promoted it mounted, proponents of the Enlightenment refuted Thomas Aquinas. Disillusioned, they turned to the seventeenth century for inspiration.

In *Some Thoughts concerning Education* (see Document 1), Locke tells his readers that to be truly educated, their children have to know the new science from Copernicus to Newton. The *Treatise of the Three Impostors* (see Document 2) relies on the Jewish heretic Baruch Spinoza, who was a follower of Descartes, while in *Letters concerning the English Nation* (Document 3), Voltaire worships Newton, Bacon, and the new science. He describes Bacon as "a great philosopher, a good historian, and an elegant writer . . . more esteemed after his death than in his lifetime." Denis Diderot saw his great encyclopedia of 1751 (see Document 5) as a project inspired by the English visionary Francis Bacon. In *The Social Contract* (see Document 7), Jean-Jacques Rousseau engages in a somewhat angry dialogue with Thomas Hobbes, the English founder of political science, who wrote a hundred years earlier in the 1650s. The great proponent of Jewish civil liberties Moses Mendelssohn (see Document 9) also discusses Hobbes. And in her letter of February 12, 1717, Montagu turned to Hobbes for an appropriate text to describe the carnage after the Battle of Carlowitz.

Hobbes and Descartes belonged to the same generation, which came to maturity in the 1620s. The wholesale reconstruction of the formal philosophical foundations of Western thought began with Descartes's *Discourse on Method* (1637). Published first while he was in the Netherlands and well away from the French Catholic censors, it became one of the most widely read books of the seventeenth century. With clear, simple prose, *Discourse* was accessible to anyone who was literate, and its pointed message urged readers to examine every thought for its coherence and to use skepticism not as an end but as a method to question all ideas. Having the idea of God in one's mind, Descartes explained, allowed people to postulate the existence of a knowable world outside the mind. God would not deceive. Human beings should search for clear and distinct ideas and, of course, adhere to the laws and customs of the country. But what if Descartes's readers decided that God was not an idea that was needed? What if the clear idea they formulated from observing the world included the conclusion that the clergy had far too many privileges or that they preached hocus-pocus?

Educated by French Jesuits, Descartes had no interest in undermining basic Christian beliefs. He urged his followers to obey all the laws of church and state while searching for "clear and distinct ideas." But some read him as supporting materialism, the doctrine that matter controls the universe and spiritual agencies are irrelevant.[27] These "misreadings" may not have been far off the mark. When speaking about the philosophy of Thomas Aquinas, for instance, Descartes said in private, "This is how the monks have opened the way to all the sects and heresies—I mean, through Scholastic Theology, which is something that should above all else have been stamped out."[28] The disillusioned in Europe saw in Descartes a fellow traveler. There were, however, plenty of pious Cartesians who took up Descartes's principles and methods in support of absolutism or to argue for the rights of husbands over wives, which, they said, were similar to the rights of masters over valets.[29] Such authoritarian piety did not stop the church from putting Descartes's writings on the *Index of Forbidden Books* in 1663. (The *Index* was abolished in the 1960s, and only in 1998 were the Vatican archives opened to scholars trying to understand how it worked over time.) Descartes's call to think clearly and methodically continued to be deeply threatening to institutions bent on controlling thought and belief in the twentieth century.

The church's condemnation of Descartes had little impact in Protestant countries or even in France. Undeterred by the pope, readers

[27] For one of his many detractors, see [Anon.], *L'impie convaincu, ou dissertation contre Spinoza* (Amsterdam: Jean Crell, 1685), 118 et seq. This is also an attack on Cartesianism.

[28] John Cottingham, *Descartes' Conversation with Burman* (Oxford: Clarendon Press, 1976), 46.

[29] Pierre Sylvain Regis, *Systêm de Philosophie contenant la logique, la metaphysique . . .* (Paris, 1690), 3:455–56, 467.

found further liberation in Descartes's philosophical treatise *The Passions of the Soul* (1649). According to Descartes, these passions are not inherently evil; they are simply there. He defined the passions as relational and not solitary, as occurring between a subject and an object of desire. By liberating the passions from the dictate to control them or be ashamed of them, Descartes's treatise had implications for living and for thinking about a common humanity. In effect, he said, emotions can be expressed and discussed.

Influenced by Descartes, the great French novelist Madeleine de Scudéry contributed to this "affective revolution" among readers by defining emotion, or sensibility, as a shared experience.[30] People who wrote or read novels could identify themselves as thinking and feeling beings who defined the authenticity of an idea or an emotion conveyed in print by the effect it had on their own private reason and emotions. With such assumptions in place, the novel became a silent companion of modern philosophy, and it encouraged a new individualism. Not surprisingly, it developed into the most powerful literary genre of the eighteenth century. The new novel legitimated the power of the senses—in this instance, the power of sight to transform the reader.

Cartesian thought split religious communities in half. Its influence was especially evident in the Netherlands. People in the generation after Descartes, such as the Dutch Calvinist minister Balthasar Bekker, read Descartes as justifying a world in which all bodies are like automatons, like the new push-pull mechanisms demonstrated by the English scientist Robert Boyle's new air pump. Bekker used Cartesian arguments about the push-pull motion of bodies to disprove the existence of devils and spirits in the universe. He argued that such beings could not make things in the world move or change. Bekker's *World Bewitched* (1691) did not sit well with his fellow preachers, who accused him of excess rationalism and effectively deposed him as a minister. Thus Dutch Calvinism was divided between fundamentalists, who wanted strict adherence to the Bible, ritual, and clergy, and Cartesian liberals like Bekker, who were eager to eradicate superstition, even from the minds of the faithful. The Calvinist Church did not want to encourage belief in witches, but it could not allow rationalist arguments to supersede biblical ones.

At every Dutch university by the 1650s, a battle broke out between the adherents of Thomas Aquinas and those of Descartes. Eventually,

---

[30] I am deeply indebted here to Joan Dejean, *Ancients against Moderns: Culture Wars and the Making of a Fin de Siècle* (Chicago: University of Chicago Press, 1997), 78–86.

Descartes's science and philosophy flourished in the Dutch universities, which were among the best in Europe. Only around 1700 did his ideas give way to the newer science of Newton.

The writings of just about every other major seventeenth-century philosopher sparked similar controversy. In the eighteenth century, people with an interest in science read Francis Bacon as the justifier of empirical work, of collecting and cataloging. That Bacon had also been a millenarian (a believer in the imminent end of the world and the Last Judgment) and a courtier (an architect of James I's absolutism) simply got left out of the story. In his *Letter 12* (1773), Voltaire said that Bacon was "the father of experimental philosophy." In the 1790s during the French Revolution, the new ministers in charge of encouraging commerce and industry, as well as applied science, publically invoked Bacon as their inspiration.

Thinkers like Locke, dedicated to upholding, though narrowing, the foundations of Christianity, were read as entirely secular in their orientation. Locke's *Some Thoughts concerning Education* (see Document 1), aimed largely at male children of good Protestants, was taken as a license to educate all children. Some even argued that it justified allowing women to preach.[31] Indeed, Locke should be seen as putting the issue of women's education on the Western agenda, but he had many feminist precursors, and in the eighteenth century advocates of women's education were writing in a variety of languages and settings. Again, it was *how* Locke, Descartes, or Bacon could be read by reformers looking for new solutions to old problems that created a new culture of light.[32]

It seems as if every seventeenth-century philosopher could be interpreted as supporting the superiority of science over fundamentalist religion or even justifying heresy. Locke's writings on how the mind works and his epistemology (or psychology) that made the senses, not innate ideas, the key to knowledge acquisition were turned into a justification for materialism. Forget the soul, where

---

[31]See Benjamin Coole, *Some Observations . . . relating to Women's exercising their spiritual gifts* (London, 1716); Josiah Martin, *A Letter to the Author . . .* (London, 1716); Benjamin Coole, *Reflection on the Letter . . .* (London, 1717); and Josiah Martin, *A Vindication of Women's Preaching . . .* (1717?). See also Alan Sell, *John Locke and the Divines* (Cardiff: University of Wales Press, 1997). I owe these references to Mark Goldie and John Marshall.

[32]See Karen Offen, "Was Mary Wollstonecraft a Feminist? A Contextual Re-reading of *A Vindication of the Rights of Women,* 1792–1992," in *Quilting a New Canon: Stitching Women's Words,* ed. Uma Parameswaran (Toronto: Sister Vision, 1996), 3–24.

innate ideas were thought to reside, said French materialists such as Denis Diderot. Instead, imagine only a blank slate inside the human mind on which events write. Voltaire claimed that even Descartes had the nature of the human mind wrong when he assumed that ideas (like that of God) reside in the mind innately. By mid-century, writers for Diderot's great *Encyclopédie* (see Document 5) would argue that induction, as described by Locke, offered the only convincing model of how human beings come to know themselves and the world.[33] The stage was set for the arrival of a new and virulent materialism, a stark vision that made the world and its people into atoms in motion.

The seventeenth-century philosophers produced, largely through no fault of their own, a cacophony of new opinions about human nature, the universe, and religion. Some of them even realized how others might read them. A contemporary of Newton, the Dutch scientist Christiaan Huygens, fretted in print about having his work translated out of Latin and into English: "It renders Philosophy cheap and vulgar, and, which is worse, furnishes a sort of injudicious people with a smattering of Notions, which being not able to make a proper use of, they pervert to the injury of Religion and Science."[34] His subject was the possibility of life on other planets and how rational souls might inhabit other than human shapes. He further argued that the vastness of the earth and the heavens should be "a matter of reflection, for those kings and princes who sacrifice the lives of so many people, only to flatter their ambition."[35] With such sentiments, Huygens perhaps had good reason to be worried about what his readers might conclude. Yet like him, the vast majority of seventeenth-century philosophers, writing in all the principal Western languages, had no desire to undermine ecclesiastic authority or doctrinal belief.

There were two major exceptions to the general piety of the seventeenth-century philosophers: Thomas Hobbes in England and Baruch Spinoza in the Dutch republic. Though very different in their political ideas (Spinoza believed in republics; Hobbes sought a new foundation for absolutism), both left no room for direct divine involvement in their philosophies of nature. In his *Tractatus Theologico-Politicus* (1670), Spinoza denies that God can intervene by miracles, treats the Bible as

---

[33] Jørn Schøsler, *John Locke et les philosophes français: La critique des idées innées en France au dix-huitième siècle* (Oxford: Voltaire Foundation, 1997), 68–69.

[34] Christiaan Huygens, *The Celestial Worlds discover'd: or, Conjectures concerning the Inhabitants, Plants and Productions of the Worlds in the Planets* (London: Timothy Childe, 1698); actually from an opening text said to be by the publisher to the reader.

[35] Ibid., 141.

a historical document, and says that the only point to having religious organizations is to teach people obedience to society's laws. Later, in his *Ethics* (1677, published after his death), Spinoza says that God and nature are basically the same substance. Hobbes, in his *Leviathan* (1651), relegates divine involvement to the final days of the world. In the meantime, life without authority, Hobbes wrote, would be nasty, brutish, and short. What people need is a strong, authoritarian ruler. They get him not from God, but from a contract made among themselves. By contrast, Spinoza believed that free will is an illusion, that movement and desire determine the direction of our will, and, left to our own devices, human beings can live in relative autonomy. Spinoza was a good Dutch republican.

Despite these differences, no other philosophers were considered more dangerous by the pious, and both could be used effectively by would-be philosophes.[36] For example, the freethinkers who wrote the tract about Jesus, Moses, and Muhammad being impostors (see Document 2) began the book, and their own spiritual odyssey from Protestantism to pantheism, with excerpts from Spinoza. The historian Daniel Roche sums up Spinoza's influence in France this way: "Condemned by the Church and read in secret, he turned unbelief into a social force."[37]

A CLANDESTINE UNIVERSE

Formal philosophers of the seventeenth century attracted informal readers. Some of them were bold enough to put their ideas into print, albeit anonymously, and a new genre, that of clandestine books and manuscripts, was born. The early stages of the Enlightenment were nurtured in that literature, and the persona of the philosophe took shape in that shadowy world. The first work to describe the new style of philosophizing, called *Le Philosophe* (The Philosopher, 1743), appeared anonymously, probably with a phony imprint on its title page. By 1700, thousands of people were involved in writing, printing, and selling anonymous books, as well as buying them and passing them along to friends. To this day, we know very few of their names, and the ones we do know generally come from the records of censors or police.

---

[36]Hobbes's impact on the continent can be see in Frederick Spanheim, *Den Atheist, of God-verloochenaar, Overtuycht en Vier Predicatien* (Amsterdam, 1677), with attacks on Lucretius, Hobbes (p. 104), and Selden. Compare Wiep van Bunge and Wim Klever, eds., *Disguised and Overt Spinozism around 1700* (New York: Brill, 1996).

[37]Roche, *France in the Enlightenment*, 381.

Being secretive about the more outrageous ideas associated with the Enlightenment was a form of self-preservation. In every Western country, prison loomed for those who violated the laws of blasphemy or evaded the official censors. Yet once the authorities could no longer control all the printing presses and people had enough money to buy the forbidden works, books and journals could be as outrageous and indiscreet as publishers dared. Never before in the Christian West had the beliefs of the literate and educated split so openly in matters not simply of doctrine (Protestants and Catholics had been quarreling for centuries) but also around the very status of Christian belief. By the late eighteenth century, during the lives of Immanuel Kant and Moses Mendelssohn, this same critical spirit would grip Judaism, engendering breaks that endure to this day.[38]

Take a small city like Namur, in the highly censored Austrian Netherlands (what is today Belgium). It had about a dozen bookstores. When the authorities raided them in the 1730s, they found "bad books"—French translations of works by John Locke and Niccolò Machiavelli, the great Italian Renaissance theorist who wrote that the end justifies the means. The bookstores also yielded examples of the risqué and the pornographic. Not just the wealthy bought these books. A decade later, when a merchant-tanner of Namur died, his library contained works by Voltaire and fashionable encyclopedias of the era.[39]

But Belgium could not match France or the Dutch republic for the outrageous. Near Paris in 1728, a humble parish priest was arrested for claiming that Jesus, Moses, and Muhammad were impostors.[40] He probably had gotten hold of *Treatise of the Three Impostors* (see Document 2). By 1728, the claim was actually old news. Ten years earlier, in faraway Saxony, German authorities had been searching bookstores in hopes of confiscating the very same tract.[41] But unknown to the authorities, the culprits were in neither Paris nor Saxony, but in the Dutch republic. As far as current scholarship can tell, relatively obscure

---

[38]See Shmuel Feiner, "The Pseudo-Enlightenment and the Question of Jewish Modernization," *Jewish Social Studies* (1996): 62–88.

[39]Th. Pisvin, *La Vie intellectuelle à Namur sous le Régime autrichien* (Louvain: University of Louvain, 1963), 202–3.

[40]Dossier on *Treatise of the Three Impostors,* Paris L 10, no. 6, f. 92, Archives Nationales; supplied by the kindness of Silvia Berti. See her article "Unmasking the Truth . . . ," in *Everything Connects: Essays in Honor of Richard H. Popkin,* ed. James E. Force and David Katz (New York: Brill, 1998).

[41]Loc. 7209, Geheimes Konsilium, Staatsarchiv Dresden; cited by Martin Mulsow, "Freethinking in Early Eighteenth-Century Protestant Germany: Peter Friedrich Arpe and the *Traité des trois imposteurs,*" in *Heterodoxy, Spinozism, and Free Thought in Early Eighteenth-Century Europe,* ed. Silvia Berti, François Charles-Daubert, and Richard Popkin (The Hague: Kluwer, 1996), 220.

deists and pantheists wrote the treatise in French, the international language of the day, in 1710, and Dutch publishers actually printed it in 1719. The book incurred so much hostility from the authorities that most copies just disappeared. Only in 1985, at the library of the University of California at Los Angeles, did Silvia Berti discover the first printed copy known to have survived the censors. It was not an accident that Jean Rousset de Missy, a young refugee turned iconoclastic, had a major hand in organizing, if not partially writing, *The Three Impostors* and guiding it into print. Decades after that escapade, he would help lead a revolution in the Netherlands (1747–48).

The secrecy of Freemasonry perfectly symbolizes the nature of the clandestine as it emerged in the Enlightenment. Lifting the veil of the lodges, we find old, familiar symbols and ideas reworked and given new meaning. A lodge in Strasbourg, on the French-German border, had an altar in the center of its meeting room, and a copy of its written constitution was placed in the "tabernacle." From a clerical point of view, such a usage could be interpreted as a mockery of the Eucharist and the Catholic altar. The Freemasons, however, probably meant it as a sign of respect for their lodge and for constitutional government, elections, voting, and public speech making. Later in the century, German Freemasons claimed that, glowing in the light of truth, Freemasonry may have originated with the building of Noah's ark. The lodges welcomed people of all religions—"Jews, Turks, Heathens"—they said, then claimed, somewhat incongruously, that the order was "bound together by the Christian religion."[42] In these lodges, men and some women, including the great composer Wolfgang Amadeus Mozart (see Figure 8), lounged and chatted in privacy and in an atmosphere made semireligious by costumes, rituals, and candlelight.

It is little wonder that by the 1740s, the French word *philosophe* (philosopher) took on new meaning as a war between the "godless" and their critics erupted in France. From time out of mind, a typical Western philosopher had carried himself with the arrogance of an aristocrat. Newton put it well when he said that his *Principia* had been written technically to avoid his "being baited by little Smatterers in Mathematics."[43] A true philosopher of the seventeenth century detached himself from worldly interests, even controversy, and sought contemplation and passivity. But in the 1740s, the philosophe became engagé. One of the earliest indications of this trend appears in *Le Philosophe,* dedicated to the memory of the English freethinker and republican Anthony Collins

---

[42] [Anon], *Freymaureren: Glizzirt im Lichte der Wahrheit* (Frankfurt, 1785), 19.
[43] Keynes MS 133, f. 10, King's College, Cambridge.

Figure 8. Freemasons' Ceremony, Vienna

The great composer Wolfgang Amadeus Mozart was an active Freemason in Vienna during the 1780s. Here he sits at the extreme right, engaged in avid conversation. Note the ceremonies around light and darkness, with one of the brothers being introduced to the lodge while blindfolded before being welcomed by its light.

Erich Lessing/Art Resource, New York.

and probably written in Paris. The tract defines the philosophe as one of those special people who could see through popular errors. In particular, the philosophe had figured out that God does not exist and in his place people should put "civil society . . . the only deity he will recognize on earth."[44] Hard work and honesty, coupled with a dedication to worldly concerns, befitted the new, enlightened philosophers.

[44] *Nouvelles libertés de Penser* (Amsterdam, 1743). Compare J. O'Higgins, S. J., *Anthony Collins* (The Hague: Nijhoff, 1970), 216–17. Also compare Hans Ulrich Gumbrecht, *Making Sense in Life and Literature,* vol. 79 of *Theory and History of Literature* (Minneapolis: University of Minnesota Press, 1992), 138–39; here the author assumes that the writer of *Le Philosophe* must have been speaking out of a French context. See the discussion in Margaret C. Jacob, *The Radical Enlightenment: Pantheists, Freemasons and Republicans*

By being dedicated to a notorious English republican, *Le Philosophe* signaled an international cosmopolitanism and an active engagement with change in the political order. Its anonymity confirmed that atheism still lay on the fringe of acceptable opinion, even among those who imagined themselves enlightened. The linkage between *Le Philosophe* and English freethinking confirmed what a clerical opponent had written a few years earlier: A freethinker believes "that the soul is material and mortal, Christianity an imposture, the Scriptures a forgery, the working of God superstition, hell a fable, and heaven a dream, our life without providence, and our death without hope like that of asses and dogs."[45] The philosophes being championed by the clandestine presses would probably have agreed with the cleric, except for the part about people being like asses and dogs. Human beings now had new forms of sociability and engaged in bold communication through speech and print. Therein lay the glory of their new worldly condition.

Claiming Amsterdam as the place of publication for *Le Philosophe* is also important. It reveals a basic truth about the use of French during the Enlightenment. French was the lingua franca of Huguenot refugees, business travelers, and the non-French elites, particularly in the Netherlands and German-speaking lands. Even those who spoke it poorly could almost certainly read it. The place of publication, or even the writing, of a French text, and sometimes the key to its ideas, was not necessarily France. For instance, *Treatise of the Three Impostors* (see Document 2) came out of the elite circles in the Dutch republic, where the speaking and writing of French denoted culture and civility.

To illustrate the importance of the French language, let's look at the publications of Pierre Marteau. There never was a publisher named Pierre Marteau, and he certainly never lived in France. He was pure fiction, invented by Dutch publishing houses and used as an imprint for books published anonymously as early as 1660 ("Pierre Marteau, Cologne").[46] We may legitimately doubt that even the paper or ink for such books had ever seen the outskirts of German-speaking Cologne, across the Rhine from the Dutch republic. If there was a taxpayer in

---

(London: George Allen and Unwin, 1981), 217. The evidence for Dumarsais as author is good but not conclusive; see A. W. Fairbairn, "Dumarsais and *Le Philosophe*," *Studies on Voltaire and the Eighteenth Century* 87 (1972): 375–95; and Olivier Bloch, ed., *Le Matérialisme du xviiie siècle et la litterature clandestine* (Paris: Librairie Vrin, 1982), 179–81, where once again the manuscript is reassigned to a Dutch context.

[45] Richard Bentley, *Remarks upon a Late Discourse of Freethinking* (London, 1713), 14.

[46] See Léonce Janmart de Brouillant, *La Liberté de la Presse en France aux xviie et xviiie siècles: Histoire de Pierre du Marteau* 1888; reprint (Geneva: Slatkine Reprints, 1971); and *A Short-Title Catalog of the First Two Decades of Pierre Marteau Imprints,* ISSN 0712 9297 no. 25.

Cologne by that name, he certainly had no idea that his name was being used, probably by the Amsterdam publisher Elsevier, to promote some fairly outrageous ideas. How could the censors arrest someone they could not find?

Possibly more than three hundred books came from the imprint of Pierre Marteau. With an average press run of five hundred copies, the total output comes to about one hundred fifty thousand copies. By contrast, at the end of the eighteenth century, we think that there were twenty-five thousand copies of the multivolume *Encyclopédie* by Diderot and his many reprinters. The Marteau books might be read at one sitting; encyclopedias were then, as they are now, reference works. Thus, by 1700, the number of anonymous works that came from just one publisher more than rivals the number of French encyclopedias produced a full eighty years later.

Pierre Marteau's earliest French-language publications were primarily anti-French and anti-Catholic polemics that could have been written by devout Protestants.[47] Almost immediately, Marteau's books became experimental, as if the authors were trying to write in the new fictional style we now call the novel. The precise nature of French corruption and decadence required narrative description. The sexual practices of young nuns and Jesuit priests were described in detail. The Capuchin monks were said to run a "university of cuckcoldry."[48]

According to the clandestine literature, no social group was as debauched as the Catholic clergy. In these Marteau books, monks

---

[47]Both UCLA's Young Research Library and the Library of Herzog August, Wolfenbüttel, Germany, have superb collections of the Marteau material. For Protestant themes, see *Recueil de diverses pieces servant à l'histoire de Henry III, Roy de France,* where the problem of Catholic bellicosity is traced back to Catherine de Médici. For another example, see Wolf. Gk 2174 (1), *De L'Etat de la France* (Cologne: Pierre de Marteau, 1671), a warning against French bellicosity; even earlier, see Wolf. Ge 599, [Anon.], *Recueil de plusieurs pieces servans à l'histoire moderne* (Cologne: Pierre du Marteau, 1663). See a related tract, *Drey Curiöse Tractatlein,* [sic] [Colln/Jean Marteau] 1675 (in handwritten note, "Hamburg, Heyl"), 9–10; Bible is useless to Catholics; "Pope is the author of our faith"; Mary is higher than God because she gave life to him. One of the few Marteaus in Dutch extolls William of Orange and the Revolution of 1688–89; see *De Gefalieerde Koning, en de Prins tegen Dank . . . tot Keulen* (Marteau, 1688), UCLA Z 233 M 30272. There is a not very helpful work from the former East Germany that tries to argue that Pierre Marteau was a German and that collects a number of German-language books that bore the imprint; see Karl Klaus Walther, *Die Deutschsprachige Verlagsproduktion von Pierre Marteau, Beifelt* 93 *zum Zentralblatt für Bibliothekswesen* (Leipzig, 1983). I am grateful to William Kelly for assistance with Pierre Marteau and his generally Dutch identity.

[48]See *Le moine secularisé* (Cologne, 1678), 56; the monk is also depicted as a seller of indulgences.

appeared as especially evil sorts, and their erections and mutual masturbation—"all the diverse emotions are rendered visible by the erection"—were recounted with relish for the public.[49] Sometimes women were said to be the authors of tell-all accounts of the passions of Catholic nuns, whether in Portugal or France.[50] One of Marteau's many imitators, Jean L'Ingenu, printed books about love between priests and nuns and bound them with titillating exposés of the salacious goings-on at the French court.[51] One Marteau work even claimed that the Bible is useless to Catholics, the pope is the author of their faith, and the Virgin Mary is higher than God because she gave life to him.[52]

Marteau's books also targeted the French aristocracy.[53] Illicit love among the great and the noble sold a lot of books.[54] Indeed, the very last book to be published by "the successor of Pierre Marteau" was a salacious attack on the French queen Marie Antoinette, which appeared in the first year of the French Revolution (1789).[55] Four years later, she was executed, a victim of the Terror and the reaction against the aristocracy and their clerical supporters.

Gradually, especially after 1685, Marteau and his many imitators took direct aim at Louis XIV, the persecutor of French Protestants, who, in the throes of an amorous liaison with a new mistress, had suddenly become pious and devout (see Figure 9). After the revocation of the Edict of Nantes in 1685, the attacks on Louis and his Catholic clergy became menacing. An anonymous pamphlet declared that the revocation would be his undoing. It further claimed that Louis had made an alliance with the Jesuits but that they could not be trusted, as

[49]Wolf. Lm 95h, [Marianna Alcoforado], *Lettre d'Amour d'une religieuse...* (Cologne: Pierre du Marteau, 1681), supposedly a translation from the Portuguese.

[50]Wolf. Tq 1422, *Le Rasibus, ou le proces fait à la Barbe des Capucins. Par une Moine Défroqué* (Cologne: Pasquin resuscité, 1680), 8, 27–28.

[51]Wolf. Qu N 1080a, *Nouvelles de l'Amerique ou Le Mercure ameriquain* (Cologne: Jean L'Ingenu, 1678); bound with *Le Berger gentil-homme par Chavigni* (Cologne: Pierre Gaillard, 1685) and *Mademoiselle de Benonville: Nouvelle Galante* (Liège: chez Louis Montfort, 1686); on the French court.

[52]*Drey Curiöse Tractatlein* (Colln: Jean Marteau, 1695), 10: *"Glauben wir an eine Person / die da mehr als Gott ist / an die Jungfrau Mariam."*

[53]Wolf. Qu N 1058y, [Anon.], *Eve ressuscitée ou la Belle sans chemise* (Cologne: Louis Le Sincere, 1683); bound with *Le Taureau Bannal de Paris* (Cologne: Pierre Marteau, 1689).

[54]See *Memoires amoureuses Conenants les Amours des Grands Hommes & Dames,* (Cologne: Pierre Marteau, 1676). See also *Nouvelles de l'Amerique ou Le Mercure ameriquain* on the love lives of priests and nuns; [Anon.], *Amours des Dames illustres de Notre Siecle* (Cologne: Jean Le Blanc, 1680).

[55]*Essay historique sur la vie privée de Marie-Antoinette d'Autriche, reine de France* (Rome: chez le successeur de Pierre Marteau, 1789), UCLA Z 233 M 3E78.

Figure 9. The Enjoyment of a Catholic Feast Day
In this piece of Protestant propaganda aimed at Louis XIV, a Catholic holy day
is depicted as the occasion for the king and his bishops to make war under
the banner of "One Faith, One Law, and One King." They are dressed for battle,
intent on triumph in war.
The Metropolitan Museum of Art, The Elisha Whittelsey Collection, The Elisha Whittelsey Fund, 1949.

they opposed all sovereignty but their own. Then came the book's
most telling line: "Eyes that are enlightened by the light [can see] that
France . . . is in the grip of a Catholic fury." It argued that Protestants
should do what the Jews did: When persecuted, they hid their religion
but raised their children to be faithful. Just look around Amsterdam,
the author said, to see how Judaism had survived. The author also
wrote that enemies "sent by God and the celestial powers who have
been profoundly irritated against the tyrannical Government that has
been established in France" would reduce Louis's kingdom to ashes.[56]

---

[56]*Histoire de la decadence de la France prouvée par sa conduite* (Cologne: Pierre
Marteau, 1687), 20: *"les yeux à la lumiere [sic] qui l'élaire, que la France sous les belles &
trompeuses esperances qu'on lui a fait consevoir, à laché la bride à la fureur Catholique."*
On the Jews, see p. 181. On Louis XIV, see pp. 24–25.

Ironically, sometimes the clandestine literature invoked the divine, if only as a warning to the enemies of toleration.

A PROTESTANT ODYSSEY

How did a Protestant publisher like Pierre Marteau start out as an anti-Catholic polemicist and end up an irreligious publisher of pornographic novels? To answer this question, we need to consider the complex relationship between Protestantism and the earliest stirrings of the European Enlightenment. In the lost world represented by Pierre Marteau and his readers, a gradual metamorphosis appears to have been occurring among some literate people. These people moved from a belief in the reasonableness of the Protestant version of Christianity—vividly highlighted by the obvious irrationality of injustice and persecution in the 1680s—toward a belief that simply being reasonable is the key to virtuous living. If the pilgrim got to that place, the only thing to do on a Sunday morning was to read the newspaper or write letters.

A bold imprint from the shop of Marteau documents the metamorphosis from Protestant to enlightened deist quite concretely. *Le Jesuite secularisé* (*The Secularized Jesuit*, 1683) wanted the world to know how evil the Jesuits had become. Each Jesuit should be exposed as an assassin in disguise in the employ of Spain and *"un pedagogue sodomite."* The book claims that by comparison, the Calvinists acted reasonably in their congregations. The author then considers who should be seen as reasonable. Surely all sorts of believers could be described as reasonable. It may be argued that reason also belonged to the Socinians—that is, to those who denied the divinity of Christ. Simply not being fanatical might be the key to true religious sentiment, and complex doctrines such as the Trinity, the author says, created situations ripe for intolerance. In this one book on the Jesuits, the author makes the leap from anticlericalism to the fringes of religious heresy.[57]

Not all late-seventeenth-century writers were willing to go this far. A decade after *Le Jesuite secularisé,* John Locke published *The Reasonableness of Christianity* (1695), in which he tried to pare Protestant Christianity down to the essentials. That year, Parliament removed prepublication censorship, and the following year John Toland published

---

[57] [Claude Dûpré, name handwritten in the margin], *Le Jesuite secularisé* (Cologne: Jacques Vilebard, 1683), 187–90. On the Jesuits, see pp. 223–24. Compare Silvia Berti, "At the Roots of Unbelief," *Journal of the History of Ideas,* 56, no. 4 (1995): 555–75.

Christianity not Mysterious. Why should we have religious doctrines or dogmas at all? the former Presbyterian asked. Why not find a set of reasonable principles based on nature's laws on which everyone could agree? According to Toland, religious persecution and the efforts to impose absolutism on the unwilling put pressure on all Protestants to decide how to defend the virtues of religious belief and practice. We now know that Locke wrote *The Reasonableness of Christianity* after he saw a pre-publication copy of Toland's book.[58]

Both Toland and Locke belonged to the Whig party. Toland had even trained for the Presbyterian ministry (briefly) at Leiden. Locke, like Newton, secretly did not believe in the doctrine of the Trinity. But both Newton and Locke were horrified at where excessive rationality, coupled with a grasp of the new science, could take people like Toland, especially if they had reason to be angry at the high-and-mighty.

Sorting out the twists and turns of Protestantism in the late seventeenth century can be a challenge. Partly because of tensions within its diverse doctrinal groupings, but largely because of the pressure put on Protestants by absolutism or the fear of its return, the various denominations splintered even more. It is useful to examine the conservative Protestant version of the Enlightenment that appeared in Britain, the American colonies, the Netherlands, and parts of Germany. Its advocates endorsed religious toleration, at least for Protestants, and were receptive to the new science. They had no time for deism or the bawdy escapades so beloved by the clandestine publishers. Pierre Marteau would not have been welcomed in such a group, but he might have found a home among fringe Protestant sects such as the Mennonites or the Collegiants in the Netherlands or the Quakers in England and America, especially if they could not trace the bawdy works to his print shop. Such fringe sects had roots in the radical Reformation of the sixteenth century where emphasis was laid on the "inner light" and the dictates of individual conscience. All liberal Protestants downplayed the authority of the clergy. Believing but enlightened Protestants might appear to be conservatives in comparison to deists or atheists, but in the eyes of devout Methodists or Catholics, they were on a very slippery slope. Such enlightened men and women could belong to debating societies, support freedom of the theater and press, and yet, as one Unitarian group in Birmingham put

---

[58]See Margaret C. Jacob, *The Newtonians and the English Revolution, 1689–1720* (Ithaca, N.Y.: Cornell University Press, 1976), 214–15; reprinted Gordon and Breach, 1990.

it, also believe that "want of religion is the cause of the increase of criminal offences."[59] Marteau might even have agreed with this judgment: Publishing bawdy literature did not have to mean endorsing it as a way of life. Business can sometimes just be business.

Marteau's books appealed to a wide, if still largely Protestant and continental, audience. Many of his readers may have felt a deep personal anger. Louis XIV, Charles II, and James II, aided and abetted by their loyal clergies, put rage on the Protestant agenda. Imprisonment, or even the threat of it, was a serious matter; the unsanitary conditions alone could kill a person. The threat of prison made people suspicious of all-powerful Catholic clerics and of any legally established church. The only hope for freethinkers and those who had been persecuted was to appeal to the court of *public opinion,* a term being invented as much out of necessity as out of the leisure and relative affluence that undergirded the new sociability.[60] Surely, it began to be argued, somewhere, someone must have figured out how to constitute societies where people could live their beliefs relatively unencumbered.

TRAVEL LITERATURE

Almost simultaneously, Europeans were discovering two new worlds: one in the heavens, as detailed by Copernicus, Galileo, and Newton; the other on the earth, as experienced by merchants, slave traders, and missionaries. Along with books about science, a new genre of literature appeared, one that remains a vital part of publishing and leisure time reading to this day. Travel literature described peoples and places never seen in detail before. Generally, the authors treated these peoples as exotic, inferior, or odd. But some commentators also saw the linkage between travel and empire, and they used the accounts of travel to point out the injustice that could accompany discovery. In complex ways, travel literature fed the impulse toward the light, and it allowed authors to create imaginary worlds where true enlightenment existed naturally. The impulse to create such utopias came from a simple observation: Might not the problem of religious

---

[59]From the periodical *Aris,* 1774–75, cited in John Money, "Joseph Priestley in Cultural Context: Philosophic Spectacle, Popular Belief and Popular Politics in Eighteenth-Century Birmingham," *Enlightenment and Dissent,* no. 7 (1988): 73.

[60]For an extremely early usage of "the public" in French, see Wolf. Tq 54, *L'autheur du Moine secularisé se retractant, et faisant Amande-honoraire* (Cologne: Pierre Martheau [sic], 1686), 6 et seq.

hatred be systemic, lying deep in the European consciousness, and not simply the result of a few bad monarchs and their overweening clergy? It became possible to use the imagination unlocked by travel to suggest new systems of social or political organization and to tell of these fictional worlds as if they were fact.

By 1700, the discontented in Europe had seized on a new way to imagine their world: by invoking an imaginary one. For example, *Le Nouveau Voyage de la terre australe* (A New Voyage to the Land of Australia) told of a land of androgynous (simultaneously possessing the two sexes) Australians. Among them, patriarchs were unknown and the word *father* did not exist. Hence mothers and children were not subordinated to fathers, and "the great empire that man has usurped over woman, has been rather the effect of an odious tyranny and not a legitimate authority."[61] Once tyranny came under attack, its definition could be broadened fairly easily. Whereas some writers saw the high-and-mighty as libertines, others endowed whole peoples with the right to sexual license. An earlier Marteau tract on travel to Africa said that there love was made freely, without shame.[62] In this way, travel literature may have contributed to sexual stereotypes that equated foreigners, or people of color, with libertines, but that was not its primary intention. Instead, many authors used the genre to hold a mirror up to European mores and to declare them in need of reform.

The essence of humankind, according to the Australian philosophe who narrates *Le Nouveau Voyage,* is liberty. That being so, the imaginary Australians had dispensed with the details about God. They were vague about him, believing "that this incomprehensible being is all there is and [give] him all the veneration imaginable." They never talked about religion. The Australian storyteller then turns into a European materialist and explains that the universe is composed of atoms in motion, nothing more. In the journey to an imagined new world, the passage from deism to materialism is virtually effortless.

---

[61]Wolf. Qu N 1013.2, Jacques Sadeur, *Nouveau Voyage de la terre australe* (Paris: Claude Barbin, 1693 [almost certainly a false imprint]), 70–72. Next to the Australian voice in the text someone wrote in "Gabriel de Foigny." This text, written twenty years earlier, is bound with tracts published by "Pierre Marteau," *Voyage d'Espagne* 1667, *Le Relation de l'Estat et Gouvernement d'Espagne* (Cologne: Pierre Marteau, 1667), and Madame d'Aunoy, *Mémoires de la Cour d'Espagne* (The Hague: Moetjens, 1695).

[62]*L'Infidelité convaincu, ou les avantures* [sic] *amoureuses* (Cologne: Pierre Marteau, 1676); bound with *Hattige ou les Amours du Roy de Tamaran nouvelle* (Cologne: Simon l'Africain, 1676 [attributed to Gabriel Brémond]).

In another account of an imaginary journey written around the same time, an anonymous English traveler to an imaginary Tartary discovers "death to be nothing else but a Cessation from the Motions of Action and Thought." The Tartars clearly did not believe in an afterlife. If anyone asked the traveler his religion, he should say, "I am a shepherd."[63]

By the 1720s, French philosophes such as Montesquieu, Voltaire, and Denis Diderot had taken up the genre of travel literature. Given their literary and imaginative skills, they elevated it to a great status. In *Lettres persanes* (Persian Letters, 1721), Montesquieu reversed the genre. His Persians visit Europe and find much that is irrational and comic. Voltaire became an actual traveler, and his *Letters concerning the English Nation,* published in French in 1733 and translated into English in 1734 (see Document 3), depicts England as the utopia sought by reformers—a mere twenty-two miles across the Channel. He instructs them to cross the Channel to find out how to reinvent society and government.

According to the philosophes, foreign places could also permit the bawdy and the outrageous. In *Les Bijoux indiscrets* (The Indiscreet Jewels, 1748), Diderot invented a mythical kingdom in the Congo where despots exploit the land and the people, particularly women. They fight back, and their "jewels" (their private parts) tell about perfidy, pomposity, and lavish waste—all in the service of rulers and their massive egos.[64] This book, among others, briefly landed Diderot in jail.

Undeterred, Diderot wrote another travel book many years later, in 1772. Diderot's *Supplement to Bougainville's* Voyage (see Document 6) owes a debt to countless earlier narrations about distant places. But Diderot put a twist on these generally pro-European accounts: He sought to cast the Europeans as exploiters. The *Supplement* belongs to the literary genre of utopian travel fiction that was invented decades earlier. As we have seen, utopian travel literature was originally intended to teach irreligion and to open up new vistas of disbelief. Diderot used the genre to attack the entire Western imperial enterprise.

---

[63] [M. Heliogenes], *A Voyage into Tartary* (London: T. Hodgkin, 1689), 60. Compare Gordon K. Lewis, *Main Currents in Caribbean Thought: The Historical Evolution of Caribbean Society in Its Ideological Aspects, 1492–1900* (Baltimore: Johns Hopkins University Press, 1983), 87.

[64] A good translation of the text is Denis Diderot, *The Indiscreet Jewels,* trans. Sophie Hawkes (New York: Marsilio, 1993).

Diderot and Lady Mary Wortley Montagu were among the few philosophes who actually traveled to places that may legitimately be described as exotic. He went to Russia, while she visited Turkey. Long before their travels, the descriptions given by the clandestine press laid the groundwork for the philosophes. At the turn of the eighteenth century, the Pierre Marteaus of northern Europe softened readers up for the next outrageous idea: Working in tandem and crossing national borders at will, anonymous readers, travel writers, and clandestine publishers constituted the populist roots of the Enlightenment.

ANGLOPHILIA

Because of the Revolution of 1688–89, parliamentary government and limited religious toleration existed in England, and its example fed the fantasy of enlightened society. Europeans in search of alternatives to absolutism, or simply to princely and court rule, looked to the west, across the English Channel. Figuratively, they fell in love with things English. The French Huguenot refugees were as responsible as anyone for giving England good press, particularly after the Revolution of 1688–89 removed the Catholic and absolutist monarch James II. The French-language journals coming out of the Dutch republic, edited by men such as Jean Le Clerc, praised England for its constitution, for the relative religious toleration accorded all Protestants, and for its advanced science and lively literature. When younger refugees approached their patriarch in Rotterdam, the journalist Pierre Bayle, and explained that they wanted to satisfy their curiosity about science, he urged them to go to England.

Anglophilia was not manufactured entirely out of fantasy. No other European society or government resembled that of the English. They had a monarchy, but after 1688–89 the monarch had to get down in the dirt of party politics and deal with Parliament. The government also was centralized; when it needed to get something done, it had the power to do so. By contrast, the Dutch republic was highly decentralized, and almost nothing could be accomplished on a national level. In addition, the clergy of the established church in England had been largely stripped of their secular authority. After 1689 church courts (except in the case of divorce) became largely irrelevant for non-Anglicans, and in 1695 pre-publication censorship of books disappeared. Anglicans were still the only Christians who could attend

English universities, but within a few decades non-Anglican Protestants built academies that rivaled Oxford and Cambridge, particularly in the study of applied science. The institution of habeas corpus also meant, in effect, that no one could be arbitrarily imprisoned for his or her beliefs and then left there at the will of the magistrate.

In Paris Diderot had been released from prison after his friends talked to anyone and everyone in high places and begged for his release. Similarly, the Dutch clergy could have someone imprisoned for years if they judged him sufficiently subversive. The French clergy could not be tried for crimes in secular courts, acted as censors of all publications, and were socially segregated by estate, thus rendered free from all taxation. Instead, the French church made "donations" to the state. Censorship was widespread in the German cities and states before 1750, and in Italy the clergy saw to it in the 1690s that people were put on trial for believing, in opposition to Scholasticism, that matter is composed of atoms. In Spain, the new science of Copernicus was not taught in the universities until late in the century. It is little wonder, then, that England seemed a more hospitable place for those who appreciated books and ideas and had little time for the pretensions of the clergy and the privileges of legally constituted estates.

In material and technological accomplishments, Britain was increasingly the most modern state in the West. A comparative approach helps illustrate what "modern" may mean in this context. Scientifically minded Dutch and French visitors of the eighteenth century discovered in England a set of interrelated institutions, mores, industrial inventions, and systems of work that were entirely different from what prevailed in their homelands. The division of labor at work sites was in place in Britain by the 1770s. By late in the century, the application of technology to industry, and the political power it promised, stunned a French spy of the 1790s: "[When traveling in England] I saw with dismay that a revolution in the mechanical arts, the real precursor, the true and principal cause of political revolutions was developing in a manner frightening to the whole of Europe, and particularly to France, which would receive the severest blow from it."[65] As early as the 1730s, French ministers of commerce nursed an obsession about English

---

[65]Le Turc to Citoyen, 14 Nivoise An 3 [Dec. 1794], MS U 216, Conservatoire des Arts et Metiers, Paris. Le Turc was born in 1748. In the 1780s, as an engineer and spy, he traveled extensively in England, describing techniques and recruiting workers. I owe this splendid quotation to the kindness of the late J. R. Harris.

competition.[66] Sampling British habits and importing engineers and workers, the French believed, might allow them to catch up.

Decades before British industry was imitated, British social mores captured European interest. The earliest example of self-conscious efforts to imitate British forms of social behavior comes from Freemasonry. As we have seen, the fashionable Masonic lodges that appeared on the continent originated in London around 1700 and migrated to Paris, Rotterdam, and The Hague by 1725. By the second half of the eighteenth century, no European or American city of any size was without a Masonic lodge. Literate men and some women broke bread together, sang, and orated. They gave charity to their lessors and organized concerts and reading groups. The lodges became associated with "meeting upon the level"—a pretense of equality among members from vastly different economic and social backgrounds. So powerful was the *relative* egalitarianism seen in English social circles that as late as 1790, French revolutionaries in Montpellier instituted their patriotic "club" by explaining that "the word *club* in English signifies a coterie where equality comes with membership; the first foundation of a club is thus equality."[67] What began in the 1720s as the leisured sociability of literate elites became on the continent a vehicle for reinventing social, and eventually political, institutions.

Thus, in the eighteenth century, Anglophilia was inextricably linked with the Enlightenment. It signaled an embrace of the modern and an interest in experimental science, economic development, and constitutional, representative government. Of the many voices that sang in praise of England, none was louder than Voltaire's (see Figure 10). His *Letters concerning the English Nation* (see Document 3), an international bestseller, introduced Europeans to everything from Newtonian science to English social mores. In the process, his own reputation as a philosophe was made, and by 1750 his name became a household word, associated with the avant-garde and the outrageous.

---

[66]The phrase belongs to Philippe Minard, "L'inspection des manufactures en France, de Colbert à la Révolution" (doctorat nouveau régime, Université Paris-1 Panthéon-Sorbonne, Dec. 1994), 2:467–75, referring to correspondence from Trudaine to Tolozan. Between 1740 and 1789, the government spent 5.5 million livres on subventions for inventions and 1.3 million in loans for industry. Made available through the kindness of Daniel Roche. On the early development of the division of labor in Britain, see Peter Earle, *The Making of the English Middle Class: Business, Society, Family Life in London, 1660–1730* (London: Methuen, 1989), 18–34.

[67]Meeting of Feb. 12, 1790, MS L 5498, Archives départementales, Hérault. This document was signed by more than two hundred people; within one week, more than three hundred.

Figure 10. Voltaire at Age Twenty-four
Voltaire was often represented by painters and engravers with a wry smile, which seems to suggest that he had solved a puzzle or had some special insight. Or was he just supremely happy in the world, enjoying his role as slayer of superstition, prejudice, and religious piety?
The Van Pelt Library, University of Pennsylvania.

Some philosophes were far more radical in politics and religion than the deist Voltaire, but few could match his wit or writing ability. As the earliest philosophe to acquire a major international reputation, Voltaire cut the template into which others would try to fit their literary prowess. As a senior ambassador of the Enlightenment, he became the darling of the European courts outside Paris. Voltaire's instincts for reform remained confined largely to religious issues. Absolutism seemed an acceptable alternative to social unrest, and he feared the pope and the people more than he feared the bellicosity and imperialism of the absolutist states. He journeyed to Berlin and for a time thought that Frederick the Great would bring the Enlightenment to Germany. But in the end, he abandoned that dream, while still remaining fond of all things English.

MID-CENTURY CRISIS

In the mid-1700s, France invaded the Low Countries, arriving in Brussels in 1746 and in the southern part of the Dutch republic by 1747. The ghost of Louis XIV had returned. Britain, Austria, and Prussia were caught up in this imperialist war, known as the War of Austrian Succession (1740–48), which also reverberated in the American colonies. The French king, Louis XV, had a mixed reputation for competence, and the French army fluctuated between brilliant success and dismal defeat. The king's mistress, Madame de Pompadour, was wildly unpopular, and discontent over the court's antics was palpable. In the corridor from Amsterdam to Paris, conspiracies against the king surfaced, and in Paris the prisons began to be filled with publishers, Freemasons, pornographers, critics, and would-be conspirators. By 1750, the mood within enlightened circles, particularly in France, had shifted. Wit, sarcasm, and bawdiness had given way to a search for new philosophical systems and new ways of organizing knowledge. A consensus was forming—France needed to be reformed—and as a result, Paris soon became the capital of the Enlightenment.

Voltaire had pioneered the way for philosophical commentators, and all sorts of men followed his lead. They flocked to Paris and took up with publishers hungry for a bestseller, even a clandestine one. Into this world came the impecunious sons of provincial artisans, such as Diderot, and foreigners such as Jean-Jacques Rousseau from Geneva. All had to live by their pens, and they became critics of music and art as well as of society and government.

By 1750, the Enlightenment had left its northern roots and become remarkably Parisian. Censorship had begun to lift, and after the war restlessness with the status quo replaced an earlier self-confidence. In addition, the French scientific academies, unlike the colleges run by the clergy, had taken up the new science and begun to make original contributions in Newtonian mathematics and physics. Soon their originality outstripped the more practical-minded English Newtonians.

A remarkable confluence of people and events—war without much glory, the arrogance of the French court, more liberal censors, an excess of hungry publishers, and simply a new generation—made members of the older generation such as Voltaire seem like moderates. The new direction taken by the philosophes and writers after 1750 might best be characterized as radical. They removed God and in his place inserted the blind forces of matter in motion. On both sides of the English Channel materialism became the rage. According to this view, human beings are merely matter in motion—nothing more, nothing less. According to one British radical late in the century, the phenomena of the mind are "to be explained upon principles *purely Physical.*" This view was met with a "fury of opposition."[68] To the philosophes and their followers, the human soul was irrelevant.

Roughly between 1747 and 1758, some of the most audacious works of the Enlightenment rolled off the presses. The first was *L'Homme machine* (Man the Machine, 1747), published in the Dutch republic. The author, Julien La Mettrie, argued that humans can be understood solely as mechanisms devoid of a soul. He had arrived at that conclusion from his reading of Descartes and his study of medicine. So radical and controversial was this view that his Dutch publisher had to disavow La Mettrie's ideas, explaining that he had published them only because of his belief in freedom of the press. Eventually, the publisher even wrote a book attacking La Mettrie, but by then the damage had been done.

Far more entertaining than La Mettrie's hefty tome was an anonymous French pornographic novel, *Thérèse philosophe* (1748), which preaches materialism while detailing erotic exploits. The title character, Thérèse, was invented by a consortium of publishers, distributors, bookbinders, and possibly one writer, the marquis d'Argens, a minor philosophe and Freemason who graced the court in Berlin, where irreligion had become fashionable. In the book, Thérèse runs away from a convent (where she experienced much pleasure) and takes up a life of fornication interspersed with philosophizing. She is a materialist, and a funny one to boot. She explains that human beings are only matter in motion and so should enjoy themselves while they can. Fortunately for the censors, the book was fairly expensive, and hence its influence was limited to the elite. Even so, the group that had sold the book was imprisoned.

The English equivalent to *Thérèse philosophe* was *Fanny Hill; or, Memoirs of a Woman of Pleasure* (1749) by John Cleland. One of the

---

[68] John Thelwall, *Poems Chiefly Written in Retirement: The Fairy of the Lake . . . Effusions of Relative and Social Feeling . . .* (London: R. Phillips and Jas. Ridgeway, 1801), xxiii, describing his views in the 1790s.

Figure 11. Denis Diderot
Diderot looks very solemn here, but he was a man of great sentiment who could weep or laugh at will. His intellectual range was extraordinary: art and theater critic, novelist, letter writer, encyclopedist, satirist, and above all a social being who loved polite society.
The Van Pelt Library, University of Pennsylvania.

most widely read novels in the English language (it has even been made into at least two Hollywood films), *Fanny Hill* contains the stuff of men's dreams: "Oh then! The fiery touch of his fingers determines me, and my fears melting away before the growing intolerable heat, my thighs disclose of themselves and yield all liberty to his hand." Fanny could live with wild abandon; she became matter in motion. Cleland may have intended to mock the new literary genre of the novel of sentiment, at the same time revealing its power. The novel seemed to loosen all literary and philosophical restraint in England.

In this explosive literary atmosphere, fame could be made by wit, not necessarily by birth. Denis Diderot (see Figure 11) may be taken as a model of the self-made man in a world that was still very much dominated by private wealth. Born in 1713, the child of a craftsman, Diderot came from a family notable only for its many priests and nuns. At age thirteen, he thought of becoming a cleric. Possibly with that goal in mind, the precocious, Jesuit-educated youth arrived in Paris, penniless and eager to be further educated. Diderot surfaced in 1748 with a publication about Newtonian mathematics. By then, he was a husband and father, and among his many literary friends was the young Jean-Jacques Rousseau.

Possibly inspired by Voltaire's *Letters concerning the English Nation,* Diderot taught himself English. Hard-pressed for money, he began to make his way as a translator. His early translation (really a paraphrase) of a work on merit and virtue by the third earl of Shaftesbury reveals the enormous impact of English thought and Whig writers on Diderot. From Shaftesbury he learned that human beings are endowed with an inherent moral sense, and when combined with the materialism that he picked up from other texts, this idea set him on a path toward atheism. Using a method of intellectual development closer to eclecticism than to systematic study, Diderot borrowed from the ancients and the moderns. Slowly, in the late 1740s, he migrated from an anticlerical deism to atheism and materialism.

Diderot believed that the soul is a superfluous hypothesis, that matter has existed for all eternity, and that it may even display the capacity for thought and feeling. He would spend much of his later intellectual energy working out the implications of these materialist positions. First, Diderot needed to make a living. Economic necessity and philosophical daring led him to try his hand at the outrageous and the profitable. His deistic and clandestinely published book, *Pensées philosophiques* (Philosophic Thoughts, 1746), contained aphorisms such as "What is God? A question which is asked of children, and which philosophers have a great deal of trouble answering (XXV)." Although the book was condemned by the Parlement of Paris, the main French judicial body, ten editions of it appeared in the eighteenth century. Diderot became emboldened, perhaps overly confident about how easy it was to hide his identity. His anonymous pornographic novel, *Les Bijoux indiscrets*—still his most reprinted and translated work—combined with other scandalous pieces resulted in his being imprisoned in July 1749.

Before 1789, France had no writ of habeas corpus, and Diderot could have stayed in jail for years. But his publishers and friends wrote on his behalf to anyone with any authority or influence. Among those who championed his cause were Voltaire, Fontenelle, Buffon, and d'Alembert. Diderot gave up some information about the clandestine publishing world, and in the autumn he was freed. He never forgot the experience, nor did the other philosophes. Jailing people for their ideas only deepened the crisis.

Diderot's publishers set him to work as editor of one of the largest print ventures ever undertaken—an encyclopedia of all learning. The publication of his *Encyclopédie* in 1751 (see Document 5) was the turning point in the mid-century crisis. It, too, got Diderot and his publishers in trouble with the authorities, who eventually suspended its publication. But at least no one went to jail, although a few of the contributors went to Amsterdam and Berlin to wait out the storm. One turned up as the orator in the main Amsterdam Masonic lodge, and lodges became good places to sell volumes of the controversial encyclopedia.

Encyclopedias had long been the fashion, beginning with Pierre Bayle and his *Dictionnaire* in 1697. The genre sought to capture the new learning while entertaining readers with witty asides and biting criticism of Louis XIV. Bayle's work reflected this style and made clear his dislike of clergy who entertained theocratic fantasies aimed at enhancing their power. With elaborate footnotes and marginalia, encyclopedias teased the censors and amused readers. Edition after edition came out in every European language, but Diderot's was by far the most ambitious. In the end, more than two hundred contributors were enlisted to write articles on everything from the soul to the printing press.

Arranged alphabetically, Diderot's *Encyclopédie* exhibits enlightened and reformist thought. The article on enjoyment heralds the joys of human sexuality without apology. The article on the soul uses footnotes to make clear that it probably does not exist. Written by one of Diderot's friends, the abbé Yvon, who has been described as the metaphysician of the *Encyclopédie,* the article reveals that materialism lay at the heart of the encyclopedia. Diderot himself proclaimed that "it could only belong to a philosophical age to attempt an *encyclopedia....* All things must be examined, debated, investigated without exception and without regard for anyone's feelings.... We must ... overturn the barriers that reason never erected, give back to the arts and sciences the liberty that is so precious to them" (see Document 5). The gauntlet had been thrown down, and everything once deemed sacred was now open to criticism and debate. Of course, with the more than sixty thousand entries, it was possible to learn about everything from the art of printing to textile dyeing, and in the process to ignore the skepticism and materialism at the book's core. But that did not dampen the wrath of the authorities.

When the Paris censors closed down Diderot's enterprise, he moved part of his production to the Netherlands and the firm associated with Marc Michel Rey, who became the greatest publisher of late Enlightenment texts.[69] Gradually, despite fights with the censors, each volume appeared, making its way to Paris and abroad. The foremost historian of Diderot's great venture thinks that about twenty-five thousand copies of the multivolume encyclopedia came into circulation.[70] By today's standard, that is a trivial number. But it is important to remember that dozens of people read each copy, and the effect rippled through Europe and America. One enterprising priest in the Austrian Netherlands, the abbé of the village of Saint-Hubert, even went to Brussels to buy a copy of the encyclopedia because he had heard about its emphasis on new technology. He was eager to find new ways to extract the coal on his land. Diderot was probably of little help to him, but there, in rural Flanders, could be found a copy of the most sensational book of the century.

Farther north in Holland, Jean Rousset de Missy wrote to ask his publisher friend for some of Diderot's exported volumes: "Do you realize that if . . . the 10 enormous volumes of the *Encyclopédie* [had been allowed] it would have led rapidly to Pantheism; the wits, the blue stockings, the light ladies, the dandies, all these Italian, English and French deists and atheists would have been rid of the yoke of religion."[71] That was a lot to ask of one encyclopedia, but Rousset's excitement reflects the mood at mid-century. There would be no turning back from the task of debunking the sacred. Kings, clergy, and their doctrines would be judged in the court of public opinion, no longer able to hide behind the piety of the superstitious.

ROUSSEAU

By the 1750s, Diderot and his friends had become the literary and intellectual sensation of Paris, and into this circle came the brilliant, if neurotic, Jean-Jacques Rousseau (see Figure 12). Within months of his arrival, this citizen of Calvinist Geneva began to find fault with the philosophes. In Rousseau's view, they were active participants in the

---

[69] For evidence of Rey's involvement as discovered in Dutch archives, see Jacob, *The Radical Enlightenment,* 260–62.

[70] Robert Darnton, *The Business of Enlightenment* (Cambridge: Harvard University Press, 1979), 299–323.

[71] Marchand MSS, University of Leiden; cited in Jacob, *The Radical Enlightenment,* 215.

Figure 12. Jean-Jacques Rousseau, 1754
Jean-Jacques Rousseau confronts the viewer with a penetrating stare. He cast
a cold eye on the society he encountered in France, and he longed for the sim-
plicity found only in nature. Almost single-handedly, he put democracy on the
Western intellectual agenda.
The Van Pelt Library, University of Pennsylvania.

social ills that he perceived everywhere. He complained that their
social scene was marred by hypocrisy and remote from the needs of
ordinary people. Salvation lay not in books or private salons, but in
politics, in finding the best government that would create the most
virtuous, the most enlightened, the wisest people. With their ascent

would come economic and social justice. Rousseau believed that materialism and wit were tools fit only for the intelligentsia. The entire people would have to be enlisted in transforming society in the direction of democracy.

Rousseau's break with the enlightened fraternity of the philosophes took many years and many forms. In the 1750s, he was still writing articles on music for Diderot's *Encyclopédie* and torn between wanting fame in the social world of the capital and longing for a simpler life in the country. Rousseau's *Social Contract* (see Document 7) was the most important political work written in the French language in the century. It laid the theoretical foundation for democracy, proposing that human beings left to their own are basically good and that government should be based on a contract with the governed. No more dangerous set of ideas surfaced in the Enlightenment. Out of Rousseau's mid-century crisis came a new diagnosis of what ailed French society — greed, hypocrisy, hierarchy — and hence a new and potent antidote.

Rousseau's impact quickly became international. In his political writings, he offered Europeans a radical alternative: the search for democratic transparency, for the soul-to-soul fraternity made possible only by liberty and equality. As a writer of fiction, he produced bestsellers that taught about sentiment and affection between men and women searching for a restrained freedom from repressive conventions. Written for a general audience, *Julie: ou, la nouvelle Héloïse* (Julie: or, The New Eloise, 1761) and *Émile* (1762) glory in the search for greater honesty between men and women, for the absence of duplicity and formal coldness. Yet both novels advocated self-discipline within the framework of sentiment and a longing to return to nature. As a religious thinker, Rousseau sought to create a benevolent religion of nature guided by Providence. He was imprudent enough to put his creed into print in the same year as *The Social Contract*. His *Profession de foi du vicaire savoyard* (The Profession of Faith of the Savoyard Vicar, 1762) led to his arrest and eventually his flight to England.

Rousseau's works generated ferocious criticism. The Parlement of Paris condemned *The Social Contract* in 1762, and even some of his closest friends backed away from him. He was clearly worried about his freedom and safety, knowing that on many counts his views were incompatible with those of the hierarchical state, either absolutist or oligarchic. Ironically, King George III of England eventually gave Rousseau a pension and helped cushion his exile from France. He was never entirely content anywhere, but he was treated far more cordially in England, the Dutch republic, and his hometown of Geneva than in France.

By the 1790s, political conservatives came to blame Rousseau, and particularly his novels, for fomenting the French Revolution. The British statesman and writer Edmund Burke saw the novels as part of the rot that had undermined all authority. He declared that they were "part of a systematic scheme by Rousseau to destroy all social and family relationships, thus enabling the French revolutionaries to take power."[72] Though in no sense a novel, *The Social Contract* was one of the few books to be condemned in the Dutch republic during the 1780s. By that time, the name Rousseau had come to symbolize subversion. As he put it in 1762, "Henceforth I was to be a fugitive upon the earth."[73]

Rousseau left his most shocking work for posterity. In his *Confessions,* published in 1781, he bared his soul as no one had done before. He tells of his father's anguish at the death of his mother: "I was born, a poor and sickly child, and cost my mother her life. . . . I felt before I thought."[74] He recounted his emotional development, his religious odyssey from believer to benevolent deist, his promiscuity, his abandonment of a child he fathered out of wedlock, and his quarrels with the other philosophes. He sought to bring the reader into the innermost reaches of his mind and emotions.

In *The Confessions,* Rousseau sought to practice transparency — the candor and honesty that he preached. He decried factionalism and accused the encyclopedists of being just as intolerant as the authorities who had tried to silence them. He confided in his reader as he would to an intimate friend. With more than a touch of self-pity, he recounted the suffering he experienced upon the publication of his most famous works: "A cry of execration . . . went up against me throughout Europe, a cry of unparalleled fury."[75] Rousseau saw himself as a partner of the philosophes, although he quarreled with them and disagreed with their facile irreligion. He sought communion with ordinary men and women (the latter he stereotyped as virtuous but without reason); no other philosophe followed such an ambitious dream. The democratic affect that would enable the enlightened to

---

[72]From *The Anti-Jacobin;* cited in G. J. Barker-Benfield, *The Culture of Sensibility: Sex and Society in Eighteenth-Century Britain* (Chicago: University of Chicago Press, 1992), 260.

[73]Jean-Jacques Rousseau, *The Confessions* (London: Viking Penquin, 1953), 548.

[74]Ibid., 19.

[75]Ibid., 545.

see through the disguise created by effete luxury and politeness lay at the heart of Rousseau's radical message.

By the 1780s, it was clear that embracing Rousseau's version of the Enlightenment would mean becoming a new kind of person, ready for the challenge of democracy. At century's end, James Gillray, a famous British caricaturist and opponent of the French Revolution, published an engraving aimed at exposing its abuses. He called it *Exhibition of a Democratic Transparency*.[76] Rousseau probably would have been flattered, even as he rejected Gillray's royalist and conservative message.

THE INTERNATIONAL REPUBLICAN CONVERSATION, 1775–1800

The Social Contract joined an international conversation, much of it quite heated and conducted in French, about the nature of the best form of government—the republic or the possibility of reform promoted by an enlightened "despot." The only alternative to a monarchy—both ancient and modern theorists agreed—was a republic. But how could societies based on hierarchy arrive at the egalitarian meritocracy so essential to republican life? The Enlightenment created "the republic of letters," a mental zone of relative freedom for the talented and the literate. But could such an abstraction become a model for governance, for elections, for guidance given by public discussions and not by the machinations of courtiers? By the last quarter of the eighteenth century, every European and colonial society possessed reformers who were convinced that their governments—whether at home or at the imperial center—were corrupt. That conviction united American, British, Dutch, French, German, and Italian thinkers and reformers.

Rousseau offered one republican model. His debt to classical republican thought was obvious, and he had the benefit of having actually lived in a city-state republic. Yet only occasionally did he offer his birthplace, Geneva, as the actual template. In general, he thought that his home republic had been corrupted by its elite. On the subject of religion, Rousseau was among the more acceptable political theorists among the philosophes. He entertained no hostility toward religion per se. As a result, Catholics and Protestants all over Europe imagined that a constitutional state modeled on Rousseau's ideas

[76]Prints 1180.1104 (1), BM 9369, Metropolitan Museum of Art.

would not be hostile to religion.[77] Arguably, Rousseau saved the republican ideal by detaching it from impiety and atheism.

Inspired by Rousseau, the Italian reformers Cosimo Amidei and Carlantonio Pilati came to see that reform had to take place throughout Europe; it was not simply an Italian problem. Rousseau's emphasis on purity and virtue, on the goodness of man, also resonated well with the liberal Protestantism found throughout the Western world. Thomas Jefferson in Virginia and Joseph Priestley in England found worth in this message. It also appealed to Freemasons, who had long used republican language to describe the constitutionally imposed discipline and egalitarian ideals of their lodges. As a Mason in Amsterdam put it in 1766, "The main reason why freemasonry was so well received among the enlightened: the natural state of humanity is therein restored perfectly, no disguise will be tolerated."[78] Republics required radical experimentation in frank and open conversation.

Certainly, the writings of Rousseau inspired men to embrace the once unthinkable. One example was the abbé de Mably, who had seen the workings of the French state firsthand and had grown disillusioned. Mably began his public life as an apologist for the Bourbon monarchy, serving in the 1740s as a diplomat during the War of Austrian Succession. By 1758, he was willing to contemplate violent revolution as the only remedy for the evils of French government and society. Inspired by his family friend Rousseau, he had entered the ranks of the philosophes in Paris. But unlike Rousseau, Mably found the salon liberating and a place for republican discussion. Disillusionment with the absolutist state left Mably with one rational alternative, the classical republic. Based on Rousseau and his reading of the ancients and the great English republicans of the seventeenth century, he created his own version of a radically democratic future. As a result, he landed in the middle of a republican political conversation to which he made major contributions. It would end only in the 1790s, when the French Revolution and international war made republics and their survival real—no longer the stuff of philosophical speculation, but the burning issue of the day.[79]

---

[77] See Dale K. Van Kley, *The Religious Origins of the French Revolution: From Calvin to the Civil Constitution, 1560–1791* (New Haven, Conn.: Yale University Press, 1996), 296–97.

[78] MS 41:8, f. 26, Library of the Grand Lodge, The Hague.

[79] See Johnson Kent Wright, *A Classical Republican in Eighteenth-Century France: The Political Thought of Mably* (Stanford, Calif.: Stanford University Press, 1997).

By the 1770s, the political stakes for European reformers were rising. In France, the parlements, courts with quasi-legislative power, rose in rebellion and prevented fiscal reform. This revealed the impotence of the monarchy to effect meaningful reform. In Sweden, royal authority was reasserted against the claims of an English-style parliament. The Polish commonwealth was dismantled by its imperialist neighbors, and the American colonies rose in rebellion against Britain. Everything political took on a new urgency. Letters and people traversed the Atlantic and the Channel with reports of defeats and victories.

In the German-speaking lands, absolutist princes ruled in nearly every principality, with the exception of a few free cities. Yet in both Germany and Austria, by the last quarter of the eighteenth century, the new public sphere was plainly visible. Journals, books, and newspapers, though censored, flourished. Probably close to three hundred Masonic lodges had sprung up, with a lodge found in almost every medium-size town.[80] Although the lodges often enjoyed the sponsorship of kings such as Frederick the Great of Prussia, they were controversial, especially in Catholic areas.

The association of Freemasonry with the absolutist monarchy of Frederick did not, however, make the lodges off-limits to enlightened intellectuals such as the young poet Goethe, the renegade Lutheran Lessing, and the secular but devout Jew Mendelssohn. Mendelssohn became one of the most brilliant thinkers of the age, a dedicated advocate of toleration and freedom of conscience. The relative acceptance that he found in the lodges may have partly inspired his commitment to absolute toleration for all, a major theme of his *Jerusalem: Or on Religious Power and Judaism* (see Document 9). It grappled with the central problem faced by any modern society: how to accept differences, even to allow people who do not accept the modern to live peacefully and freely. Mendelssohn had become deeply cosmopolitan, but the world that he loved also contained men and women who lived for the Sabbath and not for the salon. The Masonic lodge was not for everyone, but Mendelssohn wanted to take the lessons he learned there about acceptance and translate them into a universal code for religious freedom.

Many others in Germany found the goals of Freemasonry inspirational but limited. By the 1780s, German Freemasonry had spawned a radical offshoot, the Illuminati. Founded by Adam Weishaupt, a

---

[80] See Richard van Dülmen, *The Society of the Enlightenment: The Rise of the Middle Class and Enlightenment Culture in Germany,* trans. Anthony Williams (London: Polity Press, 1992).

Figure 13. Immanuel Kant
Kant was one of the most important philosophers in the West during the late 1700s. His writings remain basic to the study of Western philosophy in universities today. He gave us one definition of the Enlightenment.
The Van Pelt Library, University of Pennsylvania.

twenty-eight-year-old professor, in 1776, the League of the Illuminati was strongest in Munich. Its leaders wanted to use the league to reform Freemasonry and then to extend its influence throughout Germany. At the height of its fame, the league had no more than six hundred members, of which the majority were court and administrative officials, clergy, and military officers. They swore an oath to vague statutes such as "The order of the day is to put an end to the machinations of the purveyors of injustice."[81] They were deeply impressed by the American Revolution and probably favored the institution of republican values if not actual governments.

The danger the Illuminati allegedly posed enabled the authorities in every European country to conjure up fear of subversion and to crack down on the supporters of the Enlightenment. Its internationalism became deeply threatening. In the Austrian kingdom, the supposedly enlightened Emperor Joseph II closed down all but one Masonic lodge in every town, and the surviving one had to be approved by the Grand Lodge in Vienna or Brussels. In Germany, men were arrested just on the suspicion of membership in the Illuminati.

The controversy around the Illuminati, coupled with the writings of Lessing, provided the context within which Immanuel Kant (see Figure 13) cautiously tried to define the Enlightenment (see Document 8). In 1783, the newspaper *Berlinische Monatsschrift* asked, "What is enlightenment?" Kant's answer emerged as the most famous response to the newspaper's query. He knew that the Enlightenment's survival in the German-speaking lands was fragile at best. It flourished only where the local princes endorsed its goals. Hence the text that Kant produced was among the most timid of the 1780s. Elsewhere, followers of Rousseau called for democracy; abolitionists attacked slavery. Kant told his readers to be peaceful and obedient during the day and to read and think in privacy at night.

Kant's daring may seem tame—but understandable—by comparison to what was being written and said in the Atlantic world of the 1780s and 1790s. The Enlightenment returned to England, the land of its birth, largely as a result of the American Revolution. The cause of heterodoxy and reform was taken up by men with a dissenting background, such as the Unitarian Joseph Priestley. Dissenters (non-Anglican Protestants) tended to support the American Revolution, just as in the 1760s they had supported the parliamentary rebel John Wilkes. Just when the Church of England thought that it had put the twin genies of radicalism and heresy back in the bottle, "the infidel spirit of the times," as the dean of Canterbury put it, wafted out again.[82]

---

[81]See S. Abbott, ed., *Fictions of Freemasonry: Freemasonry and the German Novel* (Detroit: Wayne State University Press, 1991); and M. Neugebauer-Wölk, *Esoterische Bünde und Bürgerliche Gesellschaft: Entwicklungslinien zur modernen Welt im Geheimbundwesen des 18. Jahrhunderts* (Wolfenbüttel: Lessing Academie, 1995).

[82]Nigel Aston, "Horne and Heterodoxy: The Defence of Anglican Beliefs in the Late Enlightenment," *English Historical Review,* 108 (1993): 895–919.

No English traveler became more internationally famous than the radical advocate of republicanism Thomas Paine. Paine's writing activities, begun in Philadelphia, made him after 1789 a bridge between the American revolutionaries, their French successors, and British supporters. He told George Washington that "a share in two revolutions is living to some purpose."[83] Between 1775, the beginning of the serious troubles in the colonies, and September 1793, the commencement of the Terror in France, the enthusiasm for republicanism in enlightened circles was endemic. Hundreds of thousands of Paine's *Common Sense* (1776) and *Rights of Man* (1791–92) were sold. In Derbyshire, in the north of England, factory owners distributed copies to their workers. Only after the French Revolution turned violent in 1793–94 did the propertied and highly educated classes gradually realize that democracy in the hands of the untutored and the propertyless could spell disaster.

Decades before the conservative reaction of the 1790s in Britain, parliamentary reform (making the House of Commons more representative) had preoccupied sections of the urban middle class. In this period, Britain spawned radical agitators intent on broadening liberty and the franchise. In the throes of Anglophilia, a young visiting Frenchman, Jean-Paul Marat, decided to see for himself how "liberty" fared in the land of its birth. Marat witnessed political agitation in England firsthand during the "Wilkes and Liberty" movement of the 1760s and early 1770s. Wilkes and his followers had demanded reforms in the election system, but Wilkes was imprisoned on charges that his supporters claimed to have been fabricated. Marat turned to Rousseau to find out why liberty, even in Britain, had so many enemies. Marat produced a devastating attack on the power of princes, and on oppression and slavery: *Chains of Slavery* (1774).[84] Before his return to France, where he would be murdered during the Revolution, the ever-traveling Marat spent time in Amsterdam. We know this because he signed the visitors' book of the local Masonic lodge in 1774.[85]

Marat, and later Thomas Paine, captured the mood of British liberals and radicals. By the 1780s, they had made reform, particularly the abolition of the African slave trade, a lively subject for debate. In the

---

[83] Quoted in John Keane, *Tom Paine: A Political Life* (New York: Little, Brown, 1995), 283.

[84] See Clifford D. Conner, *Jean Paul Marat: Scientist and Revolutionary* (Atlantic Highlands, N.J.: Humanities Press, 1997), 23–24.

[85] MS 41:6, ff. 161, Grand Lodge of the Netherlands, The Hague; from the records of *La Bien Aimée*.

antislavery movement, ideas about human rights associated with the Enlightenment were augmented by a religious fervor, especially among Quakers and Methodists.[86] There was no shortage of published accounts of the slave trade and the brutality of the plantation system. Some were written by people who had been slaves. Thus, while the international republican conversation focused on concrete domestic issues such as the nature of parliamentary representation, it also reflected on global issues such as the human misery inflicted by European imperial expansion.

SLAVERY, IMPERIALISM, AND THE FRENCH REVOLUTION

In France, reading and travel had convinced Denis Diderot of the injustice and corruption of the colonial system in which his country was an active participant. He deplored European colonialism, and in a silent collaboration with the abbé Raynal, a bestseller was born: *Histoire philosophique et politique des établissements et du commerce des Européens dans les deux Indes* (Philosophical and Political History of the European Establishments and Trade in the Two Indies), first published in 1770. Along with works by Marat and others, the book addressed the racism endemic in European imperialism. Diderot was moving toward a belief in democracy for all the peoples of the world. Although their friendship had ended bitterly many decades earlier, Diderot and Rousseau had begun to walk the same path in their political theory.

By the 1780s, the new American republic had joined the international conversation at the heart of the Enlightenment. One northern American state after the other abolished slavery, turning their backs on centuries of this Western (and non-Western) practice. The move inspired European liberals. In Belfast, the republican newspaper *Northern Star* denounced the 1791 attack by a pro-king and pro-church mob on Joseph Priestley in Birmingham. Irish radicals sought to bring Protestants and Catholics together in opposition to British domination over Ireland. In the minds of these radicals, Negro slavery stood as yet another example of the imperial oppression that Priestley had experienced.[87] For a brief moment from Philadelphia to Berlin, it seemed as

---

[86]Michael Turner, "The Limits of Abolition: Government, Saints and the 'African Question,' c. 1780–1820," *English Historical Review,* 112 (1997): 319–57.

[87]"The Negroe's Complaint" (*Belfast*) *Northern Star,* Apr. 25, 1792.

if a consensus had formed around a set of universal, inalienable human rights on which all enlightened people could agree.

Not all the philosophes had a noble record on the subject of slavery, however. When British and French radicals of the 1790s emigrated to America, quite a few became slave owners. In the French Caribbean, writers of mixed racial ancestry such as Moreau de Saint-Méry, who held high office in the colonies, knew enough about the Enlightenment that they could identify with its scientific spirit and detail the abuses of the mercantilist and slave system. But they never completely denounced slavery and its injustices. In the end, they offered more criticisms of the French monarchy than they did of the planters.[88] A Spanish Jesuit, Francisco Javier Clavigero, attempted to write the history of Mexico and the enslavement of its people from an enlightened perspective. His *Historia Antigua de México* (1781–82) addressed Mexican civilization and sought to be true to it. Yet in the end, Clavigero could not embrace the moral vision of the Enlightenment. He argued that the Mexicans must accept their conquest and virtual enslavement as a punishment for their sins.[89]

Despite some caveats and backsliding, slavery came to the top of the international Enlightenment agenda by the 1780s. There was good reason for this late-century disaffection: the hardening of slave laws and institutions, particularly in the British and French slave colonies. Plantation life had become socially respectable for the often-absent owners who reaped its benefits. In the British West Indies, killing a slave was punishable only by a fine. In the French colonies, the repressive Code Noir (Black Code) had been promulgated by Louis XIV in 1685, the same year he began the persecution of French Protestants. During the eighteenth century, the situation of slaves in the French colonies had actually worsened, as more and more plantations were established and the black population vastly outnumbered the white overseers, who ruled with increasing harshness. Slavery, as well as racial stereotyping, had plenty of apologists.[90] Yet remarkably, given the bias against Africans found in much of the travel literature, around 1780 an emotional sea change occurred in literate European circles.

---

[88] Lewis, *Caribbean Thought,* 131–33.

[89] See Fernando Cervantes, *The Devil in the New World: The Impact of Diabolism in New Spain* (New Haven, Conn.: Yale University Press 1994), 153–54.

[90] E. V. Goveia, *The West Indian Slave Laws of the 18th Century* (London: Caribbean Universities Press, 1970), 20–21, 44–45.

No entirely adequate account has been offered for the emotional shift against slavery, but one piece in the puzzle must be the writings and testimonies given by blacks themselves. Men such as Ignatius Sancho and Olaudah Equiano, both freed slaves who made their way to England, vigorously opposed the slave system. Their voices were sorely needed, because many abolitionists held negative stereotypes of blacks. Abolitionists and freed slaves, inspired by the American and French revolutions, launched a moral crusade that slowly led to victory. At the same time, disillusionment with the amateurish and stereotypical quality of travel literature caused reformers to demand a more exacting and scientific account of the world's peoples.[91] Some of the new accounts hardened racial categories. Others, like Diderot's *Supplement to Bougainville's* Voyage (see Document 6), were written from the inside, based on the imagined values and assumptions of distant and foreign peoples.

By 1789, political events in Europe and globally made democratic rights a burning issue. As a British radical of the 1790s put it, "A new field of enquiry . . . was opened by the French Revolution," and in the crucible it heated, he found his "social heart."[92] More than any other event in Western history, the French Revolution galvanized international opinion against slavery and around the issue of universal human rights.[93] Street-corner lecturers harangued London and provincial audiences on the evils of the slave trade, and Quakers and Methodists prayed in their chapels for the victims of enslavement. The English writer Helen Maria Williams wrote anxiously from Paris amid the French Revolution asking whether the rumor that Parliament would finally vote against the slave trade was true.[94]

---

[91] P. J. Marshall and Glyndwr Williams, *The Great Map of Mankind: Perceptions of New Worlds in the Age of Enlightenment* (Cambridge: Harvard University Press, 1982), 300–301.

[92] Thelwall, *Poems Chiefly Written in Retirement,* xxiv.

[93] See Lynn Hunt, ed., *The French Revolution and Human Rights: A Brief Documentary History* (Boston: Bedford Books, 1996). Compare Michael Durey, *Transatlantic Radicals and the Early American Republic* (Lawrence: University of Kansas Press, 1997), 282–85.

[94] Williams to Mrs. Piozzi, Feb. 26, 1792, MS 570, John Rylands Library, Manchester: "Respecting the rights of man in Europe we shall always agree in wishing that a portion of those same rights were extended to Africa." See also June 13, 1792: "I read a confused account in a French paper lately that something had been done or at least attempted in our House of Commons in favor of the poor negroes—do my dear madam, tell me if our noble senators intend in this session of Parliament to wipe out the stains of the last."

Historians have long debated the exact relationship between the Enlightenment and the French Revolution. In the minds of contemporaries, the Enlightenment laid the groundwork for the Revolution's most important ideas and agendas. Within two years of its outbreak in 1789, it sparked radical movements in Britain, Haiti, and finally Ireland and Egypt. The Haitian slave revolt forced the French revolutionaries back in Paris to confront the meaning of the principles they had decreed. In 1794, the National Assembly abolished slavery and the slave trade in the French colonies, although Napoleon later reinstituted it. Britain finally abolished slavery in its colonies in 1833, and a new revolution in France in 1848 outlawed slavery forever.

THE LEGACY OF THE ENLIGHTENMENT

The democratic revolutions that began in America in 1776 and continued in Amsterdam, Brussels, and most spectacularly Paris in the late 1780s put every Western government on the defensive. Repression and censorship returned with a vengeance and brought the Enlightenment to a close. In France, the Revolution itself turned into "scenes of tumult and of death . . . a dark stain on the annals of the revolution," as Helen Maria Williams put it.[95] The Terror began in 1793, and even letter writing became dangerous. When it and the ensuing war with England were over, the days of the Enlightenment seemed halcyon—a war of words, a battle of books—in comparison with the reality of trying to live in a republic and keep faith with its principles.

British opponents of the Enlightenment could say "I told you so." The French Revolution had been the work of atheists, and a new generation of radicals, they said, reintroduced "the light of unbelief [that] first dawned upon this favored island by Shaftesbury, Toland, & Tindal."[96] In Britain the 1790s seemed to repeat the cultural wars between freethinkers and the church fought during the 1690s, but with one difference. As a result of the Enlightenment and the revolutions, reform, democracy, and republicanism had been placed irrevocably on the Western agenda. The backlash against the Enlightenment testifies to the enormous change in Western values witnessed in the eighteenth century.

[95] Ibid. See letters of Aug. 18, 1794, and Sept. 4, 1792, about the September massacres.
[96] [A. Scott], *Plain Reasons for Adopting the Plan of the Societies Calling Themselves the Friends of the People . . .* (Edinburgh, 1793); cited in George Claeys, ed., *Political Writings of the 1790s* (London: William Pickering, 1995), 8:24.

After 1800, every opponent of the French Revolution and its democratic implications blamed the Enlightenment for the modern egalitarian disease. Nineteenth-century conservatives vastly exaggerated both the power and the democratic impulses of the philosophes and the pundits. Yet the Enlightenment's opponents had been right about the overall tendency of its reformers and radicals: They started by criticizing the abuses of theocratic clergy and absolutist kings, and then they did not know where to stop.

Contemporaries who witnessed the democratic revolutions also linked them to enlightened beliefs. James Watt Jr., the radical son of the famous perfector of the steam engine, went to Paris in 1792. Tying the warp of the Enlightenment to the woof of Revolution, he wrote the following to his perplexed father in Birmingham:

> My hatred is not against individual kings, but against the system of Royalty, for I think kings in general far less blameable than the people that submit to them. The abolition of that source of all our evils in this country is a more deadly blow to the prejudices of mankind, than would be the destruction of all the monarchs of Europe. . . . The principles upon which their thrones were founded are now disavowed by an enlightened age and mankind awakened from their lethargy are everywhere shaking off a system founded upon force and Priestcraft.

The young Watt had cast his lot with the far left of the Revolution, the Jacobins, and in his letters home, he took to lecturing his father on the evils of monarchy and on his hatred for the "crimes of tyrants."[97] The elder Watt should not have been so perplexed. He and his Unitarian friends in the famous Lunar Society of Birmingham were distributing literature against slavery and had agitated on behalf of the American revolutionaries.

Typical among the children of the enlightened, young Watt's reading had been laden with scientific works as well as those by the philosophes. In addition, he, like so many followers of enlightened thought in England, had joined one of the many "corresponding societies" that sprang up after 1789. These societies sought to offer moral support to the revolutionaries in Paris and to import their radical spirit. Young Watt and his friends simply took the liberal politics and sociability associated with groups founded by his father like the Lunar

---

[97]James Watt Jr. to James Watt Sr., Oct. 17, 1792, James Watt Papers, Birmingham City Library, W/6, written from Nantes. See Peter M. Jones, "Living the Enlightenment and the French Revolution: James Watt, Matthew Boulton, and Their Sons," *Historical Journal,* 42, no. 1 (1999): 157–82.

Society and pushed them one step further. During the 1790s, the corresponding societies in England and the Jacobin clubs in France built ties on the foundations of civic and social life created in the eighteenth century. By 1794, British authorities had begun to imprison and try radicals for treason. When the situation became too threatening and the Sedition Act of 1798 made any meeting dangerous, British and Irish radicals fled to Boston, Philadelphia, and New York and rallied around the presidential candidacy of Thomas Jefferson, merging enlightened ideals into democratic agitation.

Late in the eighteenth century, new forms of civil society arose in almost every major town from London to Amsterdam to Berlin. Hundreds of new societies, fraternities, clubs, salons, *museés* (private academies), lending libraries, and scientific organizations appeared. They made Enlightenment ideals concrete. The groups sprang up in places where reformist and radical ideas had taken root. As early as 1750 a reading group consisting of deists and freethinkers met privately in Worcester, Massachusetts, and counted among its members the young John Adams (later to become the second president of the United States).[98] If one thread united most of these disparate, often informal organizations, it was their interest in the practical, in progress and self-improvement. The Enlightenment did not so much end as it became transformed into reformist agitation and utilitarian practices.

Most typical were the Dutch societies of "usefulness," each called *Het Nut.* They channeled discontent, inspired charitable efforts, built libraries, sponsored lectures, published weekly journals, and in general cast a cold eye on the Dutch republic. Baron van der Capellen emerged as a leader among the Dutch critics of the chief government officer, or stadtholder. In the early 1780s, a misguided war with Britain over commercial rights exposed the sad condition of the republic's army and navy. Van der Capellen seized on these failings and the need for representative institutions. The Estates General that met in The Hague represented each province, not the general population, and was dominated by old families drawn from local elites. Van der Capellen privately wrote to the sympathetic Benjamin Franklin about voting rights for all men of property. In an address titled *To the Netherlands People* (1781), which was soon translated into French, German, and

---

[98] C. Bradley Thompson, "Young John Adams and the New Philosophic Rationalism," *William and Mary Quarterly,* 55 (April 1998): 263–68.

English, Van der Capellen proclaimed himself the prophet who would lead his people out of bondage and "make them free."[99] Predictably, the new societies to promote usefulness took up Van der Capellen's call, as did the leading Masonic lodge of Amsterdam. When the French revolutionary army arrived in Amsterdam in 1795, members of the lodge celebrated their French brothers. At the same time, the French set up a national assembly in Amsterdam, which gratefully accepted a copy of Thomas Paine's *Age of Reason* (1794) sent by the author himself.

With the Dutch societies and their international ties in mind, it is possible to see why the Illuminati in Munich had aroused fear throughout the Western world. People in groups, meeting regularly to discuss public affairs, possessed the capacity to become political. But politics was supposed to be the province of blood and birth. The "public" had been conjured into rhetorical existence by the earlier "republic of letters." Late in the century, it turned concrete, embodied in hundreds of these small societies. By the 1780s, the Enlightenment had moved out of the comfortable milieu of salons, lodges, and coffeehouses and into new social and domestic spaces. True to its populist roots, it had become further democratized.

Voltaire almost certainly would not have approved of this change, but Rousseau might have. Mably would have stood up and cheered. Even the German philosopher Kant broke his daily routine when news of the uprising in Paris reached him in 1789. In the final phase of the Enlightenment, theorists indebted to its materialist tradition spelled out the implications of an ethical system derived solely from a naturalistic account of the human condition. An English writer who gloried in the French Revolution wrote that the "Religion of Nature" would encourage virtue among liberated people, who, "individually and socially, must be free to act conscientiously" and not simply expected to obey the law, regardless of its ethical flaws.[100] In France, the chemist Jean Chaptal told the revolutionary club in Montpellier of which he was president that religious fanaticism, superstition, and intolerance had been erased by the vigilance of French citizens.[101] Theoretically endowed with full civil and legal rights, the individual

[99] *Brieven van . . . van der Capellen,* 64.
[100] *The Moral World Display'd: An Expository Sequel to the Moral State of Nations* (London: J. Ridgway, 1791), 2:141–42. The copy at the Bancroft Library, University of California at Berkeley, has written on the title page "by John Stewart."
[101] Meeting of July 16, 1790, MS L 5498, Archives départmentales, Hérault.

had come to exist, if only in the dreams of visionaries. The Enlightenment had outgrown its origins as an international Protestant movement against religious persecution. It had reached maturity by turning the Euro-American age, at home and briefly in the slave colonies, into "the century of reformation."[102]

A NOTE ABOUT THE TEXT

In the case of those documents written originally in English—Locke's *Some Thoughts concerning Education* and Lady Mary Wortley Montagu's letters—wherever possible, original spellings and punctuation of texts and footnotes have been preserved. Modern translations from the original French or German have been provided for the remaining documents.

---

[102]See the magisterial work of Franco Venturi, *The End of the Old Regime in Europe,* vols. 1–3 (Princeton, N.J.: Princeton University Press, 1989–91). Compare John Robertson, "Franco Venturi's Enlightenment," *Past and Present,* no. 137 (1992): 181–206.

PART TWO

The Documents

1

JOHN LOCKE

Some Thoughts concerning Education

1693

Born in 1632, John Locke lived through the trauma of the English civil wars of the 1640s, the beheading of King Charles I in 1649, the dislocation of the 1650s when England became a republic, and finally the restoration of the church and the monarchy in the 1660s. Like Robert Boyle, Isaac Newton, and many others of his generation, Locke turned to the study of nature, specifically in his case medicine. Being a doctor opened up other possibilities, such as becoming a private tutor in the homes of the English aristocracy. In the 1670s, Locke resided in the home of the first earl of Shaftesbury and tutored his grandson. The first earl became one of the founders of the Whig party; his grandson emerged as a leading figure in the new international cultural movement identifiable by the first decade of the eighteenth century: the Enlightenment.

As a tutor, Locke sought the latest, most advanced information, especially in technical and scientific matters. He was never afraid to simplify,

The Works of John Locke (London: Thomas Davison Publishers, 1823), 9: 1–205.

*to break things down into their component parts, and he spoke plainly
and clearly. All these qualities are evident in his famous work partially
reprinted here. Locke believed that observation and experience lie at the
heart of the educational process and that tutors and lecturers need to
have direct contact with their pupils. This treatise on education originated with a series of letters Locke wrote to his friend Edward Clarke during the 1680s while Locke was in exile in the Dutch republic. Clarke was
worried about his son's education, and Locke undertook to advise him.*

§ 1. …I confess, there are some men's constitutions of body and
mind so vigorous, and well framed by nature, that they need not much
assistance from others; but, by strength of their natural genius, they
are, from their cradles, carried towards what is excellent; and, by the
privilege of their happy constitutions, are able to do wonders. But
examples of this kind are but few; and I think I may say, that, of all the
men we meet with, nine parts of ten are what they are, good or evil,
useful or not, by their education. It is that which makes the great difference in mankind. …

§ 4. The consideration I shall here have, of health, shall be, not
what a physician ought to do, with a sick or crazy child; but what the
parents, without the help of physic,* should do for the preservation
and improvement of an healthy, or, at least, not sickly constitution, in
their children: and this perhaps might be all despatched in this one
short rule, viz. that gentlemen should use their children as the honest
farmers and substantial yeomen do theirs. But because the mothers,
possibly, may think this a little too hard, and the fathers, too short, I
shall explain myself more particularly; only laying down this, as a general and certain observation for the women to consider, viz. that most
children's constitutions are either spoiled, or at least harmed, by cock-
ering† and tenderness. …

§ 9. Another thing, that is of great advantage to every one's health,
but especially children's, is to be much in the open air, and very little,
as may be, by the fire, even in winter. By this he will accustom himself
also to heat and cold, shine and rain; all which if a man's body will not
endure, it will serve him to very little purpose in this world: and when
he is grown up, it is too late to begin to use him to it: it must be got

*medicine
†spoiling

early and by degrees. Thus the body may be brought to bear almost any thing. If I should advise him to play in the wind and sun without a hat, I doubt whether it could be borne. There would a thousand objections be made against it, which at last would amount to no more, in truth, than being sunburnt. And if my young master to be kept always in the shade, and never exposed to the sun and wind, for fear of his complexion, it may be a good way to make him a beau, but not a man of business. And although greater regard be had to beauty in the daughters, yet I will take the liberty to say, that the more they are in the air, without prejudice to their faces, the stronger and healthier they will be; and the nearer they come to the hardships of their brothers in their education, the greater advantage will they receive from it, all the remaining part of their lives. . . .

§ 11. One thing the mention of the girls brings into my mind, which must not be forgot; and that is, that your son's clothes be never made strait, especially about the breast. Let nature have scope to fashion the body as she thinks best. She works of herself a great deal better and exacter than we can direct her. And if women were themselves to frame the bodies of their children in their wombs, as they often endeavour to mend their shapes when they are out, we should as certainly have no perfect children born, as we have few well-shaped, that are straitlaced, or much tampered with. This consideration should methinks keep busy people (I will not say ignorant nurses and boddicemakers) from meddling in a matter they understand not; and they should be afraid to put nature out of her way, in fashioning the parts, when they know not how the least and meanest is made. And yet I have seen so many instances of children receiving great harm from strait lacing, that I cannot but conclude, there are other creatures, as well as monkeys, who, little wiser than they, destroy their young ones by senseless fondness, and too much embracing.

§ 12. Narrow breasts, short and stinking breath, ill lungs, and crookedness, are the natural and almost constant effects of hard boddice, and clothes that pinch. That way of making slender waists, and fine shapes, serves but the more effectually to spoil them. Nor can there, indeed, but be disproportion in the parts, when the nourishment, prepared in the several offices of the body, cannot be distributed, as nature designs. And therefore, what wonder is it, if, it being where it can, or some part not so braced, it often makes a shoulder, or a hip, higher or bigger than its just proportion? It is generally known, that the women of China, (imagining I know not what kind of beauty in it) by bracing and binding them hard from their infancy, have very little feet. I saw lately a pair of China shoes, which I was told were for a grown woman; they were so exceedingly disproportioned to the feet of one of the same age amongst us, that they would scarce have been big enough for one of our little girls. Besides this, it is observed, that their women are also very little, and short-lived; whereas the men are of the ordinary stature of other men, and live to a proportionable age. These defects in the female sex of that country are by some imputed to the unreasonable binding of their feet; whereby the free circulation of the blood is hindered, and the growth and health of the whole body suffers. And how often do we see, that some small part of the foot being injured, by a wrench or a blow, the whole leg or thigh thereby loses its strength and nourishment, and dwindles away! How much greater inconveniences may we expect, when the thorax, wherein is placed the heart and seat of life, is unnaturally compressed, and hindred from its due expansion!

§ 13. As for his diet, it ought to be very plain and simple; and, if I might advise, flesh should be forborn as long as he is in coats,* or at least, till he is two or three years old. But whatever advantage this may be, to his present and future health and strength, I fear it will hardly be consented to, by parents, misled by the custom of eating too much flesh themselves; who will be apt to think their children, as they do themselves, in danger to be starved, if they have not flesh, at least twice a day. This I am sure, children would breed their teeth with much less danger, be freer from diseases, whilst they were little, and lay the foundations of an healthy and strong constitution much surer, if they were not crammed so much as they are, by fond mothers and foolish servants, and were kept wholly from flesh, the first three or four years of their lives. . . .

§ 30. And thus I have done with what concerns the body and health, which reduces itself to these few and easily observable rules. Plenty of open air, exercise, and sleep; plain diet, no wine or strong drink, and very little or no physic; not too warm and strait clothing; especially the head and feet kept cold, and the feet often used to cold water and exposed to wet.

§ 31. Due care being had to keep the body in strength and vigour, so that it may be able to obey and execute the orders of the mind; the

---

*the long coat that very young boys wore

next and principal business is, to set the mind right, that on all occasions it may be disposed to consent to nothing but what may be suitable to the dignity and excellency of a rational creature. . . .

§ 38. It seems plain to me, that the principle of all virtue and excellency lies in a power of denying ourselves the satisfaction of our own desires, where reason does not authorize them. This power is to be got and improved by custom, made easy and familiar by an early practice. If therefore I might be heard, I would advise, that, contrary to the ordinary way, children should be used to submit their desires, and go without their longings, even from their very cradles. The very first thing they should learn to know, should be, that they were not to have any thing, because it pleased them, but because it was thought fit for them. If things suitable to their wants were supplied to them, so that they were never suffered to have what they once cried for, they would learn to be content without it; would never with bawling and peevishness contend for mastery; nor be half so uneasy to themselves and others as they are, because from the first beginning they are not thus handled. If they were never suffered to obtain their desire by the impatience they expressed for it, they would no more cry for other things than they do for the moon.

§ 39. I say not this as if children were not to be indulged in any thing, or that I expected they should, in hanging-sleeves,* have the reason and conduct of counsellors. I consider them as children, who must be tenderly used, who must play, and have play things. That which I mean is, that whenever they craved what was not fit for them to have, or do, they should not be permitted it, because they were little and desired it: nay, whatever they were importunate for, they should be sure, for that very reason, to be denied.

§ 40. Those therefore that intend ever to govern their children, should begin it whilst they are very little; and look that they perfectly comply with the will of their parents. Would you have your son obedient to you, when past a child? Be sure then to establish the authority of a father, as soon as he is capable of submission, and can understand in whose power he is. If you would have him stand in awe of you, imprint it in his infancy; and, as he approaches more to a man, admit him nearer to your familiarity: so shall you have him your obedient subject (as is fit) whilst he is a child, and your affectionate friend

---

*presumably some kind of garment that only very small children wore

when he is a man. For methinks they mightily misplace the treatment due to their children, who are indulgent and familiar when they are little, but severe to them, and keep them at a distance, when they are grown up. For liberty and indulgence can do no good to children: their want of judgment makes them stand in need of restraint and discipline. And, on the contrary, imperiousness and severity is but an ill way of treating men, who have reason of their own to guide them, unless you have a mind to make your children, when grown up, weary of you; and secretly to say within themselves, "When will you die, father?"

§ 41. I imagine every one will judge it reasonable, that their children, when little, should look upon their parents as their lords, their absolute governors; and, as such, stand in awe of them: and that, when they come to riper years, they should look on them as their best, as their only sure friends: and, as such, love and reverence them. The way I have mentioned, if I mistake not, is the only one to obtain this. We must look upon our children, when grown up, to be like ourselves; with the same passions, the same desires. We would be thought rational creatures, and have our freedom; we love not to be uneasy under constant rebukes and brow-beatings; nor can we bear severe humours, and great distance, in those we converse with. Whoever has such treatment when he is a man, will look out other company, other friends, other conversation, with whom he can be at ease. If therefore a strict hand be kept over children from the beginning, they will in that age be tractable, and quietly submit to it, as never having known any other: and if, as they grow up to the use of reason, the rigour of government be, as they deserve it, gently relaxed, the father's brow more smoothed to them, and the distance by degrees abated: his former restraints will increase their love, when they find it was only a kindness for them, and a care to make them capable to deserve the favour of their parents, and the esteem of every body else.

§ 42. Thus much for the settling your authority over children in general. Fear and awe ought to give you the first power over their minds, and love and friendship in riper years to hold it: for the time must come, when they will be past the rod and correction; and then, if the love of you make them not obedient and dutiful; if the love of virtue and reputation keep them not in laudable courses; I ask, what hold will you have upon them, to turn them to it? Indeed, fear of having a scanty portion, if they displease you, may make them slaves to your estate; but they will be nevertheless ill and wicked in private, and that restraint will not last always. Every man must some time or other be trusted to himself, and his own conduct; and he that is a good, a virtuous, and able man, must be made so within. And therefore, what he is to receive from education, what is to sway and influence his life, must be something put into him betimes: habits woven into the very principles of his nature; and not a counterfeit carriage, and dissembled outside, put on by fear, only to avoid the present anger of a father, who perhaps may disinherit him. . . .

§ 46. 2. On the other side, if the mind be curbed, and humbled too much in children; if their spirits be abased and broken much, by too strict an hand over them; they lose all their vigour and industry, and are in a worse state than the former. For extravagant young fellows, that have liveliness and spirit, come sometimes to be set right, and so make able and great men: but dejected minds, timorous and tame, and low spirits, are hardly ever to be raised, and very seldom attain to any thing. To avoid the danger that is on either hand is the great art: and he that has found a way how to keep up a child's spirit, easy, active, and free; and yet, at the same time, to restrain him from many things he has a mind to, and to draw him to things that are uneasy to him; he, I say, that knows how to reconcile these seeming contradictions, has, in my opinion, got the true secret of education.

§ 47. The usual lazy and short way by chastisement, and the rod, which is the only instrument of government that tutors generally know, or ever think of, is the most unfit of any to be used in education. . . .

§ 48. 1. This kind of punishment contributes not at all to the mastery of our natural propensity to indulge corporal and present pleasure, and to avoid pain at any rate; but rather encourages it; and thereby strengthens that in us, which is the root, from whence spring all vicious actions and the irregularities of life. From what other motive, but of sensual pleasure, and pain, does a child act, who drudges at his book against his inclination, or abstains from eating unwholesome fruit, that he takes pleasure in, only out of fear of whipping? He in this only prefers the greater corporal pleasure, or avoids the greater corporal pain. And what is it to govern his actions, and direct his conduct, by such motives as these? what is it, I say, but to cherish that principle in him, which it is our business to root out and destroy? And therefore I cannot think any correction useful to a child, where the shame of suffering for having done amiss does not work more upon him than the pain. . . .

§ 52. Beating then, and all other sorts of slavish and corporal punishments, are not the discipline fit to be used in the education of those
who would have wise, good, and ingenuous men; and therefore very
rarely to be applied, and that only on great occasions, and cases of
extremity. On the other side, to flatter children by rewards of things
that are pleasant to them, is as carefully to be avoided. He that will
give to his son apples, or sugar-plums, or what else of this kind he is
most delighted with, to make him learn his book, does but authorise
his love of pleasure, and cocker up that dangerous propensity, which
he ought by all means to subdue and stifle in him. You can never hope
to teach him to master it, whilst you compound for the check you give
his inclination in one place, by the satisfaction you propose to it in
another. To make a good, a wise, and a virtuous man, it is fit he
should learn to cross his appetite, and deny his inclination to riches,
finery, or pleasing his palate, &c. whenever his reason advises the
contrary, and his duty requires it. But when you draw him to do any
thing that is fit, by the offer of money; or reward the pains of learning
his book, by the pleasure of a luscious morsel; when you promise him
a lace-cravat,* or a fine new suit, upon performance of some of his little
tasks; what do you, by proposing these as rewards, but allow them to
be the good things he should aim at, and thereby encourage his longing for them, and accustom him to place his happiness in them?. . .

[Now Locke turns to the formation of a virtuous temperament.]

§ 57. First, children (earlier perhaps than we think) are very sensible of praise and commendation. They find a pleasure in being
esteemed and valued, especially by their parents, and those whom they
depend on. If therefore the father caress and commend them, when
they do well; show a cold and neglectful countenance to them upon
doing ill; and this accompanied by a like carriage of the mother, and all
others that are about them; it will in a little time make them sensible of
the difference: and this, if constantly observed, I doubt not but will of
itself work more than threats or blows, which lose their force, when
once grown common, and are of no use when shame does not attend
them; and therefore are to be forborn, and never to be used, but in the
case hereafter mentioned, when it is brought to extremity.

§ 58. But, secondly, to make the sense of esteem or disgrace sink
the deeper, and be of the more weight, other agreeable or disagree-

*lace tie

able things should constantly accompany these different states; not as particular rewards and punishments of this or that particular action, but as necessarily belonging to, and constantly attending one, who by his carriage has brought himself into a state of disgrace or commendation. By which way of treating them, children may as much as possible be brought to conceive, that those that are commended and in esteem for doing well, will necessarily be beloved and cherished by every body, and have all other good things as a consequence of it; and, on the other side, when any one by miscarriage falls into disesteem, and cares not to preserve his credit, he will unavoidably fall under neglect and contempt: and, in that state, the want of whatever might satisfy or delight him, will follow. In this way the objects of their desires are made assisting to virtue; when a settled experience from the beginning teaches children, that the things they delight in, belong to, and are to be enjoyed by those only, who are in a state of reputation. If by these means you can come once to shame them out of their faults, (for besides that, I would willingly have no punishment) and make them in love with the pleasure of being well thought on, you may turn them as you please, and they will be in love with all the ways of virtue. . . .

§ 65. I have seen parents so heap rules on their children, that it was impossible for the poor little ones to remember a tenth part of them, much less to observe them. However, they were either by words or blows corrected for the breach of those multipled and often very impertinent precepts. Whence it naturally followed, that the children minded not what was said to them; when it was evident to them, that no attention they were capable of, was sufficient to preserve them from transgression, and the rebukes which followed it.

Let therefore your rules to your son be as few as is possible, and rather fewer than more than seem absolutely necessary. For if you burden him with many rules, one of these two things must necessarily follow, that either he must be very often punished, which will be of ill consequence, by making punishment too frequent and familiar; or else you must let the transgressions of some of your rules go unpunished, whereby they will of course grow contemptible, and your authority become cheap to him. Make but few laws, but see they be well observed, when once made. Few years require but few laws; and as his age increases, when one rule is by practice well established, you may add another. . . .

He therefore, that is about children, should well study their natures and aptitudes, and see, by often trials, what turn they easily take, and what becomes them; observe what their native stock is, how it may be improved, and what it is fit for: he should consider what they want, whether they be capable of having it wrought into them by industry, and incorporated there by practice; and whether it be worth while to endeavour it. For, in many cases, all that we can do, or should aim at, is, to make the best of what nature has given, to prevent the vices and faults to which such a constitution is most inclined, and give it all the advantages it is capable of. Every one's natural genius should be carried as far as it could; but to attempt the putting another upon him, will be but labour in vain; and what is so plaistered [plastered] on will at best sit but untowardly, and have always hanging to it the ungracefulness of constraint and affectation. . . .

Plain and rough nature, left to itself, is much better than an artificial ungracefulness, and such studied ways of being ill-fashioned. The want of an accomplishment, or some defect in our behaviour, coming short of the utmost gracefulness, often escapes observation and censure. But affectation in any part of our carriage is lighting up a candle to our defects; and never fails to make us be taken notice of, either as wanting sense, or wanting sincerity. This governors ought the more diligently to look after, because, as I above observed, it is an acquired ugliness, owing to mistaken education; few being guilty of it, but those who pretend to breeding, and would not be thought ignorant of what is fashionable and becoming in conversation: and, if I mistake not, it has often its rise from the lazy admonitions of those who give rules, and propose examples, without joining practice with their instructions, and making their pupils repeat the action in their sight, that they may correct what is indecent or constrained in it, till it be perfected into an habitual and becoming easiness. . . .

It is virtue then, direct virtue, which is the hard and valuable part to be aimed at in education; and not a forward pertness, or any little arts of shifting. All other considerations and accomplishments should give way, and be postponed, to this. This is the solid and substantial good, which tutors should not only read lectures, and talk of; but the labour and art of education should furnish the mind with, and fasten there, and never cease till the young man had a true relish of it, and placed his strength, his glory, and his pleasure in it.

The more this advances, the easier way will be made for other accomplishments in their turns. For he that is brought to submit to virtue, will not be refractory, or resty, in any thing that becomes him. And therefore I cannot but prefer breeding of a young gentleman at home in his father's sight, under a good governor, as much the best and safest way to this great and main end of education; when it can be had, and is ordered as it should be. Gentlemen's houses are seldom without variety of company: they should use their sons to all the strange faces that come there, and engage them in conversation with men of parts and breeding, as soon as they are capable of it. And why those, who live in the country, should not take them with them, when they make visits of civility to their neighbours, I know not: this I am sure, a father that breeds his son at home, has the opportunity to have him more in his own company, and there give him what encouragement he thinks fit; and can keep him better from the taint of servants, and the meaner* sort of people, than is possible to be done abroad. But what shall be resolved in the case, must in great measure be left to the parents, to be determined by their circumstances and conveniencies. Only I think it the worst sort of good husbandry for a father not to strain himself a little for his son's breeding; which, let his condition be what it will, is the best portion he can leave him. But if, after all, it shall be thought by some that the breeding at home has too little company, and that at ordinary schools not such as it should be for a young gentleman, I think there might be ways found out to avoid the conveniencies on the one side and the other. . . .

§ 77. As children should very seldom be corrected by blows; so, I think, frequent, and especially passionate chiding, of almost as ill consequence. It lessens the authority of the parents, and the respect of the child: for I bid you still remember, they distinguish early betwixt passion and reason: and as they cannot but have a reverence for what comes from the latter, so they quickly grow into a contempt of the former; or if it causes a present terror, yet it soon wears off; and natural inclination will easily learn to slight such scarecrows, which make a noise, but are not animated by reason. Children being to be restrained by the parents only in vicious (which, in their tender years, are only a few) things, a look or nod only ought to correct them, when they do amiss; or, if words are sometimes to be used, they ought to be grave, kind, and sober, representing the ill, or unbecomingness of the faults, rather than a hasty rating of the child for it, which makes him not sufficiently distinguish whether your dislike be not more directed to him than his fault. Passionate chiding usually carries rough and ill language with it, which has this further ill effect, that it teaches and justifies it in children: and the names that their parents or preceptors give

---

*of inferior status

them they will not be ashamed or backward to bestow on others, having so good authority for the use of them. . . .

§ 81. It will perhaps be wondered, that I mention reasoning with children: and yet I cannot but think that the true way of dealing with them. They understand it as early as they do language; and, if I misobserve not, they love to be treated as rational creatures sooner than is imagined. It is a pride should be cherished in them, and, as much as can be, made the greatest instrument to turn them by.

But when I talk of reasoning, I do not intend any other but such as is suited to the child's capacity and apprehension. Nobody can think a boy of three or seven years old should be argued with as a grown man. Long discourses, and philosophical reasonings, at best amaze and confound, but do not instruct, children. When I say, therefore, that they must be treated as rational creatures, I mean, that you should make them sensible, by the mildness of your carriage, and the composure, even in your correction of them, that what you do is reasonable in you, and useful and necessary for them; and that it is not out of caprice, passion, or fancy, that you command or forbid them any thing. This they are capable of understanding; and there is no virtue they should be excited to, nor fault they should be kept from, which I do not think they may be convinced of: but it must be by such reasons as their age and understanding are capable of, and those proposed always in very few and plain words. The foundations on which several duties are built, and the fountains of right and wrong, from which they spring, are not, perhaps, easily to be let into the minds of grown men, not used to abstract their thoughts from common received opinions. Much less are children capable of reasonings from remote principles. They cannot conceive the force of long deductions: the reasons that move them must be obvious, and level to their thoughts, and such as may (if I may so say) be felt and touched. But yet, if their age, temper, and inclinations, be considered, they will never want such motives as may be sufficient to convince them. If there be no other more particular, yet these will always be intelligible, and of force, to deter them from any fault fit to be taken notice of in them, viz. that it will be a discredit and disgrace to them, and displease you.

§ 82. But, of all the ways whereby children are to be instructed, and their manners formed, the plainest, easiest, and most efficacious, is to set before their eyes the examples of those things you would have them do or avoid. Which, when they are pointed out to them, in the practice of persons within their knowledge, with some reflections on their beauty or unbecomingness, are of more force to draw or deter their imitation than any discourses which can be made to them. Virtues and vices can by no words be so plainly set before their understandings as the actions of other men will show them, when you direct their observation, and bid them view this or that good or bad quality in their practice. And the beauty or uncomeliness* of many things, in good and ill breeding, will be better learnt, and make deeper impressions on them, in the examples of others, than from any rules or instructions can be given about them. . . .

§ 85. This course, if observed, will spare both father and child the trouble of repeated injunctions, and multiplied rules of doing and forbearing. For I am of opinion, that of those actions which tend to vicious habits, (which are those alone that a father should interpose his authority and commands in) none should be forbidden children, till they are found guilty of them. For such untimely prohibitions, if they do nothing worse, do at least so much towards teaching and allowing them, that they suppose that children may be guilty of them, who would possibly be safer in the ignorance of any such faults. And the best remedy to stop them, is, as I have said, to show wonder and amazement at any such action as hath a vicious tendency, when it is first taken notice of in a child. For example, when he is first found in a lie, or any ill-natured trick, the first remedy should be, to talk to him of it as a strange monstrous matter, that it could not be imagined he would have done: and so shame him out of it.

§ 86. It will be (it is like) objected, that whatsoever I fancy of the tractableness of children, and the prevalency of those softer ways of shame and commendation; yet there are many, who will never apply themselves to their books, and to what they ought to learn, unless they are scourged to it. This, I fear, is nothing but the language of ordinary schools and fashion, which have never suffered the other to be tried as it should be, in places where it could be taken notice of. Why, else, does the learning of Latin and Greek need the rod, when French and Italian need it not? Children learn to dance and fence without whipping: nay, arithmetic, drawing, &c. they apply themselves well enough to, without beating: which would make one suspect, that there is something strange, unnatural, and disagreeable to that age in the things required in grammar-schools, or in the methods used there, that children cannot be brought to, without the severity of the lash,

*unattractiveness

and hardly with that too; or else, that it is a mistake that those tongues could not be taught them without beating.

Another thing of greater consequence, which you will obtain by such a way of treating him, will be his friendship. Many fathers, though they proportion to their sons liberal allowances, according to their age and condition; yet they keep the knowledge of their estates and concerns from them with as much reservedness as if they were guarding a secret of state from a spy or an enemy. This, if it looks not like jealousy, yet it wants those marks of kindness and intimacy, which a father should show to his son; and, no doubt, often hinders or abates that cheerfulness and satisfaction, wherewith a son should address himself to, and rely upon, his father. And I cannot but often wonder to see fathers, who love their sons very well, yet so order the matter, by a constant stiffness, and a mien of authority and distance to them all their lives, as if they were never to enjoy or have any comfort from those they love best in the world till they have lost them by being removed into another. Nothing cements and establishes friendship and good-will so much as confident communication of concernments and affairs. Other kindnesses, without this, leave still some doubts; but when your son sees you open your mind to him; when he finds that you interest him in your affairs, as things you are willing should, in their turn, come into his hands, he will be concerned for them as for his own; wait his season with patience, and love you in the mean time, who keep him not at the distance of a stranger. This will also make him see, that the enjoyment you have, is not without care; which the more he is sensible of, the less will he envy you the possession, and the more think himself happy under the management of so favourable a friend, and so careful a father. There is scarce any young man of so little thought, or so void of sense, that would not be glad of a sure friend, that he might have recourse to, and freely consult on occasion. The reservedness and distance that fathers keep often deprive their sons of that refuge, which would be of more advantage to them than a hundred rebukes and chidings. Would your son engage in some frolic, or take a vagary;* were it not much better he should do it with, than without your knowledge? For since allowances for such things must be made to young men, the more you know of his intrigues and designs, the better will you be able to prevent great mischiefs; and, by letting him see what is like to follow, take the right way of prevailing with him to avoid less inconveniencies. Would you have him open his heart to you, and ask your advice? You must begin to do so with him first, and by your carriage beget that confidence. . . .

*a trifle

§ 110.   3. As to having and possessing of things, teach them to part with what they have, easily and freely to their friends; and let them find by experience, that the most liberal has always most plenty, with esteem and commendation to boot, and they will quickly learn to practise it. This, I imagine, will make brothers and sisters kinder and civiller to one another, and consequently to others, than twenty rules about good manners, with which children are ordinarily perplexed and cumbered. Covetousness, and the desire of having in our possession, and under our dominion, more than we have need of, being the root of all evil, should be early and carefully weeded out; and the contrary quality, or a readiness to impart to others, implanted. This should be encouraged by great commendation and credit, and constantly taking care, that he loses nothing by his liberality. Let all the instances he gives of such freeness be always repaid, and with interest; and let him sensibly perceive that the kindness he shows to others is no ill husbandry for himself; but that it brings a return of kindness, both from those that receive it, and those who look on. Make this a contest among children, who shall outdo one another this way. And by this means, by a constant practice, children having made it easy to themselves to part with what they have, goodnature may be settled in them into an habit, and they may take pleasure, and pique* themselves in being kind, liberal, and civil to others.

If liberality ought to be encouraged, certainly great care is to be taken that children transgress not the rules of justice: and whenever they do, they should be set right; and, if there be occasion for it, severely rebuked.

Our first actions being guided more by self-love than reason or reflection, it is no wonder that in children they should be very apt to deviate from the just measures of right and wrong, which are in the mind the result of improved reason and serious meditation. This the more they are apt to mistake, the more careful guard ought to be kept over them, and every the least slip in this great social virtue taken notice of and rectified; and that in things of the least weight and moment, both to instruct their ignorance, and prevent ill habits, which, from small beginnings, in pins and cherry-stones, will, if let alone, grow up to higher frauds, and be in danger to end at last in downright hardened dishonesty. The first tendency to any injustice that appears must be suppressed with a show of wonder and abhorrency in the parents and governors. But because children cannot well comprehend what injustice is, till they understand property, and how particular persons

*take pride in

come by it, the safest way to secure honesty, is to lay the foundations of it early in liberality, and an easiness to part with to others whatever they have, or like, themselves. This may be taught them early, before they have language and understanding enough to form distinct notions of property, and to know what is theirs by a peculiar right exclusive of others. And since children seldom have any thing but by gift, and that for the most part from their parents, they may be at first taught not to take or keep any thing, but what is given them by those whom they take to have a power over it; and, as their capacities enlarge, other rules and cases of justice, and rights concerning "meum" and "tuum,"* may be proposed and inculcated. If any act of injustice in them appears to proceed, not from mistake, but perverseness in their wills, when a gentle rebuke and shame will not reform this irregular and covetous inclination, rougher remedies must be applied: and it is but for the father or tutor to take and keep from them something that they value, and think their own; or order somebody else to do it; and by such instances make them sensible, what little advantage they are like to make, by possessing themselves unjustly of what is another's, whilst there are in the world stronger and more men than they. But if an ingenuous detestation of this shameful vice be but carefully and early instilled into them, as I think it may, that is the true and genuine method to obviate this crime; and will be a better guard against dishonesty than any considerations drawn from interest; habits working more constantly, and with greater facility, than reason: which, when we have most need of it, is seldom fairly consulted, and more rarely obeyed.

§ 111. Crying is a fault that should not be tolerated in children; not only for the unpleasant and unbecoming noise it fills the house with, but for more considerable reasons, in reference to the children themselves; which is to be our aim in education. . . .

§ 135. I place virtue as the first and most necessary of those endowments that belong to a man or a gentleman, as absolutely requisite to make him valued and beloved by others, acceptable or tolerable to himself. Without that, I think, he will be happy neither in this, nor the other world.

§ 136. As the foundation of this, there ought very early to be imprinted on his mind a true notion of God, as of the independent

---

*mine and thine (yours)

Supreme Being, Author and Maker of all things, from whom we receive all our good, who loves us, and gives us all things: and, consequent to this, instil into him a love and reverence of this Supreme Being. This is enough to begin with, without going to explain this matter any farther, for fear, lest by talking too early to him of spirits, and being unseasonably forward to make him understand the incomprehensible nature of that infinite Being, his head be either filled with false, or perplexed with unintelligible notions of him. Let him only be told upon occasion, that God made and governs all things, hears and sees every thing, and does all manner of good to those that love and obey him. You will find, that, being told of such a God, other thoughts will be apt to rise up fast enough in his mind about him; which, as you observe them to have any mistakes, you must set right. And I think it would be better, if men generally rested in such an idea of God, without being too curious in their notions about a Being, which all must acknowledge incomprehensible; whereby many, who have not strength and clearness of thought to distinguish between what they can, and what they cannot know, run themselves into superstition or atheism, making God like themselves, or (because they cannot comprehend any thing else) none at all. And I am apt to think the keeping children constantly morning and evening to acts of devotion to God, as to their Maker, Preserver, and Benefactor, in some plain and short form of prayer, suitable to their age and capacity, will be of much more use to them in religion, knowledge, and virtue, than to distract their thoughts with curious inquiries into his inscrutable essence and being.

§ 137. Having by gentle degrees, as you find him capable of it, settled such an idea of God in his mind, and taught him to pray to him, and praise him as the Author of his being, and of all the good he does or can enjoy, forbear any discourse of other spirits, till the mention of them coming in his way, upon occasion hereafter to be set down, and his reading the Scripture-history,* put him upon that inquiry.

§ 138. But even then, and always whilst he is young, be sure to preserve his tender mind from all impressions and notions of spirits and goblins, or any fearful apprehensions in the dark. This he will be in danger of from the indiscretion of servants, whose usual method is to awe children, and keep them in subjection, by telling them of raw-head and

---

*the Old and New Testaments

bloody-bones,* and such other names, as carry with them the ideas of something terrible and hurtful, which they have reason to be afraid of, when alone, especially in the dark. This must be carefully prevented; for though by this foolish way they may keep them from little faults, yet the remedy is much worse than the disease; and there are stamped upon their imaginations ideas that follow them with terror and affrightment. Such bugbear† thoughts, once got into the tender minds of children, and being set on with a strong impression from the dread that accompanies such apprehensions, sink deep, and fasten themselves so, as not easily, if ever, to be got out again; and, whilst they are there, frequently haunt them with strange visions, making children dastards‡ when alone, and afraid of their shadows and darkness all their lives after.

§ 139. Having laid the foundations of virtue in a true notion of a God, such as the creed wisely teaches, as far as his age is capable, and by accustoming him to pray to him; the next thing to be taken care of, is to keep him exactly to speaking of truth, and by all the ways imaginable inclining him to be good-natured. Let him know, that twenty faults are sooner to be forgiven than the straining of truth, to cover any one by an excuse: and to teach him betimes to love and be good-natured to others, is to lay early the true foundation of an honest man; all injustice generally springing from too great love of ourselves, and too little of others. . . .

§ 147. You will wonder, perhaps, that I put learning last, especially if I tell you I think it the least part. This may seem strange in the mouth of a bookish man: and this making usually the chief, if not only bustle and stir about children, this being almost that alone which is thought on, when people talk of education, makes it the greater paradox. When I consider what ado is made about a little Latin and Greek, how many years are spent in it, and what a noise and business it makes to no purpose, I can hardly forbear thinking, that the parents of children still live in fear of the schoolmaster's rod, which they look on as the only instrument of education; as if a language or two were its whole business. How else is it possible, that a child should be chained to the oar seven, eight, or ten of the best years of his life, to get a language or two, which I think might be had at a great deal cheaper rate of pains and time, and be learned almost in playing?

*folk stories
†fearful
‡cowards

Forgive me, therefore, if I say, I cannot with patience think, that a young gentleman should be put into the herd, and be driven with a whip and scourge, as if he were to run the gantlet through the several classes. "What then, say you, would you not have him write and read?" Not so, not so fast, I beseech you. Reading, and writing, and learning, I allow to be necessary, but yet not the chief business. I imagine you would think him a very foolish fellow, that should not value a virtuous, or a wise man, infinitely before a great scholar. Not but that I think learning a great help to both, in well disposed minds; but yet it must be confessed also, that in others not so disposed, it helps them only to be the more foolish, or worse men. I say this, that, when you consider of the breeding of your son, and are looking out for a schoolmaster, or a tutor, you would not have (as is usual) Latin and logic only in your thoughts. Learning must be had, but in the second place, as subservient only to greater qualities. Seek out somebody, that may know how discreetly to frame his manners: place him in hands, where you may, as much as possible, secure his innocence, cherish and nurse up the good, and gently correct and weed out any bad inclinations, and settle in him good habits. This is the main point; and this being provided for, learning may be had into the bargain; and that, as I think, at a very easy rate, by methods that may be thought on.

§ 178. At the same time that he is learning French and Latin, a child, as has been said, may also be entered in arithmetic, geography, chronology, history, and geometry too. For if these be taught him in French or Latin, when he begins once to understand either of these tongues, he will get a knowledge in these sciences, and the language to boot.

Geography, I think, should be begun with; for the learning of the figure of the globe, the situation and boundaries of the four parts of the world, and that of particular kingdoms and countries, being only an exercise of the eyes and memory, a child with pleasure will learn and retain them: and this is so certain, that I now live in the house with a child, whom his mother has so well instructed this way in geography, that he knew the limits of the four parts of the world, could readily point, being asked, to any country upon the globe, or any county in the map of England; knew all the great rivers, promontories, straits, and bays in the world, and could find the longitude and latitude of any place, before he was six years old. These things, that he will thus learn by sight, and have by rote in his memory, are not all, I confess, that he is to learn upon the globes. But yet it is a good step and preparation to it, and will make the remainder much easier, when his judgment is grown ripe enough for it: besides that, it gets so much time now, and by the pleasure of knowing things, leads him on insensibly to the gaining of languages.

§ 179. When he has the natural parts of the globe well fixed in his memory, it may then be time to begin arithmetic. By the natural parts of the globe, I mean several positions of the parts of the earth and sea, under different names and distinctions of countries; not coming yet to those artificial and imaginary lines, which have been invented, and are only supposed, for the better improvement of that science.

§ 180. Arithmetic is the easiest, and, consequently, the first sort of abstract reasoning, which the mind commonly bears, or accustoms itself to: and is of so general use in all parts of life and business, that scarce any thing is to be done without it. This is certain, a man cannot have too much of it, nor too perfectly; he should therefore begin to be exercised in counting, as soon, and as far, as he is capable of it; and do something in it every day, till he is master of the art of numbers. When he understands addition and subtraction, he may then be advanced farther in geography, and after he is acquainted with the poles, zones, parallel circles, and meridians, be taught longitude and latitude, and by them be made to understand the use of maps, and by the numbers placed on their sides, to know the respective situation of countries, and how to find them out on the terrestrial globe. Which when he can readily do, he may then be entered in the celestial; and there going over all the circles again, with a more particular observation of the ecliptic or zodiac, to fix them all very clearly and distinctly in his mind, he may be taught the figure and position of the several constellations, which may be showed him first upon the globe, and then in the heavens.

When that is done, and he knows pretty well the constellations of this our hemisphere, it may be time to give him some notions of this our planetary world, and to that purpose it may not be amiss to make him a draught of the Copernican system;* and therein explain to him the situation of the planets, their respective distances from the sun,

*a drawing of the sun-centered universe, which was identified by the sixteenth-century astronomer Copernicus

the centre of their revolutions. This will prepare him to understand the motion and theory of the planets, the most easy and natural way. For, since astronomers no longer doubt of the motion of the planets about the sun, it is fit he should proceed upon that hypothesis, which is not only the simplest and least perplexed for a learner, but also the likeliest to be true in itself. But in this, as in all other parts of instruction, great care must be taken with children, to begin with that which is plain and simple, and to teach them as little as can be at once, and settle that well in their heads, before you proceed to the next, or any thing new in that science. Give them first one simple idea, and see that they take it right, and perfectly comprehend it, before you go any farther; and then add some other simple idea, which lies next in your way to what you aim at; and so proceeding by gentle and insensible steps, children, without confusion and amazement, will have their understandings opened, and their thoughts extended, farther than could have been expected. And when any one has learned any thing himself, there is no such way to fix it in his memory, and to encourage him to go on, as to set him to teach it others.

§ 181. When he has once got such an acquaintance with the globes, as is above-mentioned, he may be fit to be tried a little in geometry; wherein I think the six first books of Euclid enough for him to be taught. For I am in some doubt, whether more to a man of business be necessary or useful; at least if he have a genius and inclination to it, being entered so far by his tutor, he will be able to go on of himself without a teacher. . . .

§ 182. With geography, chronology ought to go hand in hand; I mean the general part of it, so that he may have in his mind a view of the whole current of time, and the several considerable epochs that are made use of in history. Without these two, history, which is the great mistress of prudence and civil knowledge; and ought to be the proper study of a gentleman, or man of business in the world; without geography and chronology, I say, history will be very ill retained, and very little useful; but be only a jumble of matters of fact, confusedly heaped together without order or instruction. It is by these two that the actions of mankind are ranked into their proper places of times and countries; under which circumstances, they are not only much easier kept in the memory, but, in that natural order, are only capable to afford those observations, which make a man the better and the abler for reading them.

2

Treatise of the Three Impostors

1719

Most of the major philosophers of the seventeenth century were devout Christians. Many of the people who read them were not. When we speak of the populist origins of the Enlightenment, we inevitably speak about the clandestine and the heretical, about the deist, the pantheist, and even the atheist. As we saw in the discussion of the counterfeit publisher "Pierre Marteau" (see pages 37–43), hundreds of anonymous writers, publishers, and readers took the ideas of Descartes or Spinoza or Hobbes and ran with them. Some ran headlong into disbelief and a mocking scorn for the clergy. None ran any faster than the men who wrote Traité des trois imposteurs *(Treatise of the Three Impostors). For centuries, their identities were hidden, but today we believe we know who they are.*

Jean Rousset de Missy was the leading Freemason of Amsterdam and a leader of the revolution there in 1747–48 (see page 35). His letters, buried in manuscripts at the university library in Leiden, reveal that in his youth he and his friend Charles Levier, a bookseller, were involved in creating Treatise of the Three Impostors. *The actual author, or compiler, was probably Jan Vroese, a lawyer in the service of the Dutch government, about whom very little is known. One thing is clear: These men hated organized religion, did not believe in God, and thought that Jesus, Moses, and Muhammad were the greatest impostors of all time. They believed that people should abandon their belief in the devil, sin, heaven, and hell and instead find a natural religion that suits them. Circulating such ideas would have gotten them into deep trouble with the authorities, both secular and religious. The importance of this work lies in its origins: obscure, educated men who, through their reading of the great seventeenth-century philosophers, came up with their own, sometimes shocking ideas. This selection illustrates how original and outrageous those ideas could be.*

Abraham Anderson, ed., *The Treatise of the Three Impostors and the Problem of Enlightenment: A New Translation of the Traité des trois imposteurs* (1777 Edition) (New York: Rowman & Littlefield, 1997), pp. 3–9, 23–25, 33, 39–40. The author has altered the 1997 translation in places.

CHAPTER I

Of God

§ I

Although it matters to all men to know the truth, there are nevertheless very few who enjoy this advantage; some are incapable of searching it out by themselves, & others do not want to give themselves the trouble. One should therefore not be astonished that the world is filled with vain & ridiculous opinions; nothing is better able to give them currency than ignorance; it is the only source of the false ideas which men have of the Divinity, the Soul, Spirits, & of almost all the other objects which compose Religion. Custom has prevailed, men content themselves with the prejudices of birth, & rely in the most essential things on interested persons who make it a law to themselves stubbornly to uphold received opinions, & who dare not destroy them for fear of destroying themselves.

§ II

What renders the evil without remedy, is that after having established the false ideas men have of God, they omit nothing to engage the people to believe them, without permitting the people to examine them; on the contrary, they give the people an aversion for Philosophers or the truly Learned, for fear that the reason which they teach should make the people know the errors in which it is sunk. The partisans of these absurdities have succeeded so well that it is dangerous to combat them. It matters too much to these impostors that the people be ignorant, to suffer that they be disabused. Thus one is constrained to disguise the truth, or to sacrifice oneself to the rage of the falsely Learned, or to base & interested souls.

§ III

If the people could understand into what an abyss ignorance throws them, they would soon shake off the yoke of unworthy leaders, for it is impossible to let reason act without its discovering the truth.

These impostors have sensed this so well, that to prevent the good effects which it would infallibly produce, they have had the idea of painting it to us as a monster which is not capable of inspiring any good sentiment, & although they blame in a general way those who are unreasonable, they would nevertheless be much annoyed if the truth were listened to. Thus one sees these sworn enemies to good sense falling into continual contradictions; & it is difficult to know what they claim. If it is true that right reason is the only light which people should follow, & if the people are not . . . incapable of reasoning . . . it is necessary that those who seek to instruct the people apply themselves to rectifying false reasonings, & to destroying prejudices; then we will see eyes gradually opening & minds convinced of this truth, that God is not at all what is ordinarily imagined.

§ IV

To accomplish this, there is need neither for high speculations, nor to penetrate far into the secrets of nature. One needs only a little good sense to judge that God is neither angry nor jealous; that justice & mercy are false titles which are attributed to him; & that what the Prophets & Apostles have said of him teaches us neither his nature nor his essence.

In fact, to speak without disguise & to say the thing as it is, must one not agree that these teachers were neither more able nor better instructed than the rest of men; that far from it, what they said on the subject of God is so gross that one must be altogether vulgar* to believe it? Although the thing is evident enough in itself, we shall make it even more sensible,† by examining this question: If there is any likelihood that the Prophets & Apostles were otherwise formed than men?

§ V

Everyone agrees that with respect to birth & the ordinary functions of life, they had nothing to distinguish them from the rest of men; they were engendered by men, they were born of women, & they conserved their lives in the same fashion as we. As for the mind, some would have it that God animated that of the Prophets far more than of other men, that he communicated himself to them in a quite particular fashion: this is believed with as good faith as if the thing were proved; & without considering that all men resemble each other & that they all have the same origin, it is claimed that these men were of an extraordinary temper; & chosen by the Divinity to announce his oracles. Now, besides the fact that they had neither more wit than the vulgar, nor a more perfect understanding, what does one see in their writings which obliges us to adopt so high an opinion of them? The greater part of the things they have said is so obscure that one understands none of it, &

*illiterate and uneducated
†comprehensible

in such poor order that it is easy to perceive that they did not understand themselves, & that they were but ignorant scoundrels. What gave occasion for the opinion that has been conceived of them was their hardihood* in boasting that they got immediately from God whatever they announced to the people; a belief both absurd & ridiculous, since they admit themselves that God spoke to them only in dreams. There is nothing more natural to man than dreams, in consequence a man must be quite impudent, quite vain, & quite mad to say that God speaks to him by this means, & he who puts his faith in it must be very credulous & very mad to take dreams for divine oracles. . . .

§ VI

Let us examine a little the idea which the Prophets have had of God. If we are to believe them, God is a purely corporeal Being; Micah sees him seated; Daniel, clothed in white & in the form of an old man; Ezekiel sees him as a fire, so much for the Old Testament. As for the New, the Disciples of Jesus Christ imagine they see him in the form of a dove, the Apostles as tongues of fire, & finally St. Paul as a light which dazzles & blinds him. Then as to the contradiction between their opinions, Samuel believed that God never repented of what he had resolved to do; on the contrary Jeremiah tells us that God repents of the counsels he has taken. Joel teaches us that he repents only of the evil he has done to men: Jeremiah says that he does not repent it. Genesis teaches us that man is the master of sin, & that it depends upon him alone to do right, while St. Paul assures us that men have no empire over concupiscence† without a quite particular grace of God, &c. Such are the false & contradictory ideas which those pretenders to inspiration give us of God, & such as it is desired we should have, without considering that these ideas represent the Divinity to us as a sensible being, material & subject to all the human passions. Nevertheless they come along afterwards & tell us that God has nothing in common with matter, & that he is a Being incomprehensible to us. I should very much like to know how all that can be made to agree, if it is just to believe such visible & unreasonable contradictions, & if finally one should rely on the testimony of men gross enough to imagine, despite the sermons of Moses, that a Calf was their God!‡ But

---

*boldness
†sexual desire, lust
‡a reference to the event in the Old Testament where Moses's followers abandon the Hebrew God to worship a golden calf

without pausing over the dreamings of a people raised in servitude & in absurdity, let us agree that ignorance has produced the belief in all the impostures & errors which reign among us at the present day.

CHAPTER II

Of the Reasons Which Have Led Men to Imagine an Invisible Being Which Is Commonly Called God

§ I

Those who are ignorant of physical causes have a natural fear which proceeds from uneasiness & from the doubt they are in, if there exists a Being or a power which has the capacity to harm them or to preserve them. Thence the penchant which they have to feign* invisible causes, which are only the Phantoms of their imagination, which they invoke in adversity & which they praise in prosperity. They make themselves Gods out of these in the end, & this chimerical fear of invisible powers is the source of the Religions which each forms after his own fashion. Those to whom it mattered that the people be contained & arrested by such dreamings have fostered this seed of religion, have made a law of it, & have finally reduced the peoples by the terrors of the future, to obeying blindly.

§ II

The source of the Gods being found, men have believed that they resembled themselves, & that like them they did all things for some end. Thus they say & believe unanimously that God has done nothing but for man, & reciprocally that man is made for God alone. This prejudice is general, & when one reflects on the influence which it must necessarily have had on the morals & opinions of men, one sees clearly that it is thence that they have found occasion to form the false ideas of good & of evil, of merit & of demerit, of praise & of shame, of order & of confusion, of beauty & of deformity, & of the other similar things.

§ III

Everyone should agree that all men are in profound ignorance at birth, & that the only thing which is natural to them, is to seek what is

---

*pretend or invent

useful & profitable to them: thence it comes, 1°. that they think that it is enough in order to be free to feel within oneself that one can will & wish without troubling oneself in the least about the causes which dispose us to will & to wish, because one does not know them. 2°. Since men do nothing but for the sake of an end which they prefer to every other, their only aim is to know the final causes of their actions, & they imagine that after that they have no more subject for doubt, & since they find in themselves & outside themselves several means of arriving at what they propose to themselves, seeing that they have, for example, eyes for seeing, ears for hearing, a sun to light them, &c., they have concluded that there is nothing in nature which is not made for them, & which they cannot enjoy & use as they wish; but since they know that it was not they who have made all these things, they thought they were justified in imagining a supreme being the author of all, in a word, they thought that everything that exists was the work of one or several Divinities. On the other hand, the nature of the Gods which men have acknowledged being unknown to them, they judged of them by themselves, imagining that they were susceptible of the same passions as they; & since the inclinations of men are different, each rendered to his Divinity a cult according to his humor, with the view of attracting his blessings & of thereby making the whole of nature serve his own desires.

§ IV

It is in this manner that prejudice transformed itself into superstition; it rooted itself so thoroughly that the crudest people believed themselves capable of penetrating into final causes, as if they had an entire knowledge of them. Thus instead of showing that Nature does nothing in vain, they believed that God & nature thought after the fashion of men. Experience having made known that an infinite number of calamities trouble the sweetnesses of life like storms, earthquakes, diseases, hunger, thirst, &c. they attributed all these evils to celestial anger, they believed the Divinity irritated against the offenses of men, who have not been able to free their brains of such a chimera, nor disabuse themselves of these prejudices by the daily examples which prove to them that goods & evils have in all times been common to the good & the wicked. This error was due to the fact that it was easier for them to remain in their natural ignorance than to abolish a prejudice received for so many centuries & to establish something probable.

§ V

This prejudice led them to another, which is to believe that the judg-
ments of God were incomprehensible, & that for this reason the
knowledge of the truth was beyond the strength of the human mind;
an error which we would still be in, if mathematics, physics & some
other sciences had not destroyed it.

§ VI

There is no need for long speeches to show that nature never pro-
poses any end to itself, & that all final causes are but human fictions.
It suffices to prove that this doctrine removes from God the perfec-
tions that are attributed to him. That is what we are going to show.

If God acts for an end, whether for himself, or for some other, he
desires what he does not have, & one will have to agree that there is a
time at which God not having the object for which he acts, he wished
to have it: which is to make an indigent God. But not to omit any of
what can support the reasoning of those who hold the contrary opinion; let us suppose, for example, that a stone which breaks off a building, falls on a person & kills him, it must be, say our ignorant ones,
that this stone fell by design to kill this person; but this can only have
happened because God willed it. If one replies to them that it was the
wind which caused this fall at the time that this poor unhappy fellow
was passing, they will ask you in the first place, why he was passing
precisely at the moment that the wind disturbed the stone. Answer
them that he was going to dine with one of his friends who had invited
him, they will wish to know why his friend had rather invited him at
that time than at another; they will thus put you an infinity of bizarre
questions to rise from cause to cause & to make you admit that the
will of God alone, which is the refuge of the ignorant, is the first cause
of the fall of this stone. In the same way when they see the structure
of the human body, they fall into admiration; & because they do not
know the causes of the effects which seem to them so marvelous,
they conclude that it is a supernatural effect, in which the causes that
are known to us can have no part. Thence it comes that he who wants
to examine to the bottom the works of creation, & to penetrate like a
true philosopher into their natural causes without enslaving himself to
the prejudices formed by ignorance, passes for an infidel, or is soon
decried by the malice of those whom the vulgar recognize as the inter-
preters of nature & of the Gods: These mercenary souls know very

well that the ignorance which holds the people in wonderment, is what gives them subsistence & conserves their credit. . . .

CHAPTER III . . .

§ II

The fear which made the Gods also made Religion, & ever since men have got it into their heads that there were invisible Angels which were the cause of their good or bad fortune, they have renounced good sense & reason, & they have taken their chimeras for so many Divinities which were in charge of their conduct. Having thus forged themselves Gods they wanted to know what their nature was, & imagining that they ought to be of the same substance as the soul, which they believe resembles the phantoms which appear in the mirror or during sleep; they believed that their Gods were real substances; but so tenuous & so subtle that to distinguish them from Bodies they named them *Spirits,* although these bodies & these spirits are in effect but the same thing, & differ only as more from less, since to be *Spirit* or *incorporeal,* is something incomprehensible. The reason is that every Spirit has a shape which is proper to it, & is enclosed in some place; that is to say, it has its limits, & in consequence it is a body however subtle one supposes it.[1]

§ III

The Ignorant that is to say, the greater part of men, having fixed in this way the nature of the substance of their Gods, tried also to penetrate by what means these invisible Angels produced their effects; but being unable to achieve this, because of their ignorance, they believed in their conjectures; judging blindly of the future by the past: as if one could reasonably conclude from the fact that a thing happened once in such & such a manner, that it will happen, or that it should always happen in the same manner; above all when the circumstances & all the causes which necessarily influence events & human actions, & which determine their nature & actuality, are different. Thus they envisaged the past & augured well or ill from it for the future, according as the same enterprise had formerly succeeded well or badly. . . .

[1] *See* Hobbes Leviathan *de homine. Cap.* 12 & *pag.* 56, 57, 58.

§ IV

The empire of invisible Powers being established in this way, men at first revered them only as their Sovereigns; that is to say, by marks of submission & of respect, such as are presents, prayers, &c. I say, *at first,* for nature does not teach us to use bloody Sacrifices in this affair: They were only instituted for the subsistence of the Sacrificers & Ministers destined for the service of these imaginary Gods.

§ V

This germ of Religion (I mean hope & fear) seconded by the different passions & opinions of men, produced that great number of bizarre beliefs which are the causes of so many evils & of so many revolutions which happen in States.

The honors & the great revenues which have been attached to the Priesthood, or to the Ministries of the Gods, have flattered the ambition & the avarice of those cunning men who have known how to profit from the stupidity of the Peoples; the latter have fallen so thoroughly into their snares that they have insensibly made it a habit for themselves to revere the lie & to hate the truth.

VI

The lie being established, & the ambitious taken with the sweetness of being raised above their fellows, they attempted to gain reputation by feigning to be the friends of the invisible Gods that the vulgar feared. The better to succeed in this each one painted them in his own fashion & took the liberty of multiplying them to the point that one encountered them with every step one took.

§ VII

The formless matter of the world was called the God *Chaos.* In the same way they made a God of the *Sky,* of the *Earth,* of the *Sea,* of *Fire,* of the *Winds* & of the *Planets.* They did the same honor to men & to women; birds, reptiles, the crocodile, the calf, the dog, the lamb, the serpent & the pig, in a word all sorts of animals & plants were worshipped. Every river, every spring bore the name of a God, every house had its own, every man had his genius. In short all was filled, as much above as below the earth with Gods, Spirits, Shadows & Demons. It was still not enough to feign Divinities in every imaginable place; they would have believed they were offending *time,* the *day,* the *night, concord, love, peace, victory, contention, trust, honor, virtue, fever, & health;* they would, I say, have believed they were doing an outrage to such Divinities which they thought always ready to fall upon the heads of men; if they had not raised to them temples & altars. Next they had the idea of adoring one's *genius,* which some invoked under the name of *Muses;* others under the name of *Fortune* worshipped their own ignorance. Some sanctified their debauches under the name of *Cupid,* their anger under that of the *Furies,* their natural parts under the name of *Priapus;* in a word there was nothing to which they did not give the name of a God or of a Demon.[2]

§ VIII

The founders of Religions, sensing clearly that the basis of their impostures was the ignorance of the Peoples, resolved to keep them in it by the adoration of images, which they feigned that the Gods inhabited; this made fall on their Priests a rain of gold & of Benefices which were regarded as holy things, because they were destined for the use of the holy ministers, & no one had the temerity nor the audacity to pretend to them, nor even to touch them. The better to deceive the People, the Priests put themselves forward as Prophets, Diviners, Inspired persons capable of penetrating the future, they boasted of having commerce with the Gods; & as it is natural to want to know one's destiny, these impostors by no means neglected a circumstance so advantageous to their design. Some established themselves at Delos, others at Delphi* & elsewhere, where, by means of ambiguous oracles; they responded to the questions that were put to them: even the women got involved; the Romans had recourse in great calamities to the Books of the Sibyls.† The mad passed for inspired. Those who feigned that they had a familiar commerce with the dead were called Necromancers; others claimed to know the future by the flight of birds or by the entrails of beasts. In short the eyes, the hands, the face, an extraordinary object, everything seems to them of a good or bad augury, so true is it that ignorance receives whatever impression one wants, when one has found the secret of taking advantage of it.

---

[2]Hobbes ubi supra *de Homine. Cap.* 12. *pag.* 58.
*Delos and Delphi were sites of oracles in ancient Greece.
†female prophets of ancient Rome

§ IX

The ambitious who have always been great masters in the art of deceiving, have followed this route when they gave laws; & to oblige the People to submit itself voluntarily they have persuaded it that they had received them from a God or a Goddess.[3]

Whatever is the case with this multitude of Divinities, those among whom they were adored & who are called *Pagans,* had no general system of Religion. Every Republic, every State, every City & every individual had its own rites, & thought about the Divinity as it fancied. But afterwards there arose legislators trickier than the first ones, who used more studied & surer means in giving laws, cults, & ceremonies proper to nourish the fanaticism which they wanted to establish.

Among a great number, Asia has seen three born who distinguished themselves as much by their laws & the cults which they instituted, as by the idea which they gave of the Divinity, & by the manner in which they set about getting this idea accepted & rendering their laws sacred. Moses was the most ancient. Jesus Christ come after him, worked on his plan & conserving the heart of his laws, he abolished the rest. Mahomet* who appeared the last upon the scene, took from the one & from the other Religion the wherewithal to compose his own, & thereafter declared himself the enemy of both. Let us see the characters of these three legislators, let us examine their conduct, so that one can judge afterwards who are better founded, those who revere them as divine men, or those who call them tricksters & impostors.

§ X

Of Moses.   The celebrated Moses the grandson of a great Magician by the report of Justin Martyr,[†] had all the advantages proper to render him what he became afterwards. Everyone knows that the Hebrews of whom he made himself the Chief, were a nation of Shepherds, whom the Pharaoh King Osiris I received into his land in consideration of the services which he had received from one of them in the time of a great famine: He gave them some lands in the East of Egypt in a country fertile in pasturages, & by consequence proper to nourish their herds; during almost two centuries they multiplied considerably, whether because being considered as strangers, they were not obliged to serve in the

---

[3]Hobbes ubi supra *de Homine. Cap.* 12, *pag.* 58 & 59.
*Muhammad, the prophet of the Islamic religion
[†]an early church historian and philosopher of the second century

armies, or because on account of the privileges which Osiris had accorded them, several natives of the country joined themselves to them, or finally because some bands of Arabs came to join themselves to the character of their brothers, for they were of the same race. Whatever the case, they multiplied so astonishingly, that no longer able to fit themselves in the land of Goshen, they spread through all of Egypt, & gave Pharaoh a just reason to fear that they would be capable of some dangerous enterprises in case Egypt were attacked, (as happened at the time fairly often) by the Ethiopians his inveterate enemies: Thus a reason of state obliged this Prince to take away their privileges, & to seek the means of weakening them & of enslaving them. . . .

It is with similar precautions & by always characterizing his torments as divine vengeance that Moses reigned as an absolute Despot; & to finish in the manner in which he had begun, that is to say as a trickster & an impostor, he precipitated himself into an abyss which he had caused to be dug in the middle of a solitude where he retired from time to time, under the pretext of going to confer secretly with God, so as to conciliate thereby, the respect & the submission of his subjects. In short he threw himself down this precipice prepared long in advance, so that his body would not be found & so that it would be believed that God had carried him off to render him like himself: he was not ignorant that the memory of the Patriarchs who had preceded him, was in great veneration, even though their sepulchres had been found, but this did not suffice to satisfy his ambition: he had to be revered like a God, over whom death had no hold. . . .

§ XII

Of Jesus-Christ.   Jesus Christ who was ignorant neither of the maxims nor of the science of the Egyptians, gave currency to this opinion, he thought it suited his designs. Considering how much Moses had made himself famous, although he had commanded but a people of ignoramuses, he undertook to build on this foundation, & got himself followed by some imbeciles whom he persuaded that the Holy Spirit was his Father; & his Mother a Virgin: these good people, accustomed to indulge themselves in dreams & fancies, adopted his notions & believed all that he wanted, the more so because such a birth was not really anything too miraculous for them.

Being born of a Virgin by the operation of the Holy Spirit then, is no more extraordinary nor more miraculous than what the Tartars tell of their Gengiskan, of whom a Virgin was also the mother, the

Chinese say that the God Foë owed his birth to a Virgin made fecund by the rays of the sun.

This prodigy happened at a time when the Jews tired of their God, and wanted to have a visible one like the other nations. As the number of fools is infinite, Jesus Christ found Subjects everywhere; but since his extreme poverty was an invincible obstacle[4] to his elevation, the Pharisees, sometimes his admirers, sometimes jealous of his audacity, lowered him or raised him up according to the inconstant humor of the Populace. There was rumor of his Divinity; but stripped of forces as he was, it was impossible that his design succeed: Some sick persons whom he cured, some pretended dead people whom he resuscitated brought him into fashion; but having neither money nor army, he could not fail to perish: if he had had these two instruments, he would have succeeded no less than Moses or Mahomet, or than all those who have had the ambition to raise themselves above others. If he was more unhappy, he was no less adroit, & some places in his history prove that the greatest defect of his politics was not to have provided enough for his safety. For the rest, I do not find that he took his measures less well than the two others; his law has at least become the rule of belief of the Peoples who flatter themselves that they are the wisest in the world.

§ XIII

Of the Politics of Jesus-Christ.   Is there, for example, anything subtler than the reply of Jesus on the subject of the woman surprised in adultery? The Jews having asked of him if they should stone this woman, instead of replying positively to the question, which would have made him fall into the trap which his enemies held out to him, the negative being directly contrary to the law, & the affirmative convicting him of rigor & of cruelty, which would have alienated minds from him: instead, I say, of answering as an ordinary man would have, *let whoever,* he said, *of you who is without sin throw the first stone at her.* An adroit reply & one which clearly shows his presence of mind. Asked on another occasion if it was permitted to pay Caesar's tribute, & seeing the image of the Prince on the coin which was shown him, he eluded the difficulty by replying *that one had to render to Caesar what belonged to Caesar.* The difficulty consisted in this that he rendered himself guilty of the crime of Lèse-Majesté,* if he denied that

---

[4]Jesus Christ was of the sect of the Pharisees, that is to say, of the wretched, & these were all opposed to the Saducees who formed the sect of the rich &c. *See* the Talmud.
*a crime against the sovereign ruler

that was permitted, & that in saying that it had to be paid he overturned the law of Moses, which he protested he never wanted to do, at a time when he no doubt believed himself too weak to do it with impunity, for when he had made himself more famous, he overturned it almost totally: He did like those Princes who always promise to confirm the privileges of their Subjects, while their power is not yet well established, but who later on do not trouble themselves about keeping their promises. . . .

§ XIV

Such were the defeats of [Jesus] the destroyer of the ancient Law, & of the father of the new Religion, which was built on the ruins of the old, in which a disinterested mind sees nothing more divine than in the Religions which preceded it. Its founder, who was not altogether ignorant, seeing the extreme corruption of the Republic of the Jews, judged it near its end, & believed that another ought to be reborn from its ashes.

The fear of being anticipated by men more adroit than himself, made him hasten to establish himself by means opposed to those of Moses. The latter began by rendering himself terrible & formidable to the other nations; Jesus Christ on the contrary drew them to himself by the hope of the advantages of another life which one would obtain, he said, by believing in him, whereas Moses promised none but temporal goods to the followers of his law, Jesus Christ made men hope for some which would never end. The Laws of the one regarded but externals, those of the other go as far as what lies within, influence the thoughts, & take in all things a footing opposed to the Law of Moses; from which it follows that Jesus Christ believed with Aristotle that it is with Religion & with States as with all individuals which are generated & which grow corrupt; & since nothing can be made except from what has grown corrupt, no Law gives way to any other which is not entirely opposed to it. But since men find it difficult to resolve themselves to pass from one Law to another, & since the majority of minds are difficult to shake in matters of Religion, Jesus Christ, in imitation of the other innovators, had recourse to miracles which have always been the shipwreck of the ignorant, & the refuge of the adroitly ambitious.

§ XV

Christianity having been founded by this means Jesus Christ planned cleverly to profit from the errors of the politics of Moses, & to render his new Law eternal, an enterprise which succeeded for him beyond, perhaps, his hopes. The Hebrew Prophets thought to do honor to Moses in predicting a successor who would resemble him; that is to say, a Messiah great in virtues, Powerful in goods & terrible to his enemies; but their Prophecies produced an effect altogether contrary. . . .

§ XIX

After having examined the politics & the moral teaching of Jesus Christ, in which one finds nothing as useful & as sublime as in the writings of the ancient Philosophers, let us see if the reputation which he acquired after his death is a proof of his Divinity. The People are so accustomed to unreason, that I am astonished that anyone claims the right to draw any conclusions from their conduct; experience proves to us that they always run after phantoms, & that they do not do or say anything which indicates good sense. Nevertheless it is on similar chimeras, which have at all times been in fashion, despite the efforts of the learned who have always opposed them, that belief in him has been founded. Whatever care they have taken to uproot the reigning follies, the People have laid them aside only after having been sated with them.

No matter that Moses boasted of being the interpreter of God & of proving his mission & his rights by extraordinary signs, he had but to absent himself (which he did from time to time to confer, he said, with God, & which Numa Pompilius & several other legislators similarly did); he had, I say, but to absent himself, & he found on his return nothing but the traces of the cult of the Gods which the Hebrews had seen in Egypt. No matter that he kept them for 40 years in a desert to make them lose the idea of the Gods they had laid aside, they had not yet forgotten them, they still wanted visible ones that marched ahead of them, they stubbornly adored them, whatever cruelty they were made to suffer.

Only the hatred for other nations which their leaders inspired in them by means of a pride of which the most idiotic are capable, made them insensibly lose the memory of the Gods of Egypt, & attach themselves to that of Moses, they adored him for a while with all the circumstances prescribed in the Law, but they laid him aside later to follow that of Jesus Christ, by that inconstancy which makes men run after novelty.

§ XX

The most ignorant of the Hebrews had adopted the Law of Moses; it was also people of this sort who ran after Jesus; & as the number of them is infinite, & as they are fond of each other, one should not be astonished if his new errors spread easily. It is not that novelties are not dangerous for those who embrace them, but the enthusiasm which they excite annihilates fear. Thus the Disciples of Jesus Christ all wretched as they were while following him, & all dying of hunger (as one sees from the necessity they were in one day together with their leader to pluck Ears of corn in the fields to nourish themselves), the disciples of Jesus Christ, I say, did not begin to become discouraged until they saw their Master in the hands of the executioners & incapable of giving them the goods, the power & the greatness which he had made them hope for.

After his death his disciples in despair at seeing themselves frustrated of their hopes made a virtue of necessity; banished everywhere & pursued by the Jews who wanted to treat them like their Master, they spread about in the neighboring countries, where on the report of some women they retailed his resurrection, his Divine sonship & the rest of the fables of which the Gospels are so full. . . .

§ XXI

One can judge from all that we have said that Christianity like all other Religions is no more than a crudely woven imposture, whose success & progress would astonish even its inventors if they came back to the world; but without advancing farther into a labyrinth of errors & visible contradictions of which we have spoken enough, let us say something about Mahomet, who founded a law on maxims altogether opposed to those of Jesus Christ.

§ XXII

Of Mahomet.   Hardly had the Disciples of Christ extinguished the Mosaic Law, to introduce the Christian Law, than men swept along by force & by their ordinary inconstancy, followed a new legislator, who raised himself up by the same ways as Moses, he took like him the title of Prophet & Envoy of God; like him he made miracles, & knew how to profit from the passions of the people. First he found himself escorted by an ignorant populace, to which he explicated the new

Oracles of Heaven. These wretches seduced by the promises & the fables of this new Impostor, spread his renown & exalted him to the point of eclipsing that of his predecessors.

Mahomet was not a man who seemed fit to found an Empire, he excelled neither in politics nor[5] in philosophy; he knew neither how to read nor how to write. He even had so little firmness that he would often have abandoned his enterprise if he had not been forced to stand by his wager by the skill of one of his Sectaries.* As soon as he began to raise himself up & to become famous; Corais, a powerful Arab, jealous that a nobody had the audacity to deceive the people, declared himself his enemy & crossed his enterprise; but the People persuaded that Mahomet had continual conferences with God & his Angels brought it about that he defeated his enemy; the family of Corais had the worse of it, & Mahomet seeing himself followed by an imbecile crowd which believed him a divine man, judged he had no more need of his companion: but for fear that the latter would reveal his impostures, he wanted to prevent him, & in order to do it the more surely, he loaded him with promises, & swore to him that he only wanted to become great in order to share with him his power, to which he had contributed so much. "We are arriving, he said, at the time of our elevation, we are sure of a great People which we have won over, we must now assure ourselves of it by the artifice which you have so happily imagined." At the same time he persuaded him to hide himself in the ditch of the Oracles.

This was a well from which he spoke in order to make the People believe that the voice of God declared itself for Mahomet who was in the midst of his proselytes. Tricked by the caresses of this traitor, his

[5]"Mahomet says the Count de Boulainvilliers, was ignorant of vulgar Letters: I am ready to believe it; but he was assuredly not so of all the knowledge which a great traveler can acquire with a great deal of natural intelligence, when he endeavors to employ it usefully. He was by no means ignorant in his own language; of which use, & not reading, had taught him, all the finesse & the beauties. He was not ignorant in the art of knowing how to render odious what is truly worthy of condemnation, & of painting the truth with simple & lively colors, which do not allow one to mistake it. In fact, all that he said is true, in relation to the essential dogmas of Religion; but he did not say all that is true: & it is in that alone that our Religion differs from his." He adds below "that Mahomet was neither gross, nor barbarous, that he conducted his enterprise with all the art, all the delicacy, all the attention to circumstance ["toute la circonstance"], the intrepidity, the large views of which Alexander & Caesar would have been capable in his place, &c." *Vie de Mahomet, by the Count of Boulainvilliers,* Bk. 2, page 266, 267 & 268, Amsterdam Edition 1731.
*members of his sect

associate went into the ditch to counterfeit the Oracle in his usual fashion; Mahomet passing by at the head of an infatuated multitude, a voice was heard which said: "I who am your God I declare that I have established Mahomet to be the Prophet of all the nations; it will be from him that you will learn my true law which the Jews & the Christians have adulterated." This man had been playing this role for a long time, but in the end he was rewarded with the greatest & the blackest ingratitude. In fact Mahomet hearing the voice which proclaimed him a divine man turning towards the people, commanded it in the name of this God who recognized him for his Prophet, to fill with stones this ditch, from which had issued so authentic a testimony in his favor, in memory of the stone which Jacob raised up to mark the place where God had appeared to him. Thus perished the wretch who had contributed to the elevation of Mahomet; it was on this pile of stones that the last of the most famous impostors established his law: this foundation is so solid & fixed in such a manner that after more than a thousand years of reigning one does not yet see any sign that it is on the point of being shaken.

§ XXIII

Thus Mahomet raised himself up & was happier than Jesus, insofar as he saw before his death the progress of his law, which the son of Mary was not able to do because of his poverty. He was even happier than Moses, who by an excess of ambition cast himself down a precipice to finish his days; Mahomet died in peace & with all his wishes gratified, he had moreover some certainty that his Doctrine would subsist after his death, having accommodated it to the genius of his sectaries, born & raised in ignorance; which an abler man might perhaps not have been able to do.

This, Reader, is the most remarkable of what might be said touching the three celebrated Legislators whose Religions have subjugated a great part of the universe. They were such as we have painted them; it is for you to examine if they merit that you respect them, & if you are excusable if you let yourselves be led by guides whom ambition alone has raised up, & whose dreamings are eternalized by ignorance. To cure yourself of the errors with which they have blinded you, read what follows with a free & disinterested spirit, that will be the way to discover the truth.

CHAPTER IV

Truths Sensible & Evident

§ I

Moses, Jesus & Mahomet being such as we have just painted them, it is evident that it is not in their writings that one must search for a true idea of the Divinity. The apparitions & the conferrings of Moses & Mahomet, like the divine origin of Jesus, are the greatest impostures which anyone has been able to hatch, & which you should flee if you love the truth.

§ II

God, as we have seen, being but nature, or, if one wishes, the assemblage of all beings, of all properties & of all energies, is necessarily the immanent & not distinct cause of its effects. . . .

CHAPTER VI

Of the Spirits That Are Called Demons

§ I

We have elsewhere said how the notion of Spirits introduced itself among men, & we have shown that these spirits were but Phantoms which exist only in their own imagination.

The first teachers of the human race were not enlightened enough to explain to the people what these Phantoms were; but they did not fail to tell them what they thought on the matter. Some seeing that Phantoms dissipated themselves, & had no consistency called them *immaterial; incorporeal,* forms without matter, colors & shapes, without however being bodies neither colored nor shaped, adding that they could clothe themselves with air as if with a garment when they wanted to render themselves visible to the eyes of men. The others said that they were animate bodies, but that they were made of air or of another subtler matter, that they thickened at will, when they wanted to appear.

§ II

If these two sorts of Philosophers were opposed to each other in the opinion they had of Phantoms, they agreed in the names they gave them, for all called them *Demons;* in which they were as insensate, as those who believe they see in their sleep the souls of dead persons, & that it is their own soul that they see when they look at themselves in a mirror, or finally who believe that the stars which one sees in the water are the souls of the stars. In accordance with this ridiculous opinion they fell into an error no less absurd, when they believed that these Phantoms had an unlimited power, a notion destitute of reason; but usual among the ignorant, who imagine that the Beings which they do not know have a marvelous power.

§ III

This ridiculous opinion was no sooner divulged than the Legislators made use of it to support their authority. They established the belief in Spirits which they called *Religion,* hoping that the fear which the people would have of these invisible powers would keep it to its duty; & to give more weight to this dogma they distinguished the *Spirits* or *Demons* into good & bad ones: the first were meant to excite men to observe their laws, the others to restrain them & prevent them from breaking them. . . .

§ VI

This is why the Bible is completely filled with tales about Spirits, Demons & Demoniacs; but it is nowhere said how & when they were created, which is quite unpardonable in Moses who, it is said, presumed to speak of the creation of Heaven & Earth. Nor does Jesus who speaks often enough of Angels & of good or evil Spirits tell us if they are material or immaterial. This makes it clear that both of them only knew what the Greeks had taught their ancestors on the matter. Otherwise Jesus Christ would be no less blamable for his silence than for his malice in refusing to all men the grace, the faith & the piety which he assures us he could give them.

But to come back to Spirits, it is certain that these words *Demons, Satan, Devil,* are not proper names which designate some individual, & that no one but the ignorant have ever believed in them, as much among the Greeks who invented them, as among the Jews who adopted them: After the latter were infected with these ideas, they appropriated these names which signify *enemy, accuser* & *exterminator,* sometimes to invisible Powers, sometimes to visible ones, that is to say to the Gentiles who they said inhabit the Kingdom of Satan, there being none but themselves in their opinion, who inhabit that of God. . . .

The world has long been infected with these absurd opinions but in all times there have been solid intellects & sincere men, who despite persecution have decried the absurdities of their century as we have just done in this little Treatise. Those who love the truth will find there, no doubt, some consolation; it is they whom I wish to please without troubling myself about the judgment of those for whom prejudices take the place of an infallible oracle.

3

VOLTAIRE

Letters concerning the English Nation

1733

Born in 1694, François-Marie Arouet renamed himself Voltaire. The experience of being imprisoned in the Bastille in 1717, for writing a lampoon against the government, gave him the impetus to take on a new name and a new direction in his life. Voltaire rebelled against the authority of church and state. By the 1720s, he had grown to hate organized religion and had become a denizen of the Parisian cafés and of libertine circles. His restlessness led him in 1722 to visit the Dutch republic, where he associated with some of the men who had a hand in giving birth to the Treatise of the Three Impostors *(see Document 2).*

Upon his return from the Dutch republic, Voltaire got in trouble with an aristocrat and was jailed merely on the word of this man. In disgust, he left for England in the spring of 1726. There he entered the best literary and intellectual circles in London and quickly learned English. He wrote his friends back home that "this is a country where all the arts are honored and rewarded . . . where one thinks freely and nobly without being held back by any servile fear." Thus began Voltaire's love affair with England, which eventually fueled a European fascination with English institutions and cultural mores.

When it came to France and all of Catholic Europe, Voltaire emerged as the devil incarnate. In Letters concerning the English Nation

Peter Gay, ed., *The Enlightenment: A Comprehensive Anthology* (New York: Simon & Schuster, 1973), 147–73.

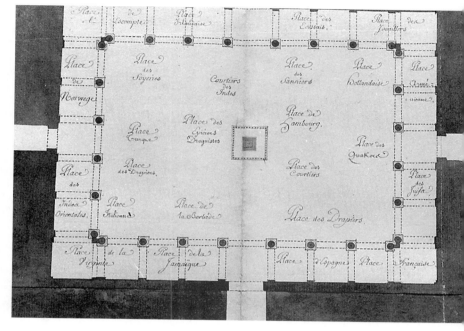

Figure 14. London Stock Exchange

This sketch was drawn by a traveling French engineer in the 1780s. It shows that men stood together based on both their national and religious identities, as well as their economic interests.
Ecole des Ponts et Chaussées.

(known in French as Lettres philosophiques*), Voltaire told the world that English society, science, politics, and religion were better than those of other countries. Protestantism was better than Catholicism, and Anglicans were more fun than Presbyterians. They also were more tolerant, as were Whigs in comparison to Tories. Indeed, Voltaire said, the Whigs seemed to be delightfully soft on orthodoxy. Science was essentially an English invention, he said; witness Francis Bacon and the great Isaac Newton.* Letters *made Voltaire an international figure, and his name became synonymous with the satire, irony, and hyperbole of the* philosophe.

To be sure, Voltaire occasionally exaggerated. For example, he said that at the Royal Exchange, Jews and Christians bartered in pacific and free assemblies. But how did Voltaire know who was on the floor of the exchange? A drawing of it from later in the century (see Figure 14) shows that men with the same religious beliefs stood together in small *clusters, partially taking their identity from their religion.* The fact that men clustered with their coreligionists may tell us more about the hedges against competition so necessary for economic survival than it does about the harmony induced by commercial transactions. Yet Voltaire did have a point: To the best of our knowledge, no one got hit or maimed on the floor of the stock exchange, whereas in other places religious debate could get very heated. Books also could be burned, as was the French edition of* Letters, *by the hangman in the courtyard of the Palais de Justice in Paris. In eighteenth-century France, being iconoclastic was a dangerous way of acquiring a reputation.*

LETTER V

On the Church of England

England is properly the country of sectarists. *Multae sunt mansiones in domo patris mei* (In my father's house are many mansions). An Englishman, as one to whom liberty is natural, may go to heaven his own way.

Nevertheless, though everyone is permitted to serve God in whatever mode of fashion he thinks proper, yet their true religion, that in which a man makes his fortune, is the sect of Episcoparians or Churchmen, called the Church of England, or simply the Church, by way of eminence. No person can possess an employment either in England or Ireland unless he be ranked among the faithful, that is, professes himself a member of the Church of England. This reason (which carries mathematical evidence with it) has converted such numbers of Dissenters of all persuasions, that not a twentieth part of the nation is out of the pale of the established church. The English clergy have retained a great number of the Romish ceremonies, and especially that of receiving, with a most scrupulous attention, their tithes. They also have the pious ambition to aim at superiority.

Moreover, they inspire very religiously their flock with a holy zeal against Dissenters of all denominations. This zeal was pretty violent under the Tories, in the four last years of Queen Anne, but was

---

*"Journal: Notes et Observation sur l'Angleterre...1784," MS 48, L'Ecole nationale des ponts et chaussées, Paris. Thomas Mortimer, *Everyman His Own Broker: Or, Guide to Exchange-Alley* (London, 1775), 43–50, 58–61, suggests that national rivalries were quite evident on the floor; see page 81 for mention of the Jews.

productive of no greater mischief than breaking the windows of some meeting-houses, and the demolishing of a few of them. For religious rage ceased in England with the Civil Wars;* and was no more under Queen Anne than the hollow noise of a sea whose billows still heaved, though so long after the storm, when the Whigs and Tories laid waste their native country, in the same manner as the Guelphs and Gibelins† formerly did theirs. It was absolutely necessary for both parties to call in religion on this occasion; the Tories declared for episcopacy, and the Whigs, as some imagined, were for abolishing it; however, after these had got the upper hand, they contented themselves with only abridging its power. . . .

With regard to the morals of the English clergy, they are more regular than those of France, and for this reason. All the clergy (a very few excepted) are educated in the universities of Oxford or Cambridge, far from the depravity and corruption which reign in the capital. They are not called to dignities till very late, in an age when men are sensible of no other passion but avarice, that is, when their ambition craves a supply. Employments are here bestowed, both in the church and the army, as a reward for long services; and we never see youngsters made bishops or colonels immediately upon their laying aside the academical gown; and besides, most of the clergy are married. The stiff and awkward air contracted by them at the university, and the little familiarity the men of this country have with the ladies, commonly oblige a bishop to confine himself to and rest contented with his own. Clergymen sometimes take a glass at the tavern, custom giving them a sanction on this occasion; and if they fuddle themselves it is in a very serious manner, and without giving the least scandal.

That sable mixed being (not to be defined) who is neither of the clergy nor of the laity, in a word, the thing called *abbé* in France, is a species quite unknown in England. All the clergy here are very much upon the reserve, and most of them pedants. When these are told that in France, young fellows famous for their dissoluteness and raised to the highest dignities of the church by female intrigues, address the fair publicly in an amorous way, amuse themselves in writing tender love songs, entertain their friends very splendidly every night at their own houses, and, after the banquet is ended, withdraw to invoke the

---

*conflicts during the 1640s
†The Guelphs were a pro-papal party in thirteenth-century Italy. The Gibelins opposed the pope.

assistance of the Holy Ghost, and call themselves boldly the successors of the Apostles, they bless God for their being Protestants. But these are shameless heretics who deserve to be blown hence through the flames to Old Nick, as Rabelais* says, and for this reason I don't trouble myself about them.

LETTER VI

On the Presbyterians

The Church of England is confined almost to the kingdom whence it received its name, and to Ireland, for Presbyterianism is the established religion in Scotland. This Presbyterianism is directly the same with Calvinism as it was established in France and is now professed at Geneva. As the priests of this sect receive but very inconsiderable stipends from their churches, and consequently cannot emulate the splendid luxury of bishops, they exclaim very naturally against honours which they can never attain to. Figure to yourself the haughty Diogenes, trampling under foot the pride of Plato. The Scotch Presbyterians are not very unlike that proud though tattered reasoner. Diogenes[†] did not use Alexander half so impertinently as these treated King Charles the Second; for when they took up arms in his cause, in opposition to Oliver,[‡] who had deceived them, they forced that poor monarch to undergo the hearing of three or four sermons every day; would not suffer him to play, reduced him to a state of penitence and mortification; so that Charles soon grew sick of these pedants, and accordingly eloped from them with as much joy as a youth does from school. . . .

These [clerical] gentlemen, who have also some churches in England, introduced there the mode of grave and severe exhortations. To them is owing the sanctification of Sunday in the three kingdoms. People are there forbid to work or take any recreation on that day, in which the severity is twice as great as that of the Romish church. No operas, plays or concerts are allowed in London on Sundays; and even cards are so expressly forbid, that none but persons of quality and those we call the genteel play on that day; the rest of the nation go either to church, to the tavern, or to see their mistresses.

---

*a sixteenth-century French satirist and humorist
†the ancient Greek Diogenes, a famous Cynic philosopher
‡Oliver Cromwell, who fought Charles I during the civil wars

Though the Episcopal and Presbyterian sects are the two prevailing ones in Great Britain, yet all others are very welcome to come and settle in it, and live very sociably together, though most of their preachers hate one another almost as cordially as a Jansenist* damns a Jesuit.

Take a view of the Royal Exchange in London, a place more venerable than many courts of justice, where the representatives of all nations meet for the benefit of mankind. There the Jew, the Mahometan,† and the Christian transact together as though they all professed the same religion, and give the name of Infidel to none but bankrupts. There the Presbyterian confides in the Anabaptist, and the Churchman depends on the Quaker's word. At the breaking up of this pacific and free assembly, some withdraw to the synagogue, and others to take a glass. This man goes and is baptized in a great tub, in the name of the Father, Son, and Holy Ghost: That man has his son's foreskin cut off, whilst a set of Hebrew words (quite unintelligible to him) are mumbled over his child. Others retire to their churches, and there wait for the inspiration of heaven with their hats on, and all are satisfied.

If one religion only were allowed in England, the government would very possibly become arbitrary; if there were but two, the people would cut one another's throats; but as there are such a multitude, they all live happy and in peace.

LETTER VII

On the Socinians, or Arians, or Antitrinitarians [Anti-Trinitarians]

There is a little sect here composed of clergymen, and of a few very learned persons among the laity, who, though they don't call themselves Arians or Socinians,‡ do yet dissent entirely from Saint Athanasius,§ with regard to their notions of the Trinity, and declare very frankly that the Father is greater than the Son.

---

*The Jansenists were a breakaway Catholic movement in France.
†Muslim
‡The Arians, followers of a movement begun under Arius, a fourth-century Christian priest, claimed that Christ the Son was not consubstantial with God the Father. The Socinians rejected the divinity of Christ and the notion of the Holy Trinity.
§St. Athanasius was a fourth-century Greek bishop who opposed Arianism. The Athanasian creed made the Holy Trinity into Orthodox doctrine.

Do you remember what is related of a certain orthodox bishop, who in order to convince an emperor of the reality of consubstantiation,* put his hand under the chin of the monarch's son, and took him by the nose in presence of his sacred majesty? The emperor was going to order his attendants to throw the bishop out of the window, when the good old man gave him this convincing reason: "Since your majesty," says he, "is angry when your son has not due respect shown him, what punishment do you think will God the father inflict on those who refuse his son Jesus the titles due to him?" The persons I just now mentioned declare that the holy bishop took a very strong step; that his argument was inconclusive, and that the emperor should have answered him thus: "Know that there are two ways by which men may be wanting in respect to me; first, in not doing honour sufficient to my son; and secondly, in paying him the same honour as to me."

Be this as it will, the principles of Arius began to revive, not only in England but in Holland and Poland. The celebrated Sir Isaac Newton honoured this opinion so far as to countenance it. This philosopher thought that the Unitarians argued more mathematically than we do. But the most sanguine stickler for Arianism is the illustrious Dr. Clarke.† This man is rigidly virtuous, and of a mild disposition; is more fond of his tenets than desirous of propagating them; and absorbed so entirely in problems and calculations, that he is a mere reasoning machine.

It is he who wrote a book which is much esteemed and little understood, on the existence of God; and another more intelligible, but pretty much condemned, on the truth of the Christian religion.

He never engaged in scholastic disputes, which our friend calls venerable trifles. He only published a work containing all the testimonies of the primitive ages, for and against the Unitarians, and leaves to the reader the counting of the voices, and the liberty of forming a judgment. This book won the doctor a great number of partisans, and lost him the See of Canterbury: But in my humble opinion, he was out in his calculation, and had better have been Primate of all England than merely an Arian parson.

You see that opinions are subject to revolutions as well as empires. Arianism, after having triumphed during three centuries, and then having been forgot twelve, rises at last out of its own ashes; but it has chosen a very improper season to make its appearance in, the present age being quite cloyed with disputes and sects. The members of this

*the belief that in the Eucharist both bread and the body of Christ are present
†Samuel Clarke, an Anglican clergyman who was a private Unitarian

sect are, besides, too few to be indulged the liberty of holding public assemblies, which, however, they will doubtless be permitted to do in case they spread considerably. But people are now so very cold with respect to all things of this kind, that there is little probability any new religion, or old one that may be revived, will meet with favour. Is it not whimsical enough that Luther, Calvin and Zwinglius,* all of them wretched authors, should have founded sects which are now spread over a great part of Europe; that Mahomet, though so ignorant, should have given a religion to Asia and Africa; and that Sir Isaac Newton, Dr. Clarke, Mr. Locke, Mr. Le Clerc, etc., the greatest philosophers as well as the ablest writers of their ages, should scarce have been able to raise a little flock, which even decreases daily? . . .

Were Oliver Cromwell, he who beheaded his sovereign and seized upon the kingly dignity, to rise from the dead, he would be a wealthy city trader, and no more.

LETTER VIII

On the Parliament

The Members of the English Parliament are fond of comparing themselves to the old Romans.

Not long since, Mr. Shippen† opened a speech in the House of Commons with these words: "The majesty of the people of England would be wounded." The singularity of the expression occasioned a loud laugh; but this gentleman, so far from being disconcerted, repeated the same words with a resolute tone of voice, and the laugh ceased. In my opinion, the majesty of the people of England has nothing in common with that of the people of Rome, much less is there any affinity between their governments. There is in London a senate, some of the members whereof are accused (doubtless very unjustly) of selling their voices on certain occasions, as was done in Rome; this is the only resemblance. Besides, the two nations appear to me quite opposite in character with regard both to good and evil. The Romans never knew the dreadful folly of religious wars, an abomination reserved for devout preachers of patience and humility. . . . The sects of the Episcoparians and Presbyterians quite distracted these very serious heads for a time. But I fancy they'll hardly ever be so silly

---

*Latinized named for Ulrich Zwingli, a sixteenth-century Swiss Protestant reformer
†a member of the English Parliament

again, they seeming to be grown wiser at their own expence; and I don't perceive the least inclination in them to murder one another merely about syllogisms, as some zealots among them once did.

But here follows a more essential difference between Rome and England, which gives the advantage entirely to the latter, *viz.* that the civil wars of Rome ended in slavery, and those of the English in liberty. The English are the only people upon earth who have been able to prescribe limits to the power of kings by resisting them; and who, by a series of struggles, have at last established that wise government where the prince is all powerful to do good, and at the same time is restrained from committing evil; where the nobles are great without insolence, though there are no vassals; and where the people share in the government without confusion.

The House of Lords and that of the Commons divide the legislative power under the King, but the Romans had no such balance. The Patricians and Plebeians in Rome were perpetually at variance, and there was no intermediate power to reconcile them. The Roman Senate, who were so unjustly, so criminally proud, as not to suffer the Plebeians to share with them in anything, could find no other artifice to keep the latter out of the Administration than by employing them in foreign wars. They considered the Plebeians as a wild beast, whom it behooved them to let loose upon their neighbours, for fear they should devour their masters. Thus the greatest defect in the government of the Romans raised them to be conquerors. By being unhappy at home, they triumphed over and possessed themselves of the world, till at last their divisions sank them to slavery.

The government of England will never rise to so exalted a pitch of glory, nor will its end be so fatal. The English are not fired with the splendid folly of making conquests, but would only prevent their neighbours from conquering. They are not only jealous of their own liberty, but even of that of other nations. The English were exasperated against Louis the Fourteenth for no other reason but because he was ambitious; and declared war against him merely out of levity, not from any interested motives.

The English have doubtless purchased their liberties at a very high price, and waded through seas of blood to drown the idol of arbitrary power. Other nations have been involved in as great calamities, and have shed as much blood; but then the blood they spilt in defence of their liberties only enslaved them the more.

That which rises to a revolution in England is no more than a sedition in other countries. A city in Spain, in Barbary, or in Turkey takes up arms in defence of its privileges, when immediately it is stormed by mercenary troops, it is punished by executioners, and the rest of the nation kiss the chains they are loaded with. The French are of the opinion that the government of this island is more tempestuous than the sea which surrounds it, which indeed is true; but then it is never so but when the King raises the storm, when he attempts to seize the ship of which he is only the chief pilot. The civil wars of France lasted longer; were more cruel, and productive of greater evils than those of England: But none of these civil wars had a wise and prudent liberty for their object. . . .*

That for which the French chiefly reproach the English nation is the murder of King Charles the First, whom his subjects treated exactly as he would have treated them had his reign been prosperous. After all, consider, on one side, Charles the First defeated in a pitched battle, imprisoned, tried, sentenced to die in Westminster Hall, and then beheaded; and on the other, the Emperor Henry the Seventh, poisoned by his chaplain at his receiving the sacrament; Henry the Third stabbed by a monk; thirty assassinations projected against Henry the Fourth; several of them put in execution, and the last bereaving that great monarch of his life. Weigh, I say, all these wicked attempts, and then judge.

LETTER X

On Trade

As trade enriched the citizens in England, so it contributed to their freedom, and this freedom on the other side extended their commerce, whence arose the grandeur of the state. Trade raised by insensible degrees the naval power, which gives the English a superiority over the Seas, and they are now masters of very near two hundred ships of war. Posterity will very possibly be surprised to hear that an island whose only produce is a little lead, tin, fuller's earth,† and coarse wood, should become so powerful by its commerce as to be able to send, in 1723, three fleets at the same time to three different and far distanced parts of the globe: one before Gibraltar, conquered and still possessed by the English; a second to Porto Bello, to dispossess the King of Spain of the treasures of the West Indies; and a third into the Baltic, to prevent the Northern Powers from coming to an engagement.

---

*Here Voltaire gives examples of violence against French monarchs.
†an absorbent clay used for removing grease from fabrics

At the time when Louis XIV made all Italy tremble, and his armies, which had already possessed themselves of Savoy and Piedmont, were upon the point of taking Turin, Prince Eugene was obliged to march from the middle of Germany in order to succour Savoy. Having no money, without which cities cannot be either taken or defended, he addressed himself to some English merchants. These, at an hour and a half's warning, lent him five millions, whereby he was enabled to deliver Turin and to beat the French; after which he wrote the following short letter to the persons who had disbursed him the abovementioned sums: "Gentlemen, I have received your money, and flatter myself that I have laid it out to your satisfaction." Such a circumstance as this raises a just pride in an English merchant, and makes him presume (not without some reason) to compare himself to a Roman citizen; and indeed a peer's brother does not think traffic beneath him. When the Lord Townshend was Minister of State, a brother of his was content to be a city merchant; and at the time that the Earl of Oxford governed Great Britain, his younger brother was no more than a factor in Aleppo, where he chose to live, and where he died. This custom, which begins, however, to be laid aside, appears monstrous to Germans, vainly puffed up with their extraction. These think it morally impossible that the son of an English peer should be no more than a rich and powerful citizen, for all are princes in Germany. There have been thirty highnesses of the same name, all whose patrimony consisted only in their escutcheons and their pride.

In France the title of marquis is given *gratis* to any one who will accept of it; and whosoever arrives at Paris from the midst of the most remote provinces with money in his purse and a name terminating in *ac* or *ille,* may strut about, and cry, "Such a man as I! A man of my rank and figure!" And may look down upon a trader with sovereign contempt; whilst the trader, on the other side, by thus often hearing his profession treated so disdainfully, is fool enough to blush at it. However, I cannot say which is most useful to a nation: a lord, powdered in the tip of the mode, who knows exactly at what o'clock the King rises and goes to bed, and who gives himself airs of grandeur and state, at the same time that he is acting the slave in the antechamber of a Prime Minister; or a merchant, who enriches his country, dispatches orders from his counting-house to Surat and Grand Cairo, and contributes to the felicity of the world.

LETTER XII

On the Lord Bacon

Not long since, the trite and frivolous question following was debated in a very polite and learned company, *viz.* who was the greatest man, Caesar, Alexander, Tamerlane, Cromwell, etc.

Somebody answered that Sir Isaac Newton excelled them all. The gentleman's assertion was very just; for if true greatness consists in having received from Heaven a mighty genius, and in having employed it to enlighten our own minds and that of others, a man like Sir Isaac Newton, whose equal is hardly found in a thousand years, is the truly great man. And those politicians and conquerors (and all ages produce some) were generally so many illustrious wicked men. That man claims our respect who commands over the minds of the rest of the world by the force of truth, not those who enslave their fellow creatures; he who is acquainted with the universe, not they who deface it.

Since therefore you desire me to give you an account of the famous personages which England has given birth to, I shall begin with Lord Bacon, Mr. Locke, Sir Isaac Newton, etc. Afterwards the warriors and ministers of state shall come in their order.

I must begin with the celebrated Viscount Verulam, known in Europe by the Name of Bacon,* which was that of his family. His father had been Lord Keeper, and himself was a great many years Lord Chancellor under King James the First. Nevertheless, amidst the intrigues of a court, and the affairs of his exalted employment, which alone were enough to engross his whole time, he yet found so much leisure for study as to make himself a great philosopher, a good historian, and an elegant writer; and a still more surprising circumstance is that he lived in an age in which the art of writing justly and elegantly was little known, much less true philosophy. Lord Bacon, as is the fate of man, was more esteemed after his death than in his lifetime. His enemies were in the British court, and his admirers were foreigners. . . .

You know that this great man was accused of a crime very unbecoming a philosopher, I mean bribery and extortion. You know that he was sentenced by the House of Lords to pay a fine of about four hundred thousand French livres; to lose his peerage and his dignity of Chancellor. But in the present age, the English revere his memory to

---

*Francis Bacon, an early seventeenth-century English philosopher. He published *Novum Organum* in 1620.

such a degree that they will scarce allow him to have been guilty. In case you should ask what are my thoughts on this head, I shall answer you in the words which I heard the Lord Bolingbroke use on another occasion. Several gentlemen were speaking, in his company, of the avarice with which the late Duke of Marlborough had been charged; some examples whereof being given, the Lord Bolingbroke was appealed to (who, having been in the opposite party, might perhaps, without the imputation of indecency, have been allowed to clear up that Matter). "He was so great a man," replied his Lordship, "that I have forgot his vices."

I shall therefore confine my self to those things which so justly gained Lord Bacon the esteem of all Europe.

The most singular, and the best of all his pieces, is that which, at this time, is the most useless and the least read. I mean his *Novum Scientiarum Organum.** This is the scaffold with which the new philosophy was raised; and when the edifice was built, part of it at least, the Scaffold, was no longer of Service.

The Lord Bacon was not yet acquainted with nature, but then he knew, and pointed out, the several paths that lead to it. He had despised in his younger years the thing called philosophy in the universities, and did all that lay in his power to prevent those societies of men, instituted to improve human reason, from depraving it by their quiddities,† their horrors of the vacuum, their substantial forms, and all those impertinent terms which not only ignorance had rendered venerable, but which had been sacred by their being ridiculously blended with religion.

He is the father of experimental philosophy. It must indeed be confessed that very surprising secrets had been found out before his time. The sea-compass, printing, engraving on copper plates, oil-painting, looking-glasses; the art of restoring, in some measure, old men to their sight by spectacles; gunpowder, etc., had been discovered. A New World had been sought for, found, and conquered. Would not one suppose that these sublime discoveries had been made by the greatest philosophers, and in ages much more enlightened than the present? But it was far otherwise; all these great changes happened in the most stupid and barbarous times. Chance only gave birth to most of those inventions; and it is very probable that what is called chance contributed very much to the discovery of America; at least it has

---

*A New Method for Restoring Knowledge
†*quid* is a Latin term used in debate, a reference to the Scholastics

been always thought that Christopher Columbus undertook his voyage merely on the relation of a captain of a ship which a storm had driven as far westward as the Caribee Islands. Be this as it will, Men had sailed round the world, and could destroy cities by an artificial thunder more dreadful than the real one. But then they were not acquainted with the circulation of the blood, the weight of the air, the laws of motion, light, the number of our planets, etc. . . .

In a word, no one, before the Lord Bacon, was acquainted with experimental philosophy, nor with the several physical experiments which have been made since his time. Scarce one of them but is hinted at in his work, and he himself had made several. He made a kind of pneumatic engine by which he guessed the elasticity of the air. He approached, on all sides as it were, to the discovery of its weight, and had very near attained it, but some time after *Torricelli* seized upon this truth. In a little time experimental philosophy began to be cultivated on a sudden in most parts of Europe. It was a hidden treasure which the Lord Bacon had some notion of, and which all the philosophers, encouraged by his promises, endeavoured to dig up.

But that which surprised me most was to read in his work, in express terms, the new attraction, the invention of which is ascribed to Sir Isaac Newton.* . . .

LETTER XIII

On Mr. Locke

Perhaps no man ever had a more judicious or more methodical genius or was a more acute logician than Mr. Locke, and yet he was not deeply skilled in the mathematics. This great man could never subject himself to the tedious fatigue of calculations, nor to the dry pursuit of mathematical truths, which do not at first present any sensible objects to the mind; and no one has given better proofs than he that it is possible for a man to have a geometrical head without the assistance of geometry. Before his time, several great philosophers had declared, in the most positive terms, what the soul of man is; but as these absolutely knew nothing about it, they might very well be allowed to differ entirely in opinion from one another.

In Greece, the infant seat of arts and of errors, and where the grandeur as well as the folly of the human mind went such prodigious

*Newton's *Principia,* 1687

lengths, the people used to reason about the soul in the very same manner as we do.

The divine Anaxagoras, in whose honor an altar was erected, for his having taught mankind that the sun was greater than Peloponnesus, that snow was black, and that the heavens were of stone, affirmed that the soul was an aerial spirit, but at the same time immortal. Diogenes (not he who was a cynical philosopher after having coined base money) declared that the soul was a portion of the substance of God; an idea which we must confess was very sublime. Epicurus* maintained that it was composed of parts in the same manner as the body.

Aristotle, who has been explained a thousand ways, because he is unintelligible, was of the opinion, according to some of his disciples, that the understanding in all men is one and the same substance.

The divine Plato, master of the divine Aristotle, and the divine Socrates, master of the divine Plato, used to say that the soul was corporeal and eternal. No doubt but the demon of *Socrates* had instructed him in the nature of it. Some people, indeed, pretend that a man who boasted his being attended by a familiar genius must infallibly be either a knave or a madman, but this kind of people are seldom satisfied with anything but reason.

... Our Descartes, born not to discover the errors of antiquity, but to substitute his own in the room of them, and hurried away by the systematic spirit which throws a cloud over the minds of the greatest men, thought he had demonstrated that the soul is the same thing as thought, in the same manner as matter, in his opinion, is the same as extension. He asserted that man thinks eternally, and that the soul, at its coming into the body, is informed with the whole series of metaphysical notions; knowing God, infinite space, possessing all abstract ideas; in a word, completely endued with the most sublime lights, which it unhappily forgets at its issuing from the womb. ...

Such a multitude of reasoners having written the romance of the soul, a sage at last arose who gave, with an air of the greatest modesty, the history of it. Mr. Locke has displayed the human soul in the same manner as an excellent anatomist explains the springs of the human body. He everywhere takes the light of physics for his Guide. He sometimes presumes to speak affirmatively, but then he presumes also to doubt. Instead of concluding at once what we know not, he

---

*an ancient philosopher who claimed that the universe was composed solely of atoms in random motion

examines gradually what we would know. He takes an infant at the instant of his Birth; he traces, step by step, the progress of his understanding; examines what things he has in common with beasts, and what he possesses above them. Above all he consults himself; the being conscious that he himself thinks.

I shall leave, says he, to those who know more of this matter than myself, the examining whether the soul exists before or after the organization of our bodies. But I confess that it is my lot to be animated with one of those heavy souls which do not think always; and I am even so unhappy as not to conceive that it is more necessary the soul should think perpetually than that bodies should be for ever in motion.

With regard to myself, I shall boast that I have the honour to be as stupid in this particular as Mr. Locke. No one shall ever make me believe that I think always; and I am as little inclined as he could be to fancy that some weeks after I was conceived I was a very learned soul, knowing at that time a thousand things which I forgot at my birth, and possessing when in the womb (though to no manner of purpose) knowledge which I lost the instant I had occasion for it, and which I have never since been able to recover perfectly.

Mr. Locke, after having destroyed innate ideas; after having fully renounced the vanity of believing that we think always; after having laid down, from the most solid principles, that ideas enter the mind through the senses; having examined our simple and complex ideas; having traced the human mind through its several operations; having showed that all the languages in the world are imperfect, and the great abuse that is made of words every moment; he at last comes to consider the extent or rather the narrow limits of human knowledge. It was in this chapter he presumed to advance, but very modestly, the following words: "We shall, perhaps, never be capable of knowing, whether a Being, purely material, thinks or not." This sage assertion was, by more divines than one, looked upon as a scandalous declaration that the soul is material and mortal. Some Englishmen, devout after their way, sounded an alarm. The superstitious are the same in society as cowards in an army; they themselves are seized with a panic fear, and communicate it to others. It was loudly exclaimed that Mr. Locke intended to destroy religion; nevertheless, religion had nothing to do in the affair, it being a question purely philosophical, altogether independent of faith and revelation. Mr. Locke's opponents needed but to examine, calmly and impartially, whether the declaring that matter can think implies a contradiction, and whether God is able to communicate thought to matter. But divines are too apt to begin their declarations with saying that God is offended when people differ from them in opinion; in which they too much resemble the bad poets who used to declare publicly that Boileau spoke irreverently of Louis XIV because he ridiculed their stupid productions. . . .

Mr. Locke addressed these gentlemen in the candid, sincere manner following: At least confess yourselves to be as ignorant as I. Neither your imaginations nor mine are able to comprehend in what manner a body is susceptible of ideas; and do you conceive better in what manner a substance, of what kind soever, is susceptible of them? As you cannot comprehend either matter or spirit, why will you presume to assert anything?

The superstitious man comes afterwards, and declares that all those must be burnt for the good of their souls who so much as suspect that it is possible for the body to think without any foreign assistance. But what would these people say should they themselves be proved irreligious? And, indeed, what man can presume to assert, without being guilty at the same time of the greatest impiety, that it is impossible for the Creator to form matter with thought and sensation? Consider only, I beg you, what a dilemma you bring yourselves into, you who confine in this manner the power of the Creator. Beasts have the same organs, the same sensations, the same perceptions as we; they have memory, and combine certain ideas. In case it was not in the power of God to animate matter and inform it with sensation, the consequence would be either that beasts are mere machines or that they have a spiritual soul.

Methinks it is clearly evident that beasts cannot be mere machines, which I prove thus: God has given them the very same organs of sensation as to us: If therefore they have no sensation, God has created a useless thing; now, according to your own confession, God does nothing in vain; he therefore did not create so many organs of sensation merely for them to be uninformed with this faculty; consequently beasts are not mere machines. Beasts, according to your assertion, cannot be animated with a spiritual soul; you will therefore, in spight of yourself, be reduced to this only assertion, *viz.* that God has endued the organs of beasts, who are mere matter, with the faculties of sensation and perception, which you call instinct in them. But why may not God, if he pleases, communicate to our more delicate organs that faculty of feeling, perceiving and thinking which we call human reason? To whatever side you turn, you are forced to acknowledge your own ignorance and the boundless power of the Creator. Exclaim therefore no more against the sage, the modest philosophy of Mr. Locke, which, so far from interfering with religion, would be no use to demonstrate the truth of it, in case Religion wanted any such support. For what philosophy can be of a more religious nature than that which, affirming nothing but what it conceives clearly, and conscious of its own weakness, declares that we must always have recourse to God in our examining of the first principles.

Besides, we must not be apprehensive that any philosophical opinion will ever prejudice the religion of a country. Though our demonstrations clash directly with our mysteries, that's nothing to the purpose, for the latter are not less revered upon that account by our Christian philosophers, who know very well that the objects of reason and those of faith are of a very different nature. Philosophers will never form a religious sect, the reason of which is, their writings are not calculated for the vulgar, and they themselves are free from enthusiasm. If we divide mankind into twenty parts, it will be found that nineteen of these consist of persons employed in manual labour, who will never know that such a man as Mr. Locke existed. In the remaining twentieth part how few are readers? And among such as are so, twenty amuse themselves with romances to one who studies philosophy. The thinking part of mankind are confined to a very small number, and these will never disturb the peace and tranquillity of the world.

Neither Montaigne, Locke, Bayle, Spinoza, Hobbes, Lord Shaftesbury, Collins nor Toland lightened up the firebrand of discord in their countries; this has generally been the work of divines, who, being at first puffed up with the ambition of becoming chiefs of a sect, soon grew very desirous of being at the head of a party. But what do I say? All the works of the modern philosophers put together will never make so much noise as even the dispute which arose among the Franciscans merely about the fashion of their sleeves and of their cowls.

LETTER XIV

On Descartes and Sir Isaac Newton

A Frenchman who arrives in London will find philosophy, like everything else, very much changed there. He had left the world a *plenum,** and he now finds it a *vacuum*. At Paris the universe is seen composed of vortices of subtile matter; but nothing like it is seen in London. In France it is the pressure of the moon that causes the tides;

*a universe filled with fine matter, or an aether

but in England, it is the sea that gravitates towards the moon; so that when you think that the moon should make it flood with us, those gentlemen fancy it should be ebb, which, very unluckily, cannot be proved. For to be able to do this it is necessary the moon and the tides should have been enquired into at the very instant of the Creation.

You'll observe farther that the sun, which in France is said to have nothing to do in the affair, comes in here for very near a quarter of its assistance. According to your Cartesians, everything is performed by an impulsion, of which we have very little notion; and according to Sir Isaac Newton, it is by an attraction, the cause of which is as much unknown to us. At Paris you imagine that the earth is shaped like a melon, or of an oblique figure; at London it has an oblate one. A Cartesian declares that light exists in the air; but a Newtonian asserts that it comes from the sun in six minutes and a half. The several operations of your chemistry are performed by acids, alkalies and subtile matter; but attraction prevails even in chymistry among the English.

The very essence of things is totally changed. You neither are agreed upon the definition of the soul nor on that of matter. Descartes, as I observed in my last, maintains that the soul is the same thing with thought, and Mr. Locke has given a pretty good proof of the contrary.

Descartes asserts farther, that extension alone constitutes matter, but Sir Isaac adds solidity to it.

How furiously contradictory are these opinions!

> *Non nostrum inter vos tantas componere lites.*
> Virgil, Eclog. III.

'Tis not for us to end such great Disputes.

This famous Newton, this destroyer of the Cartesian system, died in March Anno 1727. His countrymen honoured him in his lifetime, and interred him as though he had been a king who had made his people happy.

The English read with the highest satisfaction, and translated into their tongue, the elogium of Sir Isaac Newton which Mr. de Fontenelle spoke in the Academy of Sciences. Mr. de Fontenelle presides as judge over philosophers; and the English expected his decision as a solemn declaration of the superiority of the English philosophy over that of the French. But when it was found that this gentleman had compared Descartes to Sir Isaac, the whole Royal Society in London rose up in arms. So far from acquiescing with Mr. de Fontenelle's judgment, they criticized his discourse. And even several (who, however, were not the ablest philosophers in that body) were offended at the comparison, and for no other reason but because Descartes was a Frenchman.

It must be confessed that these two great men differed very much in conduct, in fortune, and in philosophy.

Nature had indulged Descartes a shining and strong imagination, whence he became a very singular person both in private life and in his manner of reasoning. This imagination could not conceal itself even in his philosophical works, which are everywhere adorned with very shining, ingenious metaphors and figures. Nature had almost made him a poet; and indeed he wrote a piece of poetry for the entertainment of Christina, Queen of Sweden, which, however, was suppressed in honour to his memory.

He embraced a military life for some time, and afterwards becoming a complete philosopher, he did not think the passion of love derogatory to his character. He had by his mistress a daughter called *Froncine,* who died young and was very much regretted by him. Thus he experienced every passion incident to mankind.

He was a long time of the opinion that it would be necessary for him to fly from the society of his fellow creatures, and especially from his native country, in order to enjoy the happiness of cultivating his philosophical studies in full liberty.

Descartes was very right, for his contemporaries were not knowing enough to improve and enlighten his understanding, and were capable of little else than of giving him uneasiness.

He left France purely to go in search of truth, which was then persecuted by the wretched philosophy of the Schools.* However, he found that reason was as much disguised and depraved in the universities of Holland, into which he withdrew, as in his own country. For at the time that the French condemned the only propositions of his philosophy which were true, he was persecuted by the pretended philosophers of Holland, who understood him no better, and who, having a nearer view of his glory, hated his person the more, so that he was obliged to leave Utrecht. Descartes was injuriously accused of being an atheist, the last refuge of religious scandal; and he who had employed all the sagacity and penetration of his genius in searching for new proofs of the existence of a God was suspected to believe there was no such Being.

*All schools were controlled by the clergy in Catholic Europe.

Such a persecution from all sides must necessarily suppose a most exalted merit as well as a very distinguished reputation, and indeed he possessed both. Reason at that time darted a ray upon the world through the gloom of the Schools and the prejudices of popular superstition. At last his name spread so universally that the French were desirous of bringing him back into his native country by rewards, and accordingly offered him an annual pension of a thousand crowns. Upon these hopes Descartes returned to France, paid the fees of his patent, which was sold at that time, but no pension was settled upon him. Thus disappointed, he returned to his solitude in North Holland, where he again pursued the study of philosophy, whilst the great Galileo, at fourscore years of age, was groaning in the prisons of the Inquisition, only for having demonstrated the earth's motion.

At last Descartes was snatched from the world in the flower of his age at Stockholm. His death was owing to a bad regimen, and he expired in the midst of some *literati* who were his enemies, and under the hands of a physician to whom he was odious.

The progress of Sir Isaac Newton's life was quite different. He lived happy and very much honoured in his native country, to the age of fourscore and five years.

It was his peculiar felicity not only to be born in a country of liberty, but in an age when all Scholastic impertinencies were banished from the world. Reason alone was cultivated, and mankind could only be his pupil, not his enemy.

One very singular difference in the lives of these two great men is that Sir Isaac, during the long course of years he enjoyed, was never sensible to any passion, was not subject to the common frailties of mankind, nor ever had any commerce with women; a circumstance which was assured me by the physician and surgeon who attended him in his last moments.

We may admire Sir Isaac Newton on this occasion, but then we must not censure Descartes.

The opinion that generally prevails in *England* with regard to these two philosophers is that the latter was a dreamer and the former a sage.

Very few people in England read Descartes, whose works indeed are now useless. On the other side, but a small number peruse those of Sir Isaac, because to do this the students must be deeply skilled in the mathematics, otherwise those works will be unintelligible to him. But notwithstanding this, these great men are the subject of everyone's discourse. Sir Isaac Newton is allowed every advantage, whilst Descartes is not indulged a single one. According to some, it is to the former that we owe the discovery of a vacuum, that the air is a heavy body, and the invention of telescopes. In a word, Sir Isaac Newton is here as the Hercules of fabulous story, to whom the ignorant ascribed all the feats of ancient heroes. . . .

LETTER XXIII

On the Regard That Ought to Be Shown to Men of Letters

Neither the English nor any other people have foundations established in favour of the polite arts like those in France. There are universities in most countries, but it is in France only that we meet with so beneficial an encouragement for astronomy and all parts of the mathematics, for physics, for researches into antiquity, for painting, sculpture and architecture. Louis XIV has immortalized his name by these several foundations, and this immortality did not cost him two hundred thousand livres a year.

I must confess that one of the things I very much wonder at is that as the Parliament of Great Britain have promised a reward of twenty thousand pounds sterling to any person who may discover the longitude, they should never have once thought to imitate Louis XIV in his munificence with regard to the arts and sciences.

Merit indeed meets in England with rewards of another kind, which redound more to the honour of the nation. The English have so great a veneration for exalted talents that a man of merit in their country is always sure of making his fortune. Mr. Addison in France would have been elected a member of one of the academies, and, by the credit of some women, might have obtained a yearly pension of twelve hundred livres; or else might have been imprisoned in the Bastille, upon pretence that certain strokes in his tragedy of *Cato* had been discovered which glanced at the porter of some man in power. Mr. Addison was raised to the Post of Secretary of State in England. Sir Isaac Newton was made Warden of the Royal Mint. Mr. Congreve had a considerable employment. Mr. Prior was Plenipotentiary. Dr. Swift is Dean of St. Patrick in Dublin, and is more revered in Ireland than the Primate himself. The religion which Mr. Pope professes excludes him indeed from preferments of every kind, but then it did not prevent his gaining two hundred thousand livres by his excellent translation of Homer.* . . .

---

*Joseph Addison, William Congreve, Matthew Prior, Jonathan Swift, and Alexander Pope were famous English writers and poets.

But the circumstance which mostly encourages the arts in England is the great veneration which is paid them. The picture of the Prime Minister hangs over the chimney of his own closet, but I have seen that of Mr. Pope in twenty noblemen's houses. Sir Isaac Newton was revered in his lifetime, and had a due respect paid to him after his death, the greatest men in the nation disputing who should have the honour of holding up his pall. Go into Westminster Abbey and you'll find that what raises the admiration of the spectator is not the mausoleums of the English Kings, but the monuments which the gratitude of the nation has erected to perpetuate the memory of those illustrious men who contributed to its glory. We view their statues in that Abbey in the same manner as those of Sophocles, Plato and other immortal personages were viewed in Athens; and I am persuaded that the bare sight of those glorious monuments has fired more than one breast, and been the occasion of their becoming great men.

The English have even been reproached with paying too extravagant honours to mere merit, and censured for interring the celebrated actress Mrs. Oldfield in Westminster Abbey, with almost the same pomp as Sir Isaac Newton. Some pretend that the English had paid her these great funeral honours purposely to make us more strongly sensible of the barbarity and injustice which they object to us for having buried Mademoiselle Lecouvreur* ignominiously in the fields.

But be assured from me that the English were prompted by no other principle, in burying Mrs. Oldfield in Westminster Abbey, than their good sense. They are far from being so ridiculous as to brand with infamy an art which has immortalized an Euripides and a Sophocles; or to exclude from the body of their citizens a set of people whose business is to set off with the utmost grace of speech and action those pieces which the nation is proud of.

Under the reign of Charles I, and in the beginning of the Civil Wars raised by a number of rigid fanatics, who at last were the victims to it, a great many pieces were published against theatrical and other shows, which were attacked with the greater virulence because that monarch and his Queen, daughter to Henry IV of France, were passionately fond of them.

One Mr. Prynne, a man of most furiously scrupulous principles, who would have thought himself damned had he worn a cassock instead of a short cloak, and have been glad to see one half of mankind cut the

---

*a famous French actress. In France actors and actresses were regarded as being of very low social position.

other to pieces for the glory of God and the *Propaganda Fide,** took it into his head to write a most wretched satire against some pretty good comedies which were exhibited very innocently every night before their Majesties. He quoted the authority of the rabbis, and some passages from Saint Bonaventure, to prove that the *Oedipus* of Sophocles was the work of the Evil Spirit; that Terence was excommunicated *ipso facto;* and added that doubtless Brutus, who was a very severe Jansenist, assassinated Julius Caesar for no other reason but because he, who was *Pontifex Maximus,* presumed to write a tragedy the subject of which was Oedipus. Lastly, he declared that all who frequented the theatre were excommunicated, as they thereby renounced their baptism. This was casting the highest insult on the King and all the Royal Family; and as the English loved their Prince at that time, they could not bear to hear a writer talk of excommunicating him, though they themselves afterwards cut his head off. Prynne was summoned to appear before the Star Chamber; his wonderful book...was sentenced to be burnt by the common hangman, and himself to lose his ears. His trial is now extant.

*religious orthodoxy, or the propagation of the faith

4

LADY MARY WORTLEY MONTAGU

Letters
1716–1718

When Voltaire encountered English society in the 1720s, he was enraptured by its fluidity—the ease with which men of letters mixed with the highborn and the titled. Had he come over from Paris a mere ten years earlier, he might have had the pleasure of meeting the young Lady Mary Wortley Montagu (1689–1762), who was then a rising star in London society. He did come to know her eventually, as did many of the finest writers, poets, and statesmen of her day. It was an age of relative freedom

W. May Thomas, *Letters and Works of Mary Wortley Montagu* (New York: G. Bell and Sons, 1893), 227–370 (inter alia).

of the press and Whig ascendancy, both made possible by the revolution of 1689 — the year of Lady Montagu's birth. Though not born into great wealth, she managed, by a financially secure marriage to Edward Montagu, grandson of the earl of Sandwich, to live a genteel, if lonely, life and to become (after her death) recognized as one of the great letter writers of her time.

In 1716, Edward Montagu was appointed ambassador to the Turkish court, and Lady Mary, along with their children and servants, accompanied him to Turkey. Within a year, Montagu was recalled, but not before his wife had seen a world she had never even imagined. Other Westerners would learn about the world from books; Lady Mary got to see it firsthand.

The opportunity to travel gave Lady Montagu the chance to exercise her extraordinary powers of observation and literary talent. She embodied the nascent Enlightenment by her openness and willingness to explore the foreign and the strange. She likened Arabic poetry to the Song of Solomon, and she saw the Turks as kinder than Christians. The habit of Muslim women wearing a veil neither shocked nor offended her. In her letters, she wittily pointed out that it might make illicit trysts easier to carry out.

Lady Montagu was very much of her age. The Turks could be admired because they appeared to possess learning and civilization; not so the dark people of North Africa. She also could cast a cold eye on her fellow countrymen. Slander and innuendo against outspoken women was common, and Montagu gave as good as she got. She heaped scorn on her English enemies and often wasted her time in frivolous and quite public quarrels. Yet she had a clear understanding of why women were the objects of male scorn. It was sheer prejudice. Anonymously, she advised other "ladies" to treat with contempt those who "would throw you below the dignity of the human species." Unlike many women of the time, Montagu wore religion lightly and hinted that the libertine greatly pleased her. Like the good Whig that she was, she also had little positive to say about the princes of Europe. That republican conviction makes her appreciation for the authoritarian Turks all the more remarkable. In this selection, as she travels from England to the Dutch republic, Germany, Austria, and finally Turkey, Montagu has interesting and perceptive comments to make every step of the way.

TO MRS. SMITH*

HAGUE, AUG. 5, O.S.† 1716.

I make haste to tell you, dear madam, that, after all the dreadful fatigues you threatened me with, I am hitherto very well pleased with my journey. We take care to make such short stages every day, that I rather fancy myself upon parties of pleasure, than upon the road; and sure nothing can be more agreeable than travelling in Holland. The whole country appears a large garden; the roads are well paved, shaded on each side with rows of trees, and bordered with large canals, full of boats, passing and repassing. Every twenty paces gives you the prospect of some villa, and every four hours that of a large town, so surprisingly neat, I am sure you would be charmed with them. The place I am now at is certainly one of the finest villages in the world. Here are several squares finely built, and, what I think a particular beauty, the whole set with thick large trees. The *Vor-hout*‡ is, at the same time, the Hyde-Park and Mall of the people of quality; for they take the air in it both on foot and in coaches. There are shops for wafers, cool liquors, etc.

I have been to see several of the most celebrated gardens, but I will not teaze [tease] you with their descriptions. I dare say you think my letter already long enough. But I must not conclude without begging your pardon, for not obeying your commands, in sending the lace you ordered me. Upon my word, I can yet find none, that is not dearer than you may buy it at London. If you want any India goods, here are great variety of pennyworths; and I shall follow your orders with great pleasure and exactness; being,   Dear Madam, etc., etc.

TO THE COUNTESS OF BRISTOL§

NUREMBERG, AUG. 22, O.S. 1716.

After five days travelling post, I could not sit down to write on any other occasion, than tell my dear Lady Bristol, that I have not forgotten her obliging command, of sending her some account of my travels.

I have already passed a large part of Germany, have seen all that is remarkable in Cologne, Frankfort, Wurtsburg, and this place. 'Tis

---

*the second wife of the earl of Oxford and a friend of Montagu
†old style; dates reckoned according to the Julian calendar
‡a street in The Hague
§Elizabeth Felton Harvey, a friend of Montagu

impossible not to observe the difference between the free towns and those under the government of absolute princes, as all the little sovereigns of Germany are. In the first, there appears an air of commerce and plenty. The streets are well built, and full of people, neatly and plainly dressed. The shops are loaded with merchandise, and the commonalty are clean and cheerful. In the other, you see a sort of shabby finery, a number of dirty people of quality tawdered out;* narrow nasty streets, out of repair, wretchedly thin of inhabitants, and above half of the common sort asking alms. I cannot help fancying one under the figure of a clean Dutch citizen's wife, and the other like a poor town lady of pleasure, painted and ribboned out in her headdress, with tarnished silver-laced shoes, a ragged under-petticoat, a miserable mixture of vice and poverty.

They have sumptuary laws in this town, which distinguish their rank by their dress, prevent the excess which ruins so many other cities, and has a more agreeable effect to the eye of a stranger than our fashions. I think after the Archbishop of Cambray having declared for them, I need not be ashamed to own, that I wish these laws were in force in other parts of the world. When one considers impartially the merit of a rich suit of clothes in most places, the respect and the smiles of favour it procures, not to speak of the envy and the sighs it occasions, (which is very often the principal charm to the wearer), one is forced to confess, that there is need of an uncommon understanding to resist the temptation of pleasing friends and mortifying rivals; and that it is natural to young people to fall into a folly, which betrays them to that want of money which is the source of a thousand basenesses. What numbers of men have begun the world with generous inclinations, that have afterwards been the instruments of bringing misery on a whole people, being led by vain expense into debts, that they could clear no other way but by the forfeit of their honour, and which they never could have contracted, if the respect the many pay to habits, was fixed by law, only to a particular colour or cut of plain cloth! These reflections draw after them others that are too melancholy. I will make haste to put them out of your head by the farce of relicks [relics], with which I have been entertained in all the Romish churches.

The Lutherans are not quite free from these follies. I have seen here, in the principal church, a large piece of the cross set in jewels, and the point of the spear, which they told me, very gravely, was the

*showing themselves off although they are wearing cheap and gaudy garments

same that pierced the side of our Saviour. But I was particularly diverted in a little Roman-catholic church which is permitted here, where the professors of that religion are not very rich, and consequently cannot adorn their images in so rich a manner as their neighbours. For, not to be quite destitute of all finery, they have dressed up an image of our Saviour over the altar, in a fair full-bottomed wig very well powdered. I imagine I see your ladyship stare at this article, of which you very much doubt the veracity; but, upon my word, I have not yet made use of the privilege of a traveller; and my whole account is written with the same sincerity of heart, with which I assure you that I am, dear madam, yours, etc.

TO MR. POPE*

VIENNA, SEPT. 14, O.S. 1716.

Perhaps you'll laugh at me for thanking you very gravely for all the obliging concern you express for me. 'Tis certain that I may, if I please, take the fine things you say to me for wit and raillery; and, it may be, it would be taking them right. But I never, in my life, was half so well disposed to believe you in earnest as I am at present; and that distance, which makes the continuation of your friendship improbable, has very much increased my faith in it.

I find that I have (as well as the rest of my sex), whatever face I sent on't, a strong disposition to believe in miracles. Don't fancy, however, that I am infected by the air of these popish countries; I have, indeed, so far wandered from the discipline of the church of England, as to have been last Sunday at the opera, which was performed in the garden of the Favorita; and I was so pleased with it, I have not yet repented my seeing it. Nothing of that kind ever was more magnificent; and I can easily believe what I am told, that the decorations and habits cost the emperor thirty thousand pounds sterling. The stage was built over a very large canal, and, at the beginning of the second act, divided into two parts, discovering the water, on which there immediately came, from different parts, two fleets of little gilded vessels, that gave the representation of a naval fight. It is not easy to imagine the beauty of this scene, which I took particular notice of. But all the rest were perfectly fine in their kind. The story of the opera is the enchantment of Alcina, which gives opportunities for a

*Alexander Pope, a leading eighteenth-century English poet

great variety of machines, and changes of the scenes, which are performed with a surprising swiftness. The theatre is so large, that it is hard to carry the eye to the end of it, and the habits in the utmost magnificence, to the number of one hundred and eight. No house could hold such large decorations; but the ladies all sitting in the open air, exposes them to great inconveniences; for there is but one canopy for the imperial family; and, the first night it was represented, a shower of rain happening, the opera was broken off, and the company crowded away in such confusion, that I was almost squeezed to death.

But if their operas are thus delightful, their comedies are in as high a degree ridiculous. They have but one playhouse, where I had the curiosity to go to a German comedy, and was very glad it happened to be the story of Amphitrion.* As that subject has been already handled by a Latin, French, and English poet, I was curious to see what an Austrian author would make of it. I understand enough of that language to comprehend the greatest part of it; and besides, I took with me a lady, who had the goodness to explain to me every word. The way is, to take a box, which holds four, for yourself and company. The fixed price is a gold ducat. I thought the house very low and dark; but I confess, the comedy admirably recompensed that defect. I never laughed so much in my life. It began with Jupiter's falling in love out of a peep-hole in the clouds, and ended with the birth of Hercules. But what was most pleasant, was the use Jupiter made of his metamorphosis; for you no sooner saw him under the figure of Amphitrion, but, instead of flying to Alcmena, with the raptures Mr. Dryden† puts into his mouth, he sends for Amphitrion's taylor, and cheats him of a laced coat, and his banker of a bag of money, a Jew of a diamond ring, and bespeaks a great supper in his name; and the greatest part of the comedy turns upon poor Amphitrion's being tormented by these people for their debts. Mercury uses Sosia in the same manner. But I could not easily pardon the liberty the poet has taken of larding his play with, not only indecent expressions, but such gross words, as I don't think our mob would suffer from a mountebank.‡ Besides, the two Sosias very fairly let down their breeches in the direct view of the boxes, which were full of people of the first rank, that seemed very pleased with their entertainment, and assured me this was a celebrated piece....

*a Greek myth
†John Dryden, a seventeenth-century English poet and dramatist
‡huckster or charlatan

TO THE LADY RICH*

Vienna, Sept. 20, O.S. 1716.

I am extremely pleased, but not at all surprized, at the long delightful letter you have had the goodness to send me. I know that you can think of an absent friend even in the midst of a court, and you love to oblige, where you can have no view of a return; and I expect from you that you should love me, and think of me, when you don't see me.

I have compassion for the mortifications that you tell me befel[l] our little friend, and I pity her much more, since I know that they are only owing to the barbarous customs of our country. Upon my word, if she were here, she would have no other fault but that of being something too young for the fashion, and she has nothing to do but to transplant herself hither about seven years hence, to be again a young and blooming beauty. I can assure you that wrinkles, or a small stoop in the shoulders, nay, even gray hairs, are no objection to the making [of] new conquests. I know you cannot easily figure to yourself a young fellow of five-and-twenty ogling my Lady Suffolk with passion, or pressing to hand the Countess of Oxford from an opera. But such are the sights I see every day, and I don't perceive any body surprised at them but myself. A woman, till five-and-thirty, is only looked upon as a raw girl, and can possibly make no noise in the world till about forty. I don't know what your ladyship may think of this matter; but 'tis a considerable comfort to me, to know there is upon earth such a paradise for old women; and I am content to be insignificant at present, in the design of returning when I am fit to appear nowhere else. I cannot help lamenting on this occasion, the pitiful case of too many good English ladies, long since retired to prudery and ratafia,† whom, if their stars had luckily conducted hither, would shine in the first rank of beauties. Besides, that perplexing word *reputation* has quite another meaning here than what you give it at London; and getting a lover is so far from losing, that 'tis properly getting reputation; ladies being much more respected in regard to the rank of their lovers, than that of their husbands.

But what you'll think very odd, the two sects that divide our whole nation of petticoats, are utterly unknown in this place. Here are neither coquettes nor prudes. No woman dares appear coquette enough to encourage two lovers at a time. And I have not seen any such

---

*Lady Charlotte Rich
†a liqueur flavored with almonds or fruit

prudes as to pretend fidelity to their husbands, who are certainly the best natured set of people in the world, and look upon their wives' gallants as favourably as men do upon their deputies, that take the troublesome part of their business off their hands. They have not however the less to do on that account: for they are generally deputies in another place themselves; in one word, 'tis the established custom for every lady to have two husbands, one that bears the name, and another that performs the duties and these engagements are so well known, that it would be a downright affront, and publicly resented, if you invited a woman of quality to dinner, without, at the same time, inviting her two attendants of lover and husband, between whom she sits in state with great gravity. The sub-marriages generally last twenty years together, and the lady often commands the poor lover's estate, even to the utter ruin of his family.

These connections, indeed, are as seldom begun by any real passion as other matches; for a man makes but an ill figure that is not in some commerce of this nature; and a woman looks out for a lover as soon as she's married, as part of her equipage,* without which she could not be genteel; and the first article of the treaty is establishing the pension, which remains to the lady, in case the gallant should prove inconstant. This chargeable point of honour I look upon as the real foundation of so many wonderful instances of constancy. I really know some women of the first quality, whose pensions are as well known as their annual rents, and yet nobody esteems them the less; on the contrary, their discretion would be called in question, if they should be suspected to be mistresses for nothing. A great part of their emulation consists in trying who shall get most; and having no intrigue at all, is so far a disgrace, that, I'll assure you, a lady, who is very much my friend here, told me but yesterday, how much I was obliged to her for justifying my conduct in a conversation relating to me, where it was publicly asserted, that I could not possibly have common sense, since I had been in town above a fortnight, and had made no steps toward commencing an amour. My friend pleaded for me, that my stay was uncertain, and she believed that was the cause of my seeming stupidity; and this was all she could find to say in my justification.

But one of the pleasantest adventures I ever met with in my life was last night, and it will give you a just idea in what a delicate manner the *belles passions*† are managed in this country. I was at the assembly of

*retinue
†sweet passions

the Countess of————, and the young Count of————leading me down stairs, asked me how long I was to stay at Vienna? I made answer, that my stay depended on the emperor, and it was not in my power to determine it. Well, madam, (said he,) whether your time here is to be long or short, I think you ought to pass it agreeably, and to that end you must engage in a *little affair of the heart.*—My heart, answered I gravely enough, does not engage very easily, and I have no design of parting with it. I see, madam, (said he sighing,) by the ill nature of that answer, I am not to hope for it, which is a great mortification to me that am charmed with you. But, however, I am still devoted to your service; and since I am not worthy of entertaining you myself, do me the honour of letting me know whom you like best among us, and I'll engage to manage the affair entirely to your satisfaction.—You may judge in what manner I should have received this compliment in my own country; but I was well enough acquainted with the way of this, to know that he really intended me an obligation, and I thanked him with a very grave courtesy for his zeal to serve me, and only assured him I had no occasion to make use of it.

Thus you see, my dear, that gallantry and good breeding are as different, in different climates, as morality and religion. Who have the rightest notions of both, we shall never know till the day of judgment; for which great day of *éclaircissement,** I own there is very little impatience in your, etc., etc.

TO MR. POPE

BELGRADE, FEB. 12, O.S. 1717.

I did verily intend to write you a long letter from Peterwaradin, where I expected to stay three or four days; but the pasha here was in such haste to see us, that he dispatched the courier back, which Mr. Wortley had sent to know the time he would send the convoy to meet us, without suffering him to pull off his boots.

My letters were not thought important enough to stop our journey; and we left Peterwaradin the next day, being waited on by the chief officers of the garrison, and a considerable convoy of Germans and Rascians.† The Emperor has several regiments of these people; but, to say the truth, they are rather plunderers than soldiers; having no pay,

*enlightenment
†Turks

and being obliged to furnish their own arms and horses; they rather look like vagabond gipsies, or stout beggars, then regular troops.

I cannot forbear speaking a word of this race of creatures, who are very numerous all over Hungary. They have a patriarch of their own at Grand Cairo, and are really of the Greek church; but their extreme ignorance gives their priests occasion to impose several new notions upon them. These fellows, letting their hair and beard grow inviolate, make exactly the figure of the Indian bramins. They are heirs-general to all the money of the laity; for which, in return, they give them formal passports signed and sealed for heaven; and the wives and children only inherit the house and cattle. In most other points they follow the Greek church.

This little digression has interrupted my telling you we passed over the fields of Carlowitz, where the last great victory was obtained by Prince Eugene over the Turks. The marks of that glorious bloody day are yet recent, the field being yet strewed with the skulls and carcases of unburied men, horses, and camels. I could not look, without horror, on such numbers of mangled human bodies, nor without reflecting on the injustice of war, that makes murder not only necessary but meritorious. Nothing seems to be a plainer proof of the *irrationality* of mankind, whatever fine claims we pretend to reason, than the rage with which they contest for a small spot of ground, when such vast parts of fruitful earth lie quite uninhabited. It is true, custom has now made it unavoidable; but can there be a greater demonstration of want of reason, than a custom being firmly established, so plainly contrary to the interest of man in general? I am a good deal inclined to believe Mr. Hobbes, that the *state of nature* is a *state of war;* but thence I conclude human nature not rational, if the word reason means common sense, as I suppose it does. I have a great many admirable arguments to support this reflection; I won't however trouble you with them, but return, in a plain style, to the history of my travels.

We were met at Betsko (a village in the midway between Belgrade and Peterwaradin) by an aga of the janisaries [janissaries], with a body of Turks, exceeding the Germans by one hundred men, though the pasha had engaged to send exactly the same number. You may judge by this of their fears. I am really persuaded, that they hardly thought the odds of one hundred men set them even with the Germans; however, I was very uneasy till they were parted, fearing some quarrel might arise, notwithstanding the parole given.

We came late to Belgrade, the deep snows making the ascent to it very difficult. It seems a strong city, fortified on the east side by the

Danube, and on the south by the river Save, and was formerly the barrier of Hungary. It was first taken by Solyman the Magnificent, and since by the Emperor's forces, led by the Elector of Bavaria. The Emperor held it only two years, it being retaken by the Grand Vizier. It is now fortified with the utmost care and skill the Turks are capable of, and strengthened by a very numerous garrison of their bravest janisaries, commanded by a pasha seraskiér (*i.e.* general), though this last expression is not very just; for, to say truth, the seraskiér is commanded by the janisaries. These troops have an absolute anthority here, and their conduct carries much more the aspect of rebellion, than the appearance of subordination. You may judge of this by the following story, which, at the same time, will give you an idea of the *admirable* intelligence of the governor of Peterwaradin, though so few hours distant. We were told by him at Peterwaradin, that the garrison and inhabitants of Belgrade were so weary of the war, they had killed their pasha about two months ago, in a mutiny, because he had suffered himself to be prevailed upon, by a bribe of five purses (five hundred pounds sterling), to give permission to the Tartars to ravage the German frontiers. We were very well pleased to hear of such favourable dispositions in the people: but when we came hither, we found that the governor had been ill-informed, and the real truth of the story to be this. The late pasha fell under the displeasure of his soldiers, for no other reason, but restraining their incursions on the Germans. They took it into their heads, from that mildness, that he had intelligence with the enemy, and sent such information to the Grand Signior at Adrianople; but, redress not coming quick enough from thence, they assembled themselves in a tumultuous manner, and by force dragged their pasha before the cadi and mufti,* and there demanded justice in a mutinous way; one crying out, Why he protected the infidels? Another, Why he squeezed them of their money? The pasha easily guessing their purpose, calmly replied to them, that they asked him too many questions, and that he had but one life, which must answer for all. They then immediately fell upon him with their scimitars, without waiting the sentence of their heads of the law, and in a few moments cut him in pieces. The present pasha has not dared to punish the murder; on the contrary, he affected to applaud the actors of it, as brave fellows, that knew to do themselves justice. He takes all pretences of throwing money among the garrison, and suffers them to make little excursions into Hungary, where they burn some poor Rascian houses.

*Islamic judges and religious authorities

You may imagine, I cannot be very easy in a town which is really under the government of an insolent soldiery.—We expected to be immediately dismissed, after a night's lodging here; but the pasha detains us till he receives orders from Adrianople, which may, possibly, be a month a-coming. In the mean time, we are lodged in one of the best houses, belonging to a very considerable man amongst them, and have a whole chamber of janisaries to guard us. My only diversion is the conversation of our host, Achmet Bey, a title something like that of count in Germany. His father was a great pasha, and he has been educated in the most polite eastern learning, being perfectly skilled in the Arabic and Persian languages, and an extraordinary scribe, which they call *effendi*. This accomplishment makes way to the greatest preferments; but he has had the good sense to prefer an easy, quiet, secure life, to all the dangerous honours of the Porte.* He sups with us every night, and drinks wine very freely. You cannot imagine how much he is delighted with the liberty of conversing with me. He has explained to me many pieces of Arabian poetry, which, I observe, are in numbers not unlike ours, generally of an alternate verse, and of a very musical sound. Their expressions of love are very passionate and lively. I am so much pleased with them, I really believe I should learn to read Arabic, if I was to stay here a few months. He has a very good library of their books of all kinds; and, as he tells me, spends the greatest part of his life there. I pass for a great scholar with him, by relating to him some of the Persian tales, which I find are genuine. At first he believed I understood Persian. I have frequent disputes with him concerning the difference of our customs, particularly the confinement of women. He assures me, there is nothing at all in it; only, says he, we have the advantage, that when our wives cheat us, nobody knows it. He has wit, and is more polite than many Christian men of quality. I am very much entertained with him. He has had the curiosity to make one of our servants set him an alphabet of our letters, and can already write a good roman hand....

TO THE COUNTESS OF MAR

ADRIANOPLE, APRIL 1, O.S. 1717.

I wish to God, dear sister, that you were as regular in letting me know what passes on your side of the globe, as I am careful in endeavouring

*the Ottoman Turkish imperial administration in Constantinople

to amuse you by the account of all I see here that I think worth your notice. You content yourself with telling me over and over, that the town is very dull: it may possibly be dull to you, when every day does not present you with something new; but for me that am in arrears at least two months' news, all that seems very stale with you would be very fresh and sweet here. Pray let me into more particulars, and I will try to awaken your gratitude, by giving you a full and true relation of the novelties of this place, none of which would surprise you more than a sight of my person, as I am now in my Turkish habit, though I believe you would be of my opinion, that 'tis admirably becoming.—I intend to send you my picture; in the mean time accept of it here.

The first part of my dress is a pair of drawers, very full, that reach to my shoes, and conceal the legs more modestly than your petticoats. They are of a thin rose-coloured damask, brocaded with silver flowers. My shoes are of white kid leather, embroidered with gold. Over this hangs my smock, of a fine white silk gauze, edged with embroidery. This smock has wide sleeves, hanging half way down the arm, and is closed at the neck with a diamond button; but the shape and colour of the bosom are very well to be distinguished through it. The *antery* is a waistcoat, made close to the shape, of white and gold damask, with very long sleeves falling back, and fringed with deep gold fringe, and should have diamond or pearl buttons. My *caftan,* of the same stuff with my drawers, is a robe exactly fitted to my shape, and reaching to my feet, with very long strait [straight] falling sleeves. Over this is my girdle, of about four fingers broad, which all that can afford it have entirely of diamonds or other precious stones; those who will not be at that expence, have it of exquisite embroidery on satin; but it must be fastened before with a clasp of diamonds. The *curdee* is a loose robe they throw off or put on according to the weather, being of a rich brocade (mine is green and gold), either lined with ermine or sables; the sleeves reach very little below the shoulders. The head dress is composed of a cap, called *talpock,* which is in winter of fine velvet embroidered with pearls or diamonds, and in summer of a light shining silver stuff. This is fixed on one side of the head, hanging a little way down with a gold tassel, and bound on, either with a circle of diamonds (as I have seen several) or a rich embroidered handkerchief. On the other side of the head, the hair is laid flat; and here the ladies are at liberty to show their fancies; some putting flowers, others a plume of heron's feathers, and, in short, what they please; but the most general fashion is a large *bouquet* of jewels, made like natural flowers; that is, the buds, of pearl; the roses, of different coloured rubies; the jessamines, of diamonds; the jonquils, of topazes, etc., so well set and enamelled, 'tis hard to imagine any thing of that kind so beautiful. The hair hangs at its full length behind, divided into tresses braided with pearl or ribbon, which is always in great quantity.

I never saw in my life so many fine heads of hair. In one lady's, I have counted a hundred and ten of the tresses, all natural; but it must be owned, that every kind of beauty is more common here than with us. 'Tis surprising to see a young woman that is not very handsome. They have naturally the most beautiful complexion in the world, and generally large black eyes. I can assure you with great truth, that the court of England (though I believe it the fairest in Christendom) does not contain so many beauties as are under our protection here. They generally shape their eye-brows, and both Greeks and Turks have the custom of putting round their eyes a black tincture, that, at a distance, or by candle-light, adds very much to the blackness of them. I fancy many of our ladies would be overjoyed to know this secret; but 'tis too visible by day. They dye their nails a rose colour; but, I own, I cannot enough accustom myself to this fashion to find any beauty in it.

As to their morality or good conduct, I can say, like Harlequin,* that 'tis just as it is with you; and the Turkish ladies don't commit one sin the less for not being Christians. Now that I am a little acquainted with their ways, I cannot forbear admiring, either the exemplary discretion or extreme stupidity of all the writers that have given accounts of them. 'Tis very easy to see, they have in reality more liberty than we have. No woman, of what rank soever, is permitted to go into the streets without two *murlins;* one that covers her face all but her eyes, and another that hides the whole dress of her head, and hangs half way down her back. Their shapes are also wholly concealed, by a thing they call a *ferigee,* which no woman of any sort appears without; this has strait sleeves, that reach to their finger-ends, and it laps all round them, not unlike a riding-hood. In winter 'tis of cloth, and in summer of plain stuff or silk. You may guess then how effectually this disguises them, so that there is no distinguishing the great lady from her slave. 'Tis impossible for the most jealous husband to know his wife when he meets her; and no man dare touch or follow a woman in the street.

*famous jester

This perpetual masquerade gives them entire liberty of following their inclinations without danger of discovery. The most usual method of intrigue is, to send an appointment to the lover to meet the lady at a Jew's shop, which are as notoriously convenient as our Indian-houses; and yet, even those who don't make use of them, do not scruple to go to buy pennyworths, and tumble over rich goods, which are chiefly to be found amongst that sort of people. The great ladies seldom let their gallants know who they are; and 'tis so difficult to find it out, that they can very seldom guess at her name, whom they have corresponded with for above half a year together. You may easily imagine the number of faithful wives very small in a country where they have nothing to fear from a lover's indiscretion, since we see so many have the courage to expose themselves to that in this world, and all the threatened punishment of the next, which is never preached to the Turkish damsels. Neither have they much to apprehend from the resentment of their husbands; those ladies that are rich having all their money in their own hands.

Upon the whole, I look upon the Turkish women as the only free people in the empire: the very divan pays respect to them; and the Grand-Signior himself, when a pasha is executed, never violates the privileges of the *harem* (or women's apartment), which remains unsearched and entire to the widow. They are queens of their slaves, whom the husband has no permission so much as to look upon, except it be an old woman or two that his lady chooses. 'Tis true their law permits them four wives; but there is no instance of a man of quality that makes use of this liberty, or of a woman of rank that would suffer it. When a husband happens to be inconstant (as those things will happen), he keeps his mistress in a house apart, and visits her as privately as he can, just as it is with you. Amongst all the great men here, I only know the *tefterdar* (*i.e.* treasurer) that keeps a number of she slaves for his own use (that is, on his own side of the house; for a slave once given to serve a lady is entirely at her disposal), and he is spoken of as a libertine, or what we should call a rake, and his wife won't see him, though she continues to live in his house.

Thus you see, dear sister, the manners of mankind do not differ so widely as our voyage writers would make us believe. Perhaps it would be more entertaining to add a few surprising customs of my own invention; but nothing seems to me so agreeable as truth, and I believe nothing so acceptable to you. I conclude therefore with repeating the great truth of my being.   Dear sister, etc.

TO MRS. S. C. [MISS SARAH CHISWELL]

ADRIANOPLE, APRIL 1, O.S.

In my opinion, dear S, I ought rather to quarrel with you for not answering my Nimeguen* letter of August till December, than to excuse my not writing again till now. I am sure there is on my side a very good excuse for silence, having gone such tiresome land-journeys, though I don't find the conclusion of them so bad as you seem to imagine. I am very easy here, and not in the solitude you fancy me. The great number of Greeks, French, English, and Italians, that are under our protection, make their court to me from morning till night; and, I'll assure you, are many of them very fine ladies; for there is no possibility for a Christian to live easily under this government but by the protection of an ambassador—and the richer they are, the greater is their danger.

Those dreadful stories you have heard of the *plague* have very little foundation in truth. I own I have much ado to reconcile myself to the sound of a word which has always given me such terrible ideas, though I am convinced there is little more in it than in a fever. As a proof of this, let me tell you that we passed through two or three towns most violently infected. In the very next house where we lay (in one of those places) two persons died of it. Luckily for me I was so well deceived that I knew nothing of the matter; and I was made believe, that our second cook had only a great cold. However, we left our doctor to take care of him, and yesterday they both arrived here in good health; and I am now let into the secret that he has had the *plague*. There are many that escape it; neither is the air ever infected. I am persuaded that it would be as easy a matter to root it out here as out of Italy and France; but it does so little mischief, they are not very solicitous about it, and are content to suffer this distemper instead of our variety, which they are utterly unacquainted with.

A propos of distempers, I am going to tell you a thing that will make you wish yourself here. The small-pox, so fatal, and so general amongst us, is here entirely harmless by the invention of *ingrafting,* which is the term they give it. There is a set of old women who make it their business to perform the operation every autumn, in the month of September, when the great heat is abated. People send to one another to know if any of their family has a mind to have the small-pox: they make parties for this purpose, and when they are met (commonly fifteen or

*a town in the Dutch republic

sixteen together), the old woman comes with a nut-shell full of the matter of the best sort of small-pox, and asks what vein you please to have opened. She immediately rips open that you offer to her with a large needle (which gives you no more pain than a common scratch), and puts into the vein as much matter as can lye [lie] upon the head of her needle, and after that binds up the little wound with a hollow bit of shell; and in this manner opens four or five veins. The Grecians have commonly the superstition of opening one in the middle of the forehead, one in each arm, and one on the breast, to mark the sign of the cross; but this has a very ill effect, all these wounds leaving little scars, and is not done by those that are not superstitious, who choose to have them in the legs, or that part of the arm that is concealed. The children or young patients play together all the rest of the day, and are in perfect health to the eighth. Then the fever begins to seize them, and they keep their beds two days, very seldom three. They have very rarely above twenty or thirty in their faces, which never mark; and in eight days' time they are as well as before their illness. Where they are wounded, there remain running sores during the distemper, which I don't doubt is a great relief to it. Every year thousands undergo this operation; and the French ambassador says pleasantly, that they take the small-pox here by way of diversion, as they take the waters in other countries. There is no example of any one that has died in it; and you may believe I am well satisfied of the safety of this experiment, since I intend to try it on my dear little son.

I am patriot enough to take pains to bring this useful invention into fashion in England; and I should not fail to write to some of our doctors very particularly about it, if I knew any one of them that I thought had virtue enough to destroy such a considerable branch of their revenue for the good to mankind. But that distemper is too beneficial to them, not to expose to all their resentment the hardy wight that should undertake to put an end to it. Perhaps, if I live to return, I may, however, have courage to war with them. Upon this occasion admire the heroism in the heart of your friend, etc., etc.

TO THE ABBÉ——[ABBÉ CONTI]

Constantinople, May 19, O.S. 1718.

I am extremely pleased with hearing from you, and my vanity (the darling frailty of mankind) not a little flattered by the uncommon questions you ask me, though I am utterly incapable of answering them.

And, indeed, were I as good a mathematician as Euclid himself, it requires an age's stay to make just observations on the air and vapours. I have not been yet a full year here, and am on the point of removing. Such is my rambling destiny. This will surprise you, and can surprise nobody so much as myself.

Perhaps you will accuse me of laziness, or dulness, or both together, that can leave this place without giving you some account of the Turkish court. I can only tell you, that if you please to read Sir Paul Rycaut, you will there find a full and true account of the vizier's, the *beglerbeys'*, the civil and spiritual government, the officers of the seraglio, etc., things that 'tis very easy to procure lists of, and therefore may be depended on; though other stories, God knows—I say no more—every body is at liberty to write their own remarks; the manners of people may change, or some of them escape the observation of travellers, but 'tis not the same of the government; and for that reason, since I can tell you nothing new, I will tell you nothing of it.

In the same silence shall be passed over the arsenal and seven towers; and for mosques; I have already described one of the noblest to you very particularly. But I cannot forbear taking notice to you of a mistake of Gemelli (though I honour him in a much higher degree than any other voyage writer): he says that there are no remains of Calcedon; this is certainly a mistake: I was there yesterday, and went across the canal in my galley, the sea being very narrow between that city and Constantinople. 'Tis still a large town, and has several mosques in it. The Christians still call it Calcedonia, and the Turks give it a name I forgot, but which is only a corruption of the same word.[1] I suppose this is an error of his guide, which his short stay hindered him from rectifying; or I have, in other matters, a very just esteem for his veracity. Nothing can be pleasanter than the canal, and the Turks are so well acquainted with its beauties, that all their pleasure-seats are built on its banks, where they have, at the same time, the most beautiful prospects in Europe and Asia; there are, near one another, some hundreds of magnificent palaces.

Human grandeur being here yet more unstable than anywhere else, 'tis common for the heirs of a great three-tailed pasha not to be rich enough to keep in repair the house he built; thus, in a few years, they all fall to ruin. I was yesterday to see that of the late Grand-Vizier, who was killed at Peterwaradin. It was built to receive his royal bride; daughter of the present Sultan, but he did not live to see her there. I

---

[1] Cádykúy, or the Town of Judges, from the great Christian Council held there.

have a great mind to describe it to you; but I check that inclination, knowing very well that I cannot give you, with my best description, such an idea of it as I ought. It is situated on one of the most delightful parts of the canal, with a fine wood on the side of a hill behind it. The extent of it is prodigious; the guardian assured me there are eight hundred rooms in it; I will not, however, answer for that number, since I did not count them; but 'tis certain the number is very large, and the whole adorned with a profusion of marble, gilding, and the most exquisite painting of fruit and flowers. The windows are all sashed with the finest crystalline glass brought from England; and here is all the expensive magnificence that you can suppose in a palace founded by a vain luxurious young man, with the wealth of a vast empire at his command. But no part of it pleased me better than the apartments destined for the bagnios. There are two, built exactly in the same manner, answering to one another; the baths, fountains, and pavements, all of white marble, the roofs gilt, and the walls covered with Japan china. Adjoining to them are two rooms, the uppermost of which is divided into a sofa, and in the four corners are falls of water from the very roof, from shell to shell, of white marble, to the lower end of the room, where it falls into a large basin, surrounded with pipes, that throw up the water as high as the roof. The walls are in the nature of lattices; and on the outside of them, there are vines and woodbines planted, that form a sort of green tapestry, and give an agreeable obscurity to those delightful chambers.

I should go on and let you into some of the other apartments (all worthy your curiosity); but 'tis yet harder to describe a Turkish palace than any other, being built entirely irregular. There is nothing that can be properly called front or wings; and though such a confusion is, I think, pleasing to the sight, yet it would be very unintelligible in a letter. I shall only add, that the chamber destined for the Sultan, when he visits his daughter, is wainscotted with mother of pearl fastened with emeralds like nails. There are others of mother of pearl and olive wood inlaid, and several of Japan china. The galleries, which are numerous and very large, are adorned with jars of flowers, and porcelain dishes of fruit of all sorts, so well done in plaster, and coloured in so lively a manner, that it has an enchanting effect. The garden is suitable to the house, where arbours, fountains, and walks, are thrown together in an agreeable confusion. There is no ornament wanting, except that of statues. Thus, you see, sir, these people are not so unpolished as we represent them. 'Tis true their magnificence is of a very different taste from ours, and perhaps of a better. I am almost of opinion they have a right notion of life. They consume it in music, gardens, wine, and delicate eating, while we are tormenting our brains with some scheme of politics, or studying some science to which we can never attain, or, if we do, cannot persuade other people to set that value upon it we do ourselves. 'Tis certain what we feel and see is properly (if any thing is properly) our own; but the good of fame, the folly of praise, are hardly purchased, and, when obtained, a poor recompence for loss of time and health. We die or grow old before we can reap the fruit of our labours. Considering what short-liv'd weak animals men are, is there any study so beneficial as the study of present pleasure? I dare not pursue this theme; perhaps I have already said too much, but I depend upon the true knowledge you have of my heart. I don't expect from you the insipid railleries I should suffer from another in answer to this letter. You know how to divide the idea of pleasure from that of vice, and they are only mingled in the heads of fools.—But I allow you to laugh at me for the sensual declaration in saying, that I had rather be a rich *effendi* with all his ignorance, then Sir Isaac Newton with all his knowledge.   I am, sir, etc., etc.

5

DENIS DIDEROT

Encyclopedia

1751

Denis Diderot (1713–1784) began life as a relatively poor youth in the French provinces. By the 1730s, he had made his way to Paris. He gradually left the Catholicism of his youth and even briefly made a living writing risqué novels. But he had grander plans and abilities. By the 1740s, Diderot, allied with a consortium of publishers eager for profit, decided to compile an encyclopedia of philosophy and the mechanical arts. He had a model in the English Cyclopaedia; or, An Universal Dictionary of Arts and Sciences *(1728) by Ephraim Chambers, which*

Denis Diderot, *The Encyclopedia: Selections,* ed. and trans. Stephen Gendzier (New York: Harper & Row, 1967), 92–95.

Diderot as editor, assisted by the mathematician Jean d'Alembert, intended to redo and expand. They invented a "tree of knowledge," an elaborate chart intended to illustrate all of human knowledge. The inspiration for the chart came from the writings of Francis Bacon (see page 157). More than two hundred writers, from the famous to the obscure, were assigned articles, and more than fourteen hundred subscribers were enlisted.

In 1751, the most famous work of the French Enlightenment appeared: the first volume of Diderot's Encyclopédie, *with a preface by d'Alembert. The preface proclaimed a new era, inspired by John Locke's ideas about learning and dedicated to Bacon's investigation of nature, to improvement through the practical arts, and to skepticism toward official dogmas— an era that would be thoroughly secular. In his article "Encyclopedia," reprinted here, Diderot further explained the mission, arguing that the project aimed to enlighten the entire human race.*

ENCYCLOPEDIA *(Philosophy)*. This word means the *interrelation of all knowledge;* it is made up of the Greek prefix *en,* in, and the nouns *kyklos,* circle, and *paideia,* instruction, science, knowledge. In truth, the aim of an *encyclopedia* is to collect all the knowledge scattered over the face of the earth, to present its general outlines and structure to the men with whom we live, and to transmit this to those who will come after us, so that the work of past centuries may be useful to the following centuries, that our children, by becoming more educated, may at the same time become more virtuous and happier, and that we may not die without having deserved well of the human race. . . .

We have seen that our *Encyclopedia* could only have been the endeavor of a philosophical century; that this age has dawned, and that fame, while raising to immortality the names of those who will perfect man's knowledge in the future, will perhaps not disdain to remember our own names. We have been heartened by the ever so consoling and agreeable idea that people may speak to one another about us, too, when we shall no longer be alive; we have been encouraged by hearing from the mouths of a few of our contemporaries a certain voluptuous murmur that suggests what may be said of us by those happy and educated men in whose interests we have sacrificed ourselves, whom we esteem and whom we love, even though they have not yet been born. We have felt within ourselves the development of those seeds of emulation which have moved us to renounce the better part of ourselves to accomplish our task, and which have ravished away into the void the few moments of our existence of which we are genuinely proud. Indeed, man reveals himself to his contemporaries and is seen by them for what he is: a peculiar mixture of sublime attributes and shameful weaknesses. But our weaknesses follow our mortal remains into the tomb and disappear with them; the same earth covers them both, and there remains only the total result of our attributes immortalized in the monuments we raise to ourselves or in the memorials that we owe to public respect and gratitude—honors which a proper awareness of our own deserts enables us to enjoy in anticipation, an enjoyment that is as pure, as great, and as real as any other pleasure and in which there is nothing imaginary except, perhaps, the titles on which we base our pretensions. Our own claims are deposited in the pages of this work, and posterity will judge them.

I have said that it could only belong to a philosophical age to attempt an *encyclopedia;* and I have said this because such a work constantly demands more intellectual daring than is commonly found in ages of pusillanimous taste. All things must be examined, debated, investigated without exception and without regard for anyone's feelings....We must ride roughshod over all these ancient puerilities, overturn the barriers that reason never erected, give back to the arts and sciences the liberty that is so precious to them....We have for quite some time needed a reasoning age when men would no longer seek the rules in classical authors but in nature, when men would be conscious of what is false and true about so many arbitrary treatises on aesthetics: and I take the term *treatise on aesthetics* in its most general meaning, that of a system of given rules to which it is claimed that one must conform in any genre whatsoever in order to succeed. . . .

It would be desirable for the government to authorize people to go into the factories and shops, to see the craftsmen at their work, to question them, to draw the tools, the machines, and even the premises.

There are special circumstances when craftsmen are so secretive about their techniques that the shortest way of learning about them would be to apprentice oneself to a master or to have some trustworthy person do this. There would be few secrets that one would fail to bring to light by this method, and all these secrets would have to be divulged without any exception.

I know that this feeling is not shared by everyone. These are narrow minds, deformed souls, who are indifferent to the fate of the human race and who are so enclosed in their little group that they see nothing beyond its special interest. These men insist on being called good citizens, and I consent to this, provided that they permit me to call them *bad men*. To listen to them talk, one would say that a successful *encyclopedia,* that a general history of the mechanical arts, should only take the form of an enormous manuscript that would be carefully locked up in the king's library, inaccessible to all other eyes but his, an official document of the state, not meant to be consulted by the people. What is the good of divulging the knowledge a nation possesses, its private transactions, its inventions, its industrial processes, its resources, its trade secrets, its enlightenment, its arts, and all its wisdom? Are not these the things to which it owes a part of its superiority over the rival nations that surround it? This is what they say; and this is what they might add: would it not be desirable if, instead of enlightening the foreigner, we could spread darkness over him or even plunge all the rest of the world into barbarism so that we could dominate more securely over everyone? These people do not realize that they occupy only a single point on our globe and that they will endure only a moment in its existence. To this point and to this moment they would sacrifice the happiness of future ages and that of the entire human race.

They know as well as anyone that the average duration of empires is not more than two thousand years and that in less time, perhaps, the name *Frenchman,* a name that will endure forever in history, will be sought after in vain over the surface of the earth. These considerations do not broaden their point of view; for it seems that the word *humanity* is for them a word without meaning. All the same, they should be consistent! For they also fulminate against the impenetrability of the Egyptian sanctuaries; they deplore the loss of the knowledge of the ancients; they accuse the writers of the past for having been silent or negligent in writing so badly on an infinite number of important subjects; and these illogical critics do not see that they demand of the writers of earlier ages something they call a crime when it is committed by a contemporary, that they are blaming others for having done what they think it honorable to do.

6

DENIS DIDEROT

Supplement to Bougainville's Voyage

1772

Like all educated Europeans of the time, Diderot read avidly in the travel literature. He regarded much of it as biased against non-Europeans, and he was wise enough to know that writers build their biases into what they see abroad. Yet as a would-be traveler, Diderot was at a distinct disadvantage: He hated to travel. Even so, with much complaining, he finally did make his way to the Dutch republic and Russia.

In the turbulent 1750s, when his Encyclopédie *set off a firestorm of controversy, Diderot and his friends took to writing essays and reviews for the privately circulated, handwritten* Correspondance littéraire. *Diderot reviewed a voyage book by Louis-Antoine de Bougainville, who, after traveling around the world, published his account in 1771. It told a remarkable fable about sexual liberty among the Tahitians. In this selection, which Diderot wrote in 1772 but which was not published until 1796, he imagined an encounter with the Tahitians. The* Supplement *reveals Diderot's deep antagonism toward conquest and exploitation and toward the repressive morality he associated with Christian European societies. Although modern critics might charge that he presents a purely mythical portrayal of the Tahitians and glories in a system of sexual liberty that centers on men, the piece's daring at the time far outweighs its limitations. Diderot no doubt saw Bougainville's* Voyage *as the possible start of an entire reorganization of social mores, and some kind of reform of French laws and institutions lay at the heart of his* Supplement. *So outrageous was the* Supplement, *however, that some critics saw it as working out in moral and fictive practice the sexual license and sadism advocated by Diderot's infamous contemporary the marquis de Sade. Little wonder that during Diderot's lifetime, only his closest friends had the privilege of reading the* Supplement.

In Bougainville's account of Tahiti, an old man stands apart and watches the proceedings with disapproval. This figure ignited Diderot's

Denis Diderot, *Supplement to Bougainville's* Voyage by Jacques Barzun (Upper Saddle River, N.J.: Prentice-Hall, 1965), 187–92, 194–207, 210–11, 213.

imagination, and in the first part of the document, the man delivers a scathing indictment of conquest and slavery (a reflection of Diderot's own feelings). This oration is followed by an exchange between a European chaplain and another Tahitian, Orou. The dialogue allows Diderot to examine the hypocrisy of European mores regarding marriage, sexual freedom, and religion. Note that in this selection, the Tahitians clearly regard the Europeans as inferior in most respects.

THE OLD MAN'S FAREWELL

He was the father of a numerous family. At the time of the Europeans' arrival, he cast upon them a look that was filled with scorn, though it revealed no surprise, no alarm and no curiosity. They approached him; he turned his back on them and retired into his hut. His thoughts were only too well revealed by his silence and his air of concern, for in the privacy of his thoughts he groaned inwardly over the happy days of his people, now gone forever. At the moment of Bougainville's departure, when all the natives ran swarming onto the beach, tugging at his clothing and throwing their arms around his companions and weeping, the old man stepped forward and solemnly spoke:

"Weep, wretched Tahitians, weep—but rather for the arrival than for the departure of these wicked and grasping men! The day will come when you will know them for what they are. Someday they will return, bearing in one hand that piece of wood you see suspended from this one's belt and in the other the piece of steel that hangs at the side of his companion. They will load you with chains, slit your throats and enslave you to their follies and vices. Someday you will be slaves to them, you will be as corrupt, as vile, as wretched as they are. But I have this consolation—my life is drawing to its close, and I shall not see the calamity that I foretell. O Tahitians, O my friends! You have the means of warding off a terrible fate, but I would die before I would advise you to make use of it. Let them leave, and let them live."

Then, turning to Bougainville, he went on: "And you, leader of these brigands who obey you, take your vessel swiftly from our shores. We are innocent and happy, and you can only spoil our happiness. We follow the pure instinct of nature, and you have tried to efface her imprint from our hearts. Here all things are for all, and you have preached to us I know not what distinctions between mine and thine. Our women and girls we possess in common; you have shared this privilege with us, and your coming has awakened in them a frenzy they have never known before. They have become mad in your arms; you have become ferocious in theirs. They have begun to hate one another; you have cut one another's throats for them, and they have come home to us stained with your blood.

"We are free—but see where you have driven into our earth the symbol of our future servitude. You are neither a god nor a devil—by what right, then, do you enslave people? Orou! You who understand the speech of these men, tell every one of us, as you have told me, what they have written on that strip of metal—'This land belongs to us.' This land belongs to you! And why? Because you set foot in it? If some day a Tahitian should land on your shores, and if he should engrave on one of your stones or on the bark of one of your trees 'This land belongs to the people of Tahiti,' what would you think? You are stronger than we are! And what does that signify? When one of our lads carried off some of the miserable trinkets with which your ship is loaded, what an uproar you made, and what revenge you took! And at that very moment you were plotting, in the depths of your hearts, to steal a whole country! You are not slaves; you would suffer death rather than be enslaved, yet you want to make slaves of us! Do you believe, then, that the Tahitian does not know how to die in defense of his liberty? This Tahitian, whom you want to treat as a chattel, as a dumb animal—this Tahitian is your brother. You are both children of Nature—what right do you have over him that he does not have over you?

"You came; did we attack you? Did we plunder your vessel? Did we seize you and expose you to the arrows of our enemies? Did we force you to work in the fields alongside our beasts of burden? We respected our own image in you. Leave us our own customs, which are wiser and more decent than yours. We have no wish to barter what you call our ignorance for your useless knowledge. We possess already all that is good or necessary for our existence. Do we merit your scorn because we have not been able to create superfluous wants for ourselves? When we are hungry, we have something to eat; when we are cold, we have clothing to put on. You have been in our huts—what is lacking there, in your opinion? You are welcome to drive yourselves as hard as you please in pursuit of what you call the comforts of life, but allow sensible people to stop when they see they have nothing to gain but imaginary benefits from the continuation of their painful labors. If you persuade us to go beyond the bounds of strict necessity, when shall we come to the end of our labor? When shall we have time for enjoyment? We have reduced our daily and yearly labors to the least possible amount, because to us nothing seemed more desirable than leisure. Go and bestir yourselves in your own country; there you may torment yourselves as much as you like; but leave us in peace, and do not fill our heads with a hankering after your false needs and imaginary virtues. Look at these men—see how healthy, straight and strong they are. See these women—how straight, healthy, fresh and lovely they are. Take this bow in your hands—it is my own—and call one, two, three, four of your comrades to help you try to bend it. I can bend it myself. I work the soil, I climb mountains, I make my way through the dense forest, and I can run four leagues on the plain in less than an hour. Your young comrades have been hard put to it to keep up with me, and yet I have passed my ninetieth year. . . .

"Woe to this island! Woe to all the Tahitians now living, and to all those yet to be born, woe from the day of your arrival! We used to know but one disease, the one to which all men, all animals and all plants are subject—old age. But you have brought us a new one: you have infected our blood. We shall perhaps be compelled to exterminate with our own hands some of our young girls, some of our women, some of our children, those who have lain with your women, those who have lain with your men. Our fields will be spattered with the foul blood that has passed from your veins into ours. Or else our children, condemned to die, will nourish and perpetuate the evil disease that you have given their fathers and mothers, transmitting it forever to their descendants. Wretched men! You will bear the guilt either of the ravages that will follow your baneful caresses or of the murders we must commit to arrest the progress of the poison! You speak of crime! Can you conceive of a greater crime than the one you have committed? How do they punish, in your country, the man who has killed his neighbor? Death by the headsman's ax! How do you punish the man who has poisoned his neighbor? Burning at the stake! Compare the second crime with your own, and then tell us, you poisoner of whole nations, what tortures you deserve!

"But a little while ago, the young Tahitian girl blissfully abandoned herself to the embraces of a Tahitian youth and awaited impatiently the day when her mother, authorized to do so by her having reached the age of puberty, would remove her veil and uncover her breasts. She was proud of her ability to excite men's desires, to attract the amorous looks of strangers, of her own relatives, of her own brothers. In our presence, without shame, in the center of a throng of innocent Tahitians who danced and played the flute, she accepted the caresses of the young man whom her young heart and the secret promptings of her senses had marked out for her. The notion of crime and the fear of disease have come among us only with your coming. Now our enjoyments, formerly so sweet, are attended with guilt and terror. That man in black, who stands near to you and listens to me, has spoken to our young men, and I know not what he has said to our young girls, but our youths are hesitant and our girls blush. Creep away into the dark forest, if you wish, with the perverse companion of your pleasures, but allow the good, simple Tahitians to reproduce themselves without shame under the open sky and in broad daylight.

"What more noble or more wholesome feelings could you put in the place of the ones we have nurtured in them and by which they live? When they think the time has come to enrich the nation and the family with a new citizen, they glorify the occasion. They eat in order to live and grow; they grow in order that they may multiply, and in that they see neither vice nor shame. Listen to the consequences of your crimes. Scarcely had you shown yourselves among our people than they became thieves. Scarcely had you set foot upon our soil than it began to reek of blood. You killed the Tahitian who ran to greet you, crying 'Taïo—friend!' And why did you kill him? Because he was tempted by the glitter of your little serpent's eggs. He gave you his fruit; he offered you his wife and daughter; he gave you his hut to live in—and you killed him for taking a handful of those little glass beads without asking your permission. And the others? At the sound of your murderous weapons they fled to the hills. But you should know that had it not been for me they would soon have come down again to destroy you. Oh, why did I appease their anger? Why did I calm their fury? Why do I still restrain them, even at this moment? I do not know, for you surely have no claim to pity. Your own soul is hard and will never feel any.

"You and your men have gone where you pleased, wandered over the whole island; you have been respected; you have enjoyed everything: no barrier nor refusal has been placed in your path. You have been invited into our homes; you have sat down at our tables; our people have spread before you the abundance of our land. If you wanted one of our young women, her mother presented her to you all naked, unless she was one of those who are not yet old enough to have the privilege of showing their faces and breasts. Thus you have enjoyed possession of these tender sacrificial victims to the duty of hospitality. For the girl and for you we have strewn the ground with leaves and flowers, the musicians have put their instruments in tune; nothing has troubled the sweetness nor interfered with the freedom of her caresses and yours. We chanted the hymn, the one that urges you to be a man, that urges our child to be a woman, a compliant and voluptuous woman. We danced around your couch. Yet you had hardly left this girl's embrace, having experienced in her arms the sweetest intoxication, than you killed her brother, her friend, or perhaps her father.

"And you have done worse still—look yonder at that enclosure, bristling with arrows, with weapons that heretofore have threatened only our foes—see them now turned against our own children. Look now upon the unhappy companions of your pleasures! See their sorrow! See the distress of their fathers and the despair of their mothers! That is where they are condemned to die at our hands or from the disease you gave them. So leave this place, unless your cruel eyes delight in the spectacle of death! Go! And may the guilty sea, that spared your lives when you came here, now absolve itself and avenge our wrongs by swallowing you up on your homeward way! And you, Tahitians, go back to your huts, go indoors, all of you, so that these unworthy strangers, as they depart, may hear nothing but the growling of the waves and may see nothing but the white spray dashing in fury on a desert coast!"

He finished speaking, and in an instant the throng of natives disappeared. A vast silence reigned over the whole extent of the island, and nothing was to be heard but the dry whistling of the wind and the dull pounding of the waves along the whole length of the coast. It was as though the winds and waters had heard the old man's voice and obeyed him.

B: Well, what do you think of that?

A: The oration strikes me as forceful enough, but in the midst of so much that is unmistakably abrupt and savage I seem to detect a few European ideas and turns of phrase.

B: You must remember that it is a translation from Tahitian into Spanish and from Spanish into French. The previous night, the old man made a visit to Orou, the one to whom he appealed while speaking, in whose family the knowledge of Spanish had been preserved for several generations. Orou wrote down the old man's harangue in Spanish, and Bougainville had a copy of it in his hand while the old man was speaking. . . .

CONVERSATION BETWEEN
THE CHAPLAIN AND OROU

B: When the members of Bougainville's expedition were shared out among the native families, the ship's chaplain fell to the lot of Orou. The Tahitian and the chaplain were men of about the same age, that is, about thirty-five years old. At that time, Orou's family consisted of his wife and three daughters, who were called Asto, Palli and Thia. The women undressed their guest, washed his face, hands and feet, and put before him a wholesome though frugal meal. When he was about to go to bed, Orou, who had stepped outside with his family, reappeared and presented to him his wife and three girls—all naked as Eve—and said to him:

"You are young and healthy and you have just had a good supper. He who sleeps alone sleeps badly; at night a man needs a woman at his side. Here is my wife and here are my daughters. Choose whichever one pleases you most, but if you would like to do me a favor, you will give your preference to my youngest girl, who has not yet any children."

The mother said: "Poor girl! I don't hold it against her. It's no fault of hers."

The chaplain replied that his religion, his holy orders, his moral standards and his sense of decency all prevented him from accepting Orou's invitation.

Orou answered: "I don't know what this thing is that you call 'religion,' but I can only have a low opinion of it because it forbids you to partake of an innocent pleasure to which Nature, the sovereign mistress of us all, invites everybody. It seems to prevent you from bringing one of your fellow creatures into the world, from doing a favor asked of you by a father, a mother and their children, from repaying the kindness of a host, and from enriching a nation by giving it an additional citizen. I don't know what it is that you call 'holy orders,' but your chief duty is to be a man and to show gratitude. I am not asking you to take my moral standards back with you to your own country, but Orou, your host and your friend, begs you merely to lend yourself to the morality of Tahiti. Is our moral code a better or a worse one than your own? This is an easy question to answer. Does the country you were born in have more people than it can support? If it does, then your morals are neither better nor worse than ours. Or can it feed more people than it now has? Then our morals are better than yours. As for the sense of propriety that leads you to object to my proposal, that I understand, and I freely admit that I am in the wrong. I ask your pardon. I cannot ask you to do anything that might harm your health; if you are too tired, you should by all means go to sleep at once. But I hope that you will not persist in disappointing us. Look at the distress you have caused to appear on the faces of these four women—they are afraid you have noticed some defect in them that arouses your distaste. But even if that were so, would it not be possible for you to do a good deed and have the pleasure of honoring one of my daughters in the sight of her sisters and friends? Come, be generous!"

The Chaplain: You don't understand — it's not that. They are all four of them equally beautiful. But there is my religion! My holy orders!

Orou: They are mine and I offer them to you; they are all of age and they give themselves to you. However clear a conscience may be demanded of you by this thing 'religion,' or by those 'holy orders' of yours, you need have no scruples about accepting these women. I am making no abuse of my paternal authority, and you may be sure that I recognize and respect the rights of individuals to their own persons.

At this point in his account, the truthful chaplain has to admit that up to that moment Providence had never exposed him to such strong temptation. He was young, he was excited, he was in torment. He turned his eyes away from the four lovely suppliants, then let his gaze wander back to them again. He lifted his hands and his countenance to Heaven. Thia, the youngest of the three girls, threw her arms around his knees and said to him: "Stranger, do not disappoint my father and mother. Do not disappoint me! Honor me in this hut and among my own family! Raise me to the dignity enjoyed by my sisters, for they make fun of me. Asto, my eldest sister, already has three children; Palli, the second oldest of us, has two; and Thia has none! Stranger, good stranger, do not reject me! Make me a mother! Give me a child whom I can someday lead by the hand as he walks at my side, to be seen by all Tahiti — a little one to nurse at my breast nine months from now, a child of whom I can be proud, and who will be part of my dowry when I go from my father's hut into that of another. Perhaps I shall be more fortunate with you than I have been with our Tahitian young men. If you will only grant me this favor, I will never forget you; I will bless you all my life; I will write your name on my arm and on that of my child; we will always pronounce it with joy; and when you leave this shore, my prayers will go with you across the seas all the way to your own country."

The poor chaplain records that she pressed his hands, that she fastened her eyes on his with the most expressive and touching gaze, that she wept, that her father, mother and sisters went out, leaving him alone with her, and that despite his repetition of "But there is my religion and my holy orders," he awoke the next morning to find the young girl lying at his side. She overwhelmed him with more caresses, and when her father, mother and sisters came in, she called upon them to add their gratitude to hers.

Asto and Palli, who had left the room briefly, soon returned bearing native food, drink and fruits. They embraced their sister and wished her good fortune. They all ate breakfast together; then, when Orou was left alone with the chaplain, he said to him: "I see that my daughter is pleased with you, and I thank you. But would you be good enough to tell me the meaning of this word 'religion' which you have spoken so frequently and so mournfully?"

After considering for a moment what to say, the chaplain replied: "Who made your hut and all the furnishings in it?"

Orou: I did.

The Chaplain: Well, we believe that this world and everything in it is the work of a maker.

Orou: Then he must have hands and feet, and a head.

The Chaplain: No.

Orou: Where is his dwelling place?

The Chaplain: Everywhere.

Orou: In this place too?

The Chaplain: In this place, too.

Orou: But we have never seen him.

The Chaplain: He cannot be seen.

Orou: He sounds to me like a father that doesn't care very much for his children. He must be an old man, because he must be at least as old as the things he made.

The Chaplain: No, he never grows old. He spoke to our ancestors and gave them laws; he prescribed to them the way in which he wishes to be honored; he ordained that certain actions are good, and others he forbade them to do as being evil.

Orou: I see. And one of these evil actions which he has forbidden is that of a man who goes to bed with a woman or girl. But in that case, why did he make two sexes?

The Chaplain: In order that they might come together—but only when certain conditions are satisfied and only after certain initial ceremonies have been performed. By virtue of these ceremonies one man belongs to one woman and only to her; one woman belongs to one man and only to him.

Orou: For their whole lives?

The Chaplain: For their whole lives.

Orou: So that if it should happen that a woman should go to bed with some man who was not her husband, or some man should go to bed with a woman that was not his wife . . . but that could never happen, because the workman would know what was going on, and since he doesn't like that sort of thing, he wouldn't let it occur.

The Chaplain: No. He lets them do as they will, and they sin against the law of God (for that is the name by which we call the great workman) and against the law of the country; they commit a crime.

Orou: I should be sorry to give offense by anything I might say, but if you don't mind, I'll tell you what I think.

The Chaplain: Go ahead.

Orou: I find these strange precepts contrary to nature, and contrary to reason. I think they are admirably calculated to increase the number of crimes and to give endless annoyance to the old workman—who made everything without hands, head or tools, who is everywhere but can be seen nowhere, who exists today and tomorrow but grows not a day older, who gives commands and is not obeyed, who can prevent what he dislikes but fails to do so. His commands are contrary to nature because they assume that a thinking being, one that has feelings and a sense of freedom, can be the property of another being like himself. On what could such a right of ownership be founded? Do you not see that in your country you have confused things that have no feelings, thoughts, desires or wills—things one takes or leaves, keeps or sells, without them suffering or complaining—with things that can neither be bought nor sold, which have freedom, volition, and desires of their own, which have the ability to give or to withhold themselves for a moment or forever, which suffer and complain? These latter things can never be treated like a trader's stock of goods unless one forgets what their true character is and does violence to nature. Furthermore, your laws seem to me to be contrary to the general order of things. For in truth is there anything so senseless as a precept that forbids us to heed the changing impulses that are inherent in our being, or commands that require a degree of constancy which is not possible, that violate the liberty of both male and female by chaining them perpetually to one another? Is there anything more unreasonable than this perfect fidelity that would restrict us, for the enjoyment of pleasures so capricious, to a single partner, than an oath of immutability taken by two individuals made of flesh and blood under a sky that is not the same for a moment, in a cavern that threatens to collapse upon them, at the foot of a cliff that is crumbling into dust, under a tree that is withering, on a bench of stone that is being worn away? Take my word for it, you have reduced human beings to a worse condition than that of the animals.

I don't know what your great workman is, but I am very happy that
he never spoke to our forefathers, and I hope that he never speaks to
our children, for if he does, he may tell them the same foolishness,
and they may be foolish enough to believe it. Yesterday, as we were
having supper, you told us all about your "magistrates" and "priests."
I do not know who these characters are whom you call magistrates
and priests and who have the authority to govern your conduct—but
tell me, are they really masters of good and evil? Can they transform
justice into injustice and contrariwise? Is it within their power to
attach the name of "good" to harmful actions or the name of "evil" to
harmless or useful deeds? One can hardly think so, because in that
case there would no longer be any difference between true and false,
between good and bad, between beautiful and ugly—only such differences as it pleased your great workman, your magistrates or your
priests to define as such. You would then have to change your ideas
and behavior from one moment to the next. One day you would be
told, on behalf of one of your three masters, "Kill," and in all good
conscience you would be obliged to kill. Another day they might say,
"Steal," and you would be bound to steal. Or: "Do not eat of this
fruit," and would not dare to eat of it; "I forbid you to eat this veg-
etable or this meat," and you would be careful never to touch them.
There is not a single good thing they could not forbid you to enjoy,
and no wickedness they could not order you to commit. And where
would you be if your three masters, disagreeing among themselves,
took it into their heads to permit, enjoin and forbid you to do the
same thing, as I am sure must occasionally happen? Then, in order to
please your priest, you would have to get yourself into hot water with
the magistrate; to satisfy the magistrate, you would have to risk the
displeasure of the great workman; and to make yourself agreeable to
the great workman, you would have to fly in the face of your own
nature. And do you know what will finally happen? You will come to
despise all three, and you will be neither man nor citizen nor pious
believer; you will be nothing at all; you will be at odds with all the
authorities, at odds with yourself, malicious, disturbed by your own
conscience, persecuted by your witless masters, and miserable, as
you were yesterday evening when I offered you my wife and daughters and you could only wail, "What about my religion? What about
my holy orders?" Would you like to know what is good and what is
bad in all times and places? Pay close attention to the nature of
things and actions, to your relations with your fellow creatures, to the
effect of your behavior on your own well-being and on the general

welfare. You are mad if you believe that there is anything in the universe, high or low, that can add or subtract from the laws of nature. Her eternal will is that good shall be chosen rather than evil, and the general welfare rather than the individual's well-being. You may decree the opposite, but you will not be obeyed. By threats, punishment and guilt you can make more wretches and rascals, make more depraved consciences and more corrupted characters. People will no longer know what they ought or ought not to do. They will feel guilty when they are doing nothing wrong and proud of themselves in the midst of crime; they will have lost the North Star that should guide their course. Give me an honest answer: in spite of the express commands of your three legislators, do the young men in your country never go to bed with a young woman without having received permission?

The Chaplain: I would be lying if I said they never do.

Orou: And the women, once they have sworn an oath to belong to only one husband, do they never give themselves to another man?

The Chaplain: Nothing happens more often.

Orou: And are your legislators severe in handing out punishment to such disobedient people, or are they not? If they are, then they are wild animals who make war against nature; if they are not severe, they are fools who risk bringing their authority into contempt by issuing futile prohibitions.

The Chaplain: The guilty ones, if they escape the rigor of the laws, are punished by public opinion.

Orou: That's like saying that justice is done by means of the whole nation's lack of common sense, and that public folly is the substitute for law.

The Chaplain: A girl who has lost her honor cannot find a husband.

Orou: Lost her honor! And for what cause?

The Chaplain: An unfaithful woman is more or less despised.

Orou: Despised! Why should that be?

The Chaplain: And the young man is called a cowardly seducer.

Orou: Coward? Seducer? Why that?

The Chaplain: The father and mother and their dishonored child are desolate. An erring husband is called a libertine; a husband who has been betrayed shares the shame of his wife.

Orou: What monstrous foolishness you're talking! And still you must be holding something back, because when people take it upon themselves to rearrange all ideas of justice and propriety to suit their own whims, to apply or remove the names of things in a completely arbitrary manner, to associate the ideas of good and evil with certain actions or to dissociate them for no reason save caprice—then of course people will blame each other, accuse each other, suspect each other, tyrannize, become jealous and envious, deceive and wound one another, conceal, dissimulate, and spy on one another, catch each other out, quarrel and tell lies. Girls will deceive their parents, husbands their wives and wives their husbands. Unmarried girls—yes, I am sure of it—unmarried girls will suffocate their babies; suspicious fathers will neglect or show contempt for their own rightful children; mothers will abandon their infants and leave them to the mercy of fate. Crime and debauchery will appear in every imaginable shape and form. I see all that as plainly as if I had lived among you. The things are so because they must be so, and your society, whose well-ordered ways your chief boasts to you about, can't be anything but a swarm of hypocrites who secretly trample the laws under foot, or a multitude of wretched beings who serve as instruments for inflicting willing torture upon themselves; or imbeciles in whom prejudice has utterly silenced the voice of nature, or ill-fashioned creatures in whom nature cannot claim her rights.

The Chaplain: That is a close likeness. But do you never marry?

Orou: Oh yes, we marry.

The Chaplain: Well, how does it work?

Orou: It consists only of an agreement to occupy the same hut and to sleep in the same bed for so long as both partners find the arrangement good.

The Chaplain: And when they find it bad?

Orou: Then they separate.

The Chaplain: But what becomes of the children?

Orou: Oh, stranger! That last question of yours finally reveals to me the last depths of your country's wretchedness. Let me tell you, my friend, that the birth of a child is always a happy event, and its death is an occasion for weeping and sorrow. A child is a precious thing because it will grow up to be a man or a woman. Therefore we take infinitely better care of our children than of our plants and animals. The birth of a child is the occasion for public celebration and a source of joy for its entire family. For the hut it means an increase in wealth, while for the nation it signifies additional strength. It means another pair of hands and arms for Tahiti—we see in the newborn baby a future farmer, fisherman, hunter, soldier, husband or father. When a woman goes from her husband's hut back to that of her family, she takes with her all the children she brought with her as her dowry; those born during the marriage are divided equally between the two spouses, and care is taken to give each an equal number of boys and girls whenever possible.

The Chaplain: But children are a burden for many years before they are old enough to make themselves useful.

Orou: We set aside for them and for the support of the aged one part in six of all our harvests; wherever the child goes, this support follows him. And so, you see, the larger the family a Tahitian has, the richer he is.

The Chaplain: One part in six!

Orou: Yes. It's a dependable method for encouraging the growth of population, for promoting respect for our old people and for safeguarding the welfare of our children.

The Chaplain: And does it ever happen that a couple who have separated decide to live together again?

Orou: Oh, yes. It happens fairly often. Also, the shortest time any marriage can last is one month.

The Chaplain: Assuming, of course, that the wife is not with child, for in that case, wouldn't the marriage have to last at least nine months?

Orou: Not at all. The child keeps the name of its mother's husband at the time it was conceived, and its paternity, like its means of support, follows it wherever it goes.

The Chaplain: You spoke about the children that a wife brings to her husband as dowry.

Orou: To be sure. Take my eldest daughter, who has three children. They are able to walk, they are healthy and attractive, and they promise to be strong when they are grown up. If she should take it into her head to get married, she would take them along, for they belong to her, and her husband would be extremely happy to have them in his hut. He would think all the better of his wife if she were carrying still a fourth child at the time of her wedding.

The Chaplain: His child?

Orou: His or another's. The more children our young women have had, the more desirable they are as wives. The stronger and lustier our young men are, the richer they become. Therefore, careful as we are to protect our young girls from male advances, and our young boys from intercourse with women, before they reach sexual maturity, once they have passed the age of puberty we exhort them all the more strongly to have as many children as possible. You probably haven't fully realized what an important service you will have rendered my daughter Thia if you have succeeded in getting her with child. Her mother will no longer plague her every month by saying, "But, Thia, what is the matter with you? You never get pregnant, and here you are nineteen years old. You should have had at least a couple of babies by this time, and you have none. Who is going to look after you in your old age if you throw away your youth in this way? Thia, I begin to think there is something wrong with you, some defect that puts men off. Find out what it is, my child, and correct it if you can. At your age, I was already three times a mother!"

The Chaplain: What precautions do you take to safeguard your boys and girls before they reach maturity?

Orou: That's the main object of our children's education within the family circle, and it's the main important point in our code of public morality. Our boys, until the age of twenty-two, that is for two to three years after they reach maturity, must wear a long tunic that covers their bodies completely, and they must wear a little chain around their loins. Before they reach nubile age, our girls would not dare to go out without white veils. The two misdeeds of taking off one's chain or of raising one's veil are rarely met with, because we teach our children at a very early age what harmful results will ensue. But when the proper time comes—when the male has attained his full strength, when the principal indication of virility lasts for a sufficient time, and when we are confirmed in our judgment by the quality and by the frequent emission of the seminal fluid—and when the young girl seems wilted and suffers from boredom, when she seems mature enough to feel passion, to inspire it and to satisfy it, then the father unfastens his son's chain and cuts the nail on the middle finger of the boy's right hand. The mother removes her daughter's veil. The young man can now ask a woman for her favors or be asked by her to grant his. The girl may walk about freely in public places with her face and breast uncovered; she may accept or reject men's caresses. All we do is to point out in advance to the boy certain girls and to the girl certain boys that they might well choose as partners. The day when a boy or girl is emancipated is a gala holiday. In the case of a girl, the young men assemble the night before around her hut and the air is filled all night long with singing and the sound of musical instruments. When the sun has risen, she is led by her father and mother into an enclosure where dancing is going on and where games of wrestling, running and jumping are in progress. A naked man is paraded in front of her, allowing her to examine his body from all aspects and in all sorts of attitudes. For a young man's initiation, the young girls do the honors of the occasion by letting him look at the nude female body unadorned and unconcealed. The remainder of the ceremony is enacted on a bed of leaves, just as you saw it on your arrival here. At sunset the girl returns to her parents' hut or else moves to the hut of the young man she has chosen and remains there as long as she pleases.

The Chaplain: But is this celebration a marriage ceremony or is it not?

Orou: Well, as you have said . . .

The Chaplain: [With such customs] how can she know who the father of her child is?

Orou: How could she not know? With us the same rule that applies to marriage applies also to love affairs—each lasts at least from one moon to the next.

The Chaplain: And is the rule strictly observed?

Orou: You can judge for yourself. First, the interval between two moons isn't long, but when it appears that two men have well-founded claims to be the father of a child, it no longer belongs to the mother.

The Chaplain: To whom does it belong?

Orou: To whichever of the two men the mother chooses to give it. This is the only right she has, and since a child is an object of both interest and value, you can understand that among us loose women are rare and that our young men keep away from them.

The Chaplain: Then you do have a few licentious women? That makes me feel better.

Orou: Yes, we have some, and more than one kind—but that is another subject. When one of our girls gets pregnant, she is twice as pleased with herself if the child's father is a handsome, well-built, brave, intelligent, industrious young man, because she has reason to hope that the child will inherit its father's good qualities. The only thing a girl would be ashamed of would be a bad choice. You have no idea how much store we set by good health, beauty, strength, industry and courage; you have no notion what a tendency there is, even without our having to pay any particular attention to it, for good physical inheritance to be passed on from generation to generation among us. You are a person who has traveled in all sorts of countries—tell me if you have seen anywhere else so many handsome men and beautiful women as in Tahiti. Look at me. What do you think of me? Well, there are ten thousand men on this island who are taller than I am and just as strong; but there is none braver, and for that reason mothers very often point me out to their girls as a good father for their children.

The Chaplain: And out of all these children you have sired outside your own hut, how many fall to your share?

Orou: Every fourth, be it a boy or a girl. You see, we have developed a kind of circulation of men, women and children—that is, of able-bodied workers of all ages and occupations—which is much more important than trade in foodstuffs (which are only the products of human labor) in your country. . . .

The Chaplain: So far as I can see, jealousy is practically unknown here in Tahiti. But tenderness between husband and wife, and maternal love, which are strong, beautiful emotions—if they exist here at all, they must be fairly lukewarm.

Orou: We have put in their place another impulse, which is more universal, powerful and lasting—self-interest. Examine your conscience in all candor, put aside the hypocritical parade of virtue which is always on the lips of your companions, though not in their hearts, and tell me if there is anywhere on the face of the earth a man who, if he were not held back by shame, would not prefer to lose his child—a husband who would not prefer to lose his wife—rather than lose his fortune and all the amenities of life? You may be sure that if ever a man can be led to care as much about his fellow men as he does about his own bed, his own health, his leisure, his house, his harvests or his fields, he can be depended upon to do his utmost to look out for the well-being of other people. Then you will see him shedding tears over the bed of a sick child or taking care of a mother when she is ill. Then you will find fruitful women, nubile girls and handsome young men highly regarded. Then you will find a great deal of attention paid to the education of the young, because the nation grows stronger with their growth, and suffers a material loss if their well-being is impaired.

The Chaplain: I am afraid there is some reason in what this savage says. The poor peasant of our European lands wears out his wife in order to spare his horse, lets his child die without help and calls the veterinary to look after his ox. . . .

The good chaplain tells us that he spent the rest of the day wandering about the island, visiting a number of huts, and that in the evening, after supper, the father and mother begged him to go to bed with Palli, the second eldest daughter. She offered herself in the same undress as Thia's, and he tells us that several times during the night he cried out, "My religion! My holy orders!" The third night he suffered the same guilty torments in the arms of Asto, the eldest, and the fourth night, not to be unfair, he devoted to his hostess. . . .

7

JEAN-JACQUES ROUSSEAU

The Social Contract

1762

Jean-Jacques Rousseau (1712–1778) remains the most famous citizen of Geneva. Rousseau delighted in describing himself by his status within his native city, which provided the framework for many of his ideas, and an overly idealized vision of the Geneva republic became a cornerstone of his republicanism. Like so many of the philosophes, Rousseau conducted a dialogue with the great philosophers of the seventeenth century. At the heart of The Social Contract *lies his radical reworking of the ideas of the English theorist Thomas Hobbes, particularly Hobbes's notion, articulated in his* Leviathan *(1651), of the contract as the foundation of the state. For men to be free and yet enjoy the protection offered by authority, they must make a contract among themselves to live in harmony, which is made possible only by obedience and liberty. Unlike Hobbes's contract, which could never be altered and guaranteed only property rights, Rousseau based his ideas on the sovereignty of the people: A free people have leaders and not masters; they obey, but they do not serve. Most important, they vote, and they have the right to depose a sovereign. If this sounds familiar, it is because the founders of the American republic knew Rousseau's writings intimately.*

Rousseau arrived at his democratic theory by a fanciful and imaginary route. First he postulated a benign state of nature where, unlike Hobbes's war of all against all, everyone is free and endowed with the possibility of self-improvement. Only warfare over property—the sport of the rich—leads to a social condition that requires a contract. Ironically, nascent society gave human beings a social contract so that they might regulate and mitigate the evils of society. Once encoded by social mores, truly virtuous people seek as much refuge from these evils as possible. They go into the country, take romantic journeys to faraway places, and dream of abrupt shocks or revolutions that will break old habits and return humankind to a more pristine, primitive state.

The Social Contract and Discourses and Other Essays by Jean-Jacques Rousseau, trans. G. D. H. Cole (New York: E. P. Dutton, 1955), 322–52.

To ensure the preservation of the social contract, Rousseau invented the concept of the general will. *This amalgam of majority opinion gives leaders the right to enforce laws, demand conformity, and mold the state in accord with the general will. Twentieth-century theorists argued that Rousseau laid the foundation for totalitarianism with this concept, but that is an anachronistic reading of his work. Rousseau placed too much emphasis on equality before the law and human liberty to make him of much use to modern architects of totalitarianism. First and foremost, Rousseau cared passionately about human freedom and equality. His use of slavery as the metaphor best describing the political order of Europe in his time was guaranteed to inflame the authorities.*

In this excerpt from The Social Contract, *Rousseau betrays his limited knowledge of the world and sends a mixed message about "the savage." On the one hand, this "savage" could be noble, a model for man in the state of nature. On the other hand, the climate and soil in some places made governance of the "savage" next to impossible. The philosophes had almost no concrete experience of the non-Western world and vice versa. But when non-Westerners read Rousseau, he provokes and fascinates, almost always being seen as a champion of democracy and human liberation.*

BOOK I

Chapter I: Subject of the First Book

Man is born free; and everywhere he is in chains. One thinks himself the master of others, and still remains a greater slave than they. How did this change come about? I do not know. What can make it legitimate? That question I think I can answer.

If I took into account only force, and the effects derived from it, I should say: "As long as a people is compelled to obey, and obeys, it does well; as soon as it can shake off the yoke, and shakes it off, it does still better; for, regaining its liberty by the same right as took it away, either it is justified in resuming it or there was no justification for those who took it away." But the social order is a sacred right which is the basis of all rights. Nevertheless, this right does not come from nature, and must therefore be founded on conventions. Before coming to that, I have to prove what I have just asserted.

Chapter II: The First Societies

The most ancient of all societies, and the only one that is natural, is the family: and even so the children remain attached to the father only so long as they need him for their preservation. As soon as this need ceases, the natural bond is dissolved. The children, released from the obedience they owed to the father, and the father, released from the care he owed his children, return equally to independence. If they remain united, they continue so no longer naturally, but voluntarily; and the family itself is then maintained only by convention.

This common liberty results from the nature of man. His first law is to provide for his own preservation, his first cares are those which he owes to himself; and, as soon as he reaches years of discretion, he is the sole judge of the proper means of preserving himself, and consequently becomes his own master.

The family, then, may be called the first model of political societies: the ruler corresponds to the father, and the people to the children; and all, being born free and equal, alienate their liberty only for their own advantage. The whole difference is that in the family the love of the father for his children repays him for the care he takes of them, while in the State the pleasure of commanding takes the place of the love which the chief cannot have for the peoples under him. . . .

As a shepherd is of a nature superior to that of his flock, the shepherds of men, i.e. their rulers, are of a nature superior to that of the peoples under them. Thus, Philo* tells us, the Emperor Caligula reasoned, concluding equally well either that kings were gods or that men were beasts.

The reasoning of Caligula agrees with that of Hobbes and Grotius.† Aristotle, before any of them, had said that men are by no means equal naturally, but that some are born for slavery, and others for dominion.

Aristotle was right; but he took the effect for the cause. Nothing can be more certain than that every man born in slavery is born for slavery. Slaves lose everything in their chains, even the desire of escaping from them: they love their servitude, as the comrades of Ulysses loved their brutish condition.[1] If, then, there are slaves by nature, it is because there have been slaves against nature. Force made the first slaves, and their cowardice perpetuated the condition.

I have said nothing of King Adam, or Emperor Noah, father of the three great monarchs who shared out the universe, like the children of Saturn, whom some scholars have recognized in them. I trust to getting due thanks for my moderation; for, being a direct descendant of one of these princes, perhaps of the eldest branch, how do I know that a verification of titles might not leave me the legitimate king of the human

*a Roman historian
†Hugo Grotius, a seventeenth-century Dutch jurist and statesman
[1]See a short treatise of Plutarch's entitled "That Animals Reason."

race? In any case, there can be no doubt that Adam was sovereign of the world, as Robinson Crusoe was of his island, as long as he was its only inhabitant; and this empire had the advantage that the monarch, safe on his throne, had no rebellions, wars, or conspirators to fear.

Chapter III: The Right of the Strongest

The strongest is never strong enough to be always the master, unless he transforms strength into right, and obedience into duty. Hence the right of the strongest, which, though to all seeming meant ironically, is really laid down as a fundamental principle. But are we never to have an explanation of this phrase? Force is a physical power, and I fail to see what moral effect it can have. To yield to force is an act of necessity, not of will—at the most, an act of prudence. In what sense can it be a duty?

Suppose for a moment that this so-called "right" exists. I maintain that the sole result is a mass of inexplicable nonsense. For, if force creates right, the effect changes with the cause: every force that is greater than the first succeeds to its right. As soon as it is possible to disobey with impunity, disobedience is legitimate; and, the strongest being always in the right, the only thing that matters is to act so as to become the strongest. But what kind of right is that which perishes when force fails? If we must obey perforce, there is no need to obey because we ought; and if we are not forced to obey, we are under no obligation to do so. Clearly, the word "right" adds nothing to force: in this connection, it means absolutely nothing.

Obey the powers that be. If this means yield to force, it is a good precept, but superfluous: I can answer for its never being violated. All power comes from God, I admit; but so does all sickness: does that mean that we are forbidden to call in the doctor? A brigand surprises me at the edge of a wood: must I not merely surrender my purse on compulsion, but, even if I could withhold it, am I in conscience bound to give it up? For certainly the pistol he holds is also a power.

Let us then admit that force does not create right, and that we are obliged to obey only legitimate powers. In that case, my original question recurs.

Chapter IV: Slavery

Since no man has a natural authority over his fellow, and force creates no right, we must conclude that conventions form the basis of all legitimate authority among men.

If an individual, says Grotius, can alienate his liberty and make himself the slave of a master, why could not a whole people do the same and make itself subject to a king? There are in this passage plenty of ambiguous words which would need explaining; but let us confine ourselves to the word *alienate*. To alienate is to give or to sell. Now, a man who becomes the slave of another does not give himself; he sells himself, at the least for his subsistence: but for what does a people sell itself? A king is so far from furnishing his subjects with their subsistence that he gets his own only from them; and, according to Rabelais, kings do not live on nothing. Do subjects then give their persons on condition that the king takes their goods also? I fail to see what they have left to preserve.

It will be said that the despot assures his subjects civil tranquillity. Granted; but what do they gain, if the wars his ambition brings down upon them, his insatiable avidity, and the vexatious conduct of his ministers press harder on them than their own dissensions would have done? What do they gain, if the very tranquillity they enjoy is one of their miseries? Tranquillity is found also in dungeons; but is that enough to make them desirable places to live in? The Greeks imprisoned in the cave of the Cyclops* lived there very tranquilly while they were awaiting their turn to be devoured.

To say that a man gives himself gratuitously is to say what is absurd and inconceivable; such an act is null and illegitimate, from the mere fact that he who does it is out of his mind. To say the same of a whole people is to suppose a people of madmen; and madness creates no right.

Even if each man could alienate himself, he could not alienate his children: they are born men and free; their liberty belongs to them, and no one but they has the right to dispose of it. Before they come to years of discretion, the father can, in their name, lay down conditions for their preservation and well-being, but he cannot give them irrevocably and without conditions: such a gift is contrary to the ends of nature, and exceeds the rights of paternity. It would therefore be necessary, in order to legitimize an arbitrary government, that in every generation the people should be in a position to accept or reject it; but, were this so, the government would be no longer arbitrary.

To renounce liberty is to renounce being a man, to surrender the rights of humanity and even its duties. For him who renounces

---

*This refers to an episode in Homer's *Odyssey* in which Odysseus and his men are held captive by the Cyclops, a one-eyed giant.

everything no indemnity is possible. Such a renunciation is incompatible with man's nature; to remove all liberty from his will is to remove all morality from his acts. Finally, it is an empty and contradictory convention that sets up, on the one side, absolute authority, and, on the other, unlimited obedience. Is it not clear that we can be under no obligation to a person from whom we have the right to exact everything? Does not this condition alone, in the absence of equivalence or exchange, in itself involve the nullity of the act? For what right can my slave have against me, when all that he has belongs to me, and, his right being mine, this right of mine against myself is a phrase devoid of meaning?

Grotius and the rest find in war another origin for the so-called right of slavery. The victor having, as they hold, the right of killing the vanquished, the latter can buy back his life at the price of his liberty; and this convention is the more legitimate because it is to the advantage of both parties.

But it is clear that this supposed right to kill the conquered is by no means deducible from the state of war. Men, from the mere fact that, while they are living in their primitive independence, they have no mutual relations stable enough to constitute either the state of peace or the state of war, cannot be naturally enemies. War is constituted by a relation between things, and not between persons; and, as the state of war cannot arise out of simple personal relations, but only out of real relations, private war, or war of man with man, can exist neither in the state of nature, where there is no constant property, nor in the social state, where everything is under the authority of the laws.

Individual combats, duels, and encounters are acts which cannot constitute a state; while the private wars authorized by the Establishments of Louis IX, King of France, and suspended by the Peace of God,* are abuses of feudalism, in itself an absurd system if ever there was one, and contrary to the principles of natural right and to all good polity.

War, then, is a relation, not between man and man, but between State and State, and individuals are enemies only accidentally, not as men, nor even as citizens,[2] but as soldiers; not as members of their

---

*In the eleventh century the Church tried to restrict warfare to only a few days a week.

[2]The Romans, who understood and respected the right of war more than any other nation on earth, carried their scruples on this head so far that a citizen was not allowed to serve as a volunteer without engaging himself expressly against the enemy, and against such and such an enemy by name. A legion in which the younger Cato was seeing his first service under Popilius having been reconstructed, the elder Cato wrote to Popilius that, if he wished his son to continue serving under him, he must administer to him a new military oath, because, the first having been annulled, he was no longer able

country, but as its defenders. Finally, each State can have for enemies only other States, and not men; for between things disparate in nature there can be no real relation.

Furthermore, this principle is in conformity with the established rules of all times and the constant practice of all civilized peoples. Declarations of war are intimations less to powers than to their subjects. The foreigner, whether king, individual, or people, who robs, kills, or detains the subjects, without declaring war on the prince, is not an enemy, but a brigand. Even in real war, a just prince, while laying hands, in the enemy's country, on all that belongs to the public, respects the lives and goods of individuals: he respects rights on which his own are founded. The object of the war being the destruction of the hostile State, the other side has a right to kill its defenders while they are bearing arms; but as soon as they lay them down and surrender, they cease to be enemies or instruments of the enemy, and become once more merely men, whose life no one has any right to take. Sometimes it is possible to kill the State without killing a single one of its members; and war gives no right which is not necessary to the gaining of its object. These principles are not those of Grotius: they are not based on the authority of poets, but derived from the nature of reality and based on reason.

The right of conquest has no foundation other than the right of the strongest. If war does not give the conqueror the right to massacre the conquered peoples, the right to enslave them cannot be based upon a right which does not exist. No one has a right to kill an enemy except when he cannot make him a slave, and the right to enslave him cannot therefore be derived from the right to kill him. It is accordingly an unfair exchange to make him buy at the price of his liberty his life, over which the victor holds no right. Is it not clear that there is a vicious circle in founding the right of life and death on the right of slavery, and the right of slavery on the right of life and death?

Even if we assume this terrible right to kill everybody, I maintain that a slave made in war, or a conquered people, is under no obligation to a master, except to obey him as far as he is compelled to do so. By taking an equivalent for his life, the victor has not done him a favor; instead of

---

to bear arms against the enemy. The same Cato wrote to his son telling him to take great care not to go into battle before taking this new oath. I know that the siege of Clusium and other isolated events can be quoted against me; but I am citing laws and customs. The Romans are the people that least often transgressed its laws; and no other people has had such good ones.

killing him without profit, he has killed him usefully. So far then is he from acquiring over him any authority in addition to that of force, that the state of war continues to subsist between them: their mutual relation is the effect of it, and the usage of the right of war does not imply a treaty of peace. A convention has indeed been made; but this convention, so far from destroying the state of war, presupposes its continuance.

So, from whatever aspect we regard the question, the right of slavery is null and void, not only as being illegitimate, but also because it is absurd and meaningless. The words *slave* and *right* contradict each other, and are mutually exclusive. It will always be equally foolish for a man to say to a man or to a people: "I make with you a convention wholly at your expense and wholly to my advantage; I shall keep it as long as I like, and you will keep it as long as I like." . . .

Chapter VI: The Social Compact

I suppose men to have reached the point at which the obstacles in the way of their preservation in the state of nature show their power of resistance to be greater than the resources at the disposal of each individual for his maintenance in that state. That primitive condition can then subsist no longer; and the human race would perish unless it changed its manner of existence.

But, as men cannot engender new forces, but only unite and direct existing ones, they have no other means of preserving themselves than the formation, by aggregation, of a sum of forces great enough to overcome the resistance. These they have to bring into play by means of a single motive power, and cause to act in concert.

This sum of forces can arise only where several persons come together: but, as the force and liberty of each man are the chief instruments of his self-preservation, how can he pledge them without harming his own interests, and neglecting the care he owes to himself? This difficulty, in its bearing on my present subject, may be stated in the following terms:

"The problem is to find a form of association which will defend and protect with the whole common force the person and goods of each associate, and in which each, while uniting himself with all, may still obey himself alone, and remain as free as before." This is the fundamental problem of which the *social contract* provides the solution.

The clauses of this contract are so determined by the nature of the act that the slightest modification would make them vain and ineffective;

so that, although they have perhaps never been formally set forth, they are everywhere the same and everywhere tacitly admitted and recognized, until, on the violation of the social compact, each regains his original rights and resumes his natural liberty, while losing the conventional liberty in favor of which he renounced it.

These clauses, properly understood, may be reduced to one—the total alienation of each associate, together with all his rights, to the whole community; for, in the first place, as each gives himself absolutely, the conditions are the same for all; and, this being so, no one has any interest in making them burdensome to others.

Moreover, the alienation being without reserve, the union is as perfect as it can be, and no associate has anything more to demand: for, if the individuals retained certain rights, as there would be no common superior to decide between them and the public, each, being on one point his own judge, would ask to be so on all; the state of nature would thus continue, and the association would necessarily become inoperative or tyrannical.

Finally, each man, in giving himself to all, gives himself to nobody; and as there is no associate over which he does not acquire the same right as he yields others over himself, he gains an equivalent for everything he loses, and an increase of force for the preservation of what he has.

If then we discard from the social compact what is not of its essence, we shall find that it reduces itself to the following terms:

"Each of us puts his person and all his power in common under the supreme direction of the general will, and, in our corporate capacity, we receive each member as an indivisible part of the whole."

At once, in place of the individual personality of each contracting party, this act of association creates a moral and collective body, composed of as many members as the assembly contains voters, and receiving from this act its unity, its common identity, its life, and its will. This public person, so formed by the union of all other persons, formerly took the name of *city,* and now takes that of *Republic* or *body politic;* it is called by its members *State* when passive, *Sovereign* when active, and *Power* when compared with others like itself. Those who are associated in it take collectively the name of *people,* and severally are called *citizens,* as sharing in the sovereign power, and *subjects,* as being under the laws of the State. But these terms are often confused and taken one for another: it is enough to know how to distinguish them when they are being used with precision.

Chapter VII: The Sovereign

This formula shows us that the act of association comprises a mutual undertaking between the public and the individuals, and that each individual, in making a contract, as we may say, with himself, is bound in a double capacity; as a member of the Sovereign he is bound to the individuals, and as a member of the State to the Sovereign. But the maxim of civil right, that no one is bound by undertakings made to himself, does not apply in this case; for there is a great difference between incurring an obligation to yourself and incurring one to a whole of which you form a part.

Attention must further be called to the fact that public deliberation, while competent to bind all the subjects to the Sovereign, because of the two different capacities in which each of them may be regarded, cannot, for the opposite reason, bind the Sovereign to itself; and that it is consequently against the nature of the body politic for the Sovereign to impose on itself a law which it cannot infringe. Being able to regard itself in only one capacity, it is in the position of an individual who makes a contract with himself; and this makes it clear that there neither is nor can be any kind of fundamental law binding on the body of the people—not even the social contract itself. This does not mean that the body politic cannot enter into undertakings with others, provided the contract is not infringed by them; for in relation to what is external to it, it becomes a simple being, an individual.

But the body politic or the Sovereign, drawing its being wholly from the sanctity of the contract, can never bind itself, even to an outsider, to do anything derogatory to the original act, for instance to alienate any part of itself, or to submit to another Sovereign. Violation of the act by which it exists would be self-annihilation; and that which is itself nothing can create nothing.

As soon as this multitude is so united in one body, it is impossible to offend against one of the members without attacking the body, and still more to offend against the body without the members resenting it. Duty and interest therefore equally oblige the two contracting parties to give each other help; and the same men should seek to combine, in their double capacity, all the advantages dependent upon that capacity.

Again, the Sovereign, being formed wholly of the individuals who compose it, neither has nor can have any interest contrary to theirs; and consequently the sovereign power need give no guarantee to its subjects, because it is impossible for the body to wish to hurt all its subjects, members. We shall also see later on that it cannot hurt any in particular. The Sovereign, merely by virtue of what it is, is always what it should be.

This, however, is not the case with the relation of the subjects to the Sovereign, which, despite the common interest, would have no security that they would fulfill their undertakings, unless it found means to assure itself of their fidelity.

In fact, each individual, as a man, may have a particular will contrary or dissimilar to the general will which he has as a citizen. His particular interest may speak to him quite differently from the common interest: his absolute and naturally independent existence may make him look upon what he owes to the common cause as a gratuitous contribution, the loss of which will do less harm to others than the payment of it is burdensome to himself; and, regarding the moral person which constitutes the State as a *persona ficta,** because not a man, he may wish to enjoy the rights of citizenship without being ready to fulfill the duties of a subject. The continuance of such an injustice could not but prove the undoing of the body politic.

In order then that the social compact may not be an empty formula, it tacitly includes the undertakings, which alone can give force to the rest, that whoever refuses to obey the general will shall be compelled to do so by the whole body. This means nothing less than that he will be forced to be free; for this is the condition which, by giving each citizen to his country, secures him against all personal dependence. In this lies the key to the working of the political machine; this alone legitimizes civil undertakings, which, without it, would be absurd, tyrannical, and liable to the most frightful abuses.

Chapter VIII: The Civil State

The passage from the state of nature to the civil state produces a very remarkable change in man, by substituting justice for instinct in his conduct, and giving his actions the morality they had formerly lacked. Then only, when the voice of duty takes the place of physical impulses and right of appetite, does man, who so far had considered only himself, find that he is forced to act on different principles, and to consult his reason before listening to his inclinations. Although, in this state, he deprives himself of some advantages which he got from nature, he gains in return others so great, his faculties are so stimulated and developed, his ideas so extended, his feelings so ennobled, and his

*a fictional person

whole soul so uplifted, that, did not the abuses of this new condition often degrade him below that which he left, he would be bound to bless continually the happy moment which took him from it forever, and, instead of a stupid and unimaginative animal, made him an intelligent being and a man.

Let us draw up the whole account in terms easily commensurable. What man loses by the social contract is his natural liberty and an unlimited right to everything he tries to get and succeeds in getting; what he gains is civil liberty and the proprietorship of all he possesses. If we are to avoid mistake in weighing one against the other, we must clearly distinguish natural liberty, which is bounded only by the strength of the individual, from civil liberty, which is limited by the general will; and possession, which is merely the effect of force or the right of the first occupier, from property, which can be founded only on a positive title.

We might, over and above all this, add, to what man acquires in the civil state, moral liberty, which alone makes him truly master of himself; for the mere impulse of appetite is slavery, while obedience to a law which we prescribe to ourselves is liberty. But I have already said too much on this head, and the philosophical meaning of the word "liberty" does not now concern us.

Chapter IX: Real Property

Each member of the community gives himself to it, at the moment of its foundation, just as he is, with all the resources at his command, including the goods he possesses. This act does not make possession, in changing hands, change its nature, and becomes property in the hands of the Sovereign; but, as the forces of the city are incomparably greater than those of an individual, public possession is also, in fact, stronger and more irrevocable, without being any more legitimate, at any rate from the point of view of foreigners. For the State, in relation to its members, is master of all their goods by the social contract, which, within the State, is the basis of all rights; but, in relation to other powers, it is so only by the right of the first occupier, which it holds from its members.

The right of the first occupier, though more real than the right of the strongest, becomes a real right only when the right of property has already been established. Every man has naturally a right to everything he needs; but the positive act which makes him proprietor of one thing excludes him from everything else. Having his share, he ought to keep to it, and can have no further right against the community. This is why the right of the first occupier, which in the state of nature is so weak, claims the respect of every man in civil society. In this right we are respecting not so much what belongs to another as what does not belong to ourselves.

In general, to establish the right of the first occupier over a plot of ground, the following conditions are necessary: first, the land must not yet be inhabited; secondly, a man must occupy only the amount he needs for his subsistence; and, in the third place, possession must be taken, not by an empty ceremony, but by labor and cultivation, the only sign of proprietorship that should be respected by others, in default of a legal title.

In granting the right of first occupancy to necessity and labor, are we not really stretching it as far as it can go? Is it possible to leave such a right unlimited? Is it to be enough to set foot on a plot of common ground, in order to be able to call yourself at once the master of it? Is it to be enough that a man has the strength to expel others for a moment, in order to establish his right to prevent them from ever returning? How can a man or a people seize an immense territory and keep it from the rest of the world except by a punishable usurpation, since all others are being robbed, by such an act, of the place of habitation and the means of subsistence which nature gave them in common? When Nuñez Balboa,* standing on the seashore, took possession of the South Seas and the whole of South America in the name of the crown of Castile, was that enough to dispossess all their actual inhabitants, and to shut out from them all the princes of the world? On such a showing, these ceremonies are idly multiplied, and the Catholic King need only take possession all at once, from his apartment, of the whole universe, merely making a subsequent reservation about what was already in the possession of other princes.

We can imagine how the lands of individuals, where they were contiguous and came to be united, became the public territory, and how the right of Sovereignty, extending from the subjects over the lands they held, became at once real and personal. The possessors were thus made more dependent, and the forces at their command used to guarantee their fidelity. The advantage of this does not seem to have been felt by ancient monarchs, who called themselves King of the Persians, Scythians, or Macedonians, and seemed to regard themselves more as rulers of men than as masters of a country. Those of

---

*a Spanish explorer of the late fifteenth and early sixteenth centuries

the present day more cleverly call themselves Kings of France, Spain, England, etc.: thus holding the land, they are quite confident of holding the inhabitants.

The peculiar fact about this alienation is that, in taking over the goods of individuals, the community, so far from despoiling them, only assures them legitimate possession, and changes usurpation into a true right and enjoyment into proprietorship. Thus the possessors, being regarded as depositaries of the public good, and having their rights respected by all the members of the State and maintained against foreign aggression by all its forces, have, by a cession which benefits both the public and still more themselves, acquired, so to speak, all that they gave up. This paradox may easily be explained by the distinction between the rights which the Sovereign and the proprietor have over the same estate, as we shall see later on.

It may also happen that men begin to unite one with another before they possess anything, and that, subsequently occupying a tract of country which is enough for all, they enjoy it in common, or share it out among themselves, either equally or according to a scale fixed by the Sovereign. However the acquisition be made, the right which each individual has to his own estate is always subordinate to the right which the community has over all: without this, there would be neither stability in the social tie nor real force in the exercise of Sovereignty.

I shall end this chapter and this book by remarking on a fact on which the whole social system should rest: i.e. that, instead of destroying natural inequality, the fundamental compact substitutes, for such physical inequality as nature may have set up between men, an equality that is moral and legitimate, and that men, who may be unequal in strength or intelligence, become every one equal by convention and legal right.

BOOK II

Chapter I: That Sovereignty Is Inalienable

The first and most important deduction from the principles we have so far laid down is that the general will alone can direct the State according to the object for which it was instituted, i.e. the common good: for if the clashing of particular interests made the establishment of societies necessary, the agreement of these very interests made it possible. The common element in these different interests is what forms the social tie; and, were there no point of agreement between them all, no society could exist. It is solely on the basis of this common interest that every society should be governed.

I hold, then, that Sovereignty, being nothing less than the exercise of the general will, can never be alienated, and that the Sovereign, who is no less than a collective being, cannot be represented except by himself: the power indeed may be transmitted, but not the will.

In reality, if it is not impossible for a particular will to agree on some point with the general will, it is at least impossible for the agreement to be lasting and constant; for the particular will tends, by its very nature, to partiality, while the general will tends to equality. It is even more impossible to have any guarantee of this agreement; for even if it should always exist, it would be the effect not of art, but of chance. The Sovereign may indeed say: "I now will actually what this man wills, or at least what he says he wills"; but it cannot say: "What he wills tomorrow, I too shall will," because it is absurd for the will to bind itself for the future, nor is it incumbent on any will to consent to anything that is not for the good of the being who wills. If then the people promises simply to obey, by that very act it dissolves itself and loses what makes it a people; the moment a master exists, there is no longer a Sovereign, and from that moment the body politic has ceased to exist.

This does not mean that the commands of the rulers cannot pass for general wills, so long as the Sovereign, being free to oppose them, offers no opposition. In such a case, universal silence is taken to imply the consent of the people. This will be explained later on. . . .

Chapter III: Whether the General Will Is Fallible

It follows from what has gone before that the general will is always right and tends to the public advantage; but it does not follow that the deliberations of the people are always equally correct. Our will is always for our own good, but we do not always see what that is; the people is never corrupted, but it is often deceived, and on such occasions only does it seem to will what is bad.

There is often a great deal of difference between the will of all and the general will; the latter considers only the common interest, while the former takes private interest into account, and is no more than a sum of particular wills: but take away from these same wills the pluses and minuses that cancel one another, and the general will remains as the sum of the differences.

If, when the people, being furnished with adequate information, held its deliberations, the citizens had no communication one with another, the grand total of the small differences would always give the general will, and the decision would always be good. But when factions arise, and partial associations are formed at the expense of the great association, the will of each of these associations becomes general in relation to its members, while it remains particular in relation to the State: it may then be said that there are no longer as many votes as there are men, but only as many as there are associations. The differences become less numerous and give a less general result. Lastly, when one of these associations is so great as to prevail over all the rest, the result is no longer a sum of small differences, but a single difference; in this case there is no longer a general will, and the opinion which prevails is purely particular.

It is therefore essential, if the general will is to be able to express itself, that there should be no partial society within the State, and that each citizen should think only his own thoughts; which was indeed the sublime and unique system established by the great Lycurgus.* But if there are partial societies, it is best to have as many as possible and to prevent them from being unequal, as was done by Solon, Numa, and Servius.† These precautions are the only ones that can guarantee that the general will shall be always enlightened, and that the people shall in no way deceive itself.

Chapter IV: The Limits of the Sovereign Power

If the State is a moral person whose life is in the union of its members, and if the most important of its cares is the care for its own preservation, it must have a universal and compelling force, in order to move and dispose each part as may be most advantageous to the whole. As nature gives each man absolute power over all his members, the social compact gives the body politic absolute power over all its members also; and it is this power which, under the direction of the general will, bears, as I have said, the name of Sovereignty.

But, besides the public person, we have to consider the private persons composing it, whose life and liberty are naturally independent of it. We are bound then to distinguish clearly between the respective rights of the citizens and the Sovereign, and between the duties the

---

*Spartan lawgiver of the ninth century B.C.
†Solon, Numa, and Servius were ancient Greek and Roman sages.

former have to fulfill as subjects and the natural rights they should enjoy as men.

Each man alienates, I admit, by the social compact, only such part of his powers, goods, and liberty as it is important for the community to control; but it must also be granted that the Sovereign is sole judge of what is important.

Every service a citizen can render the State he ought to render as soon as the Sovereign demands it; but the Sovereign, for its part, cannot impose upon its subjects any fetters that are useless to the community, nor can it even wish to do so; for no more by the law of reason than by the law of nature can anything occur without a cause.

The undertakings which bind us to the social body are obligatory only because they are mutual; and their nature is such that in fulfilling them we cannot work for others without working for ourselves. Why is it that the general will is always in the right, and that all continually will the happiness of each one, unless it is because there is not a man who does not think of "each" as meaning him, and consider himself in voting for all? This proves that equality of rights and the idea of justice which such equality creates originate in the preference each man gives to himself, and accordingly in the very nature of man. It proves that the general will, to be really such, must be general in its object as well as its essence; that it must both come from all and apply to all; and that it loses its natural rectitude when it is directed to some particular and determinate object, because in such a case we are judging of something foreign to us, and have no true principle of equity to guide us.

Indeed, as soon as a question of particular fact or right arises on a point not previously regulated by a general convention, the matter becomes contentious. It is a case in which the individuals concerned are one party, and the public the other, but in which I can see neither the law that ought to be followed nor the judge who ought to give the decision. In such a case, it would be absurd to propose to refer the question to an express decision of the general will, which can be only the conclusion reached by one of the parties and in consequence will be, for the other party, merely an external and particular will, inclined on this occasion to injustice and subject to error. Thus, just as a particular will cannot stand for the general will, the general will, in turn, changes its nature when its object is particular, and, as general, cannot pronounce on a man or a fact. When, for instance, the people of Athens nominated or displaced its rulers, decreed honors to one, and imposed penalties on another, and, by a multitude of particular decrees, exercised all the functions of government indiscriminately, it had in such cases no longer a general will in the strict sense; it was acting no longer as Sovereign, but as magistrate. This will seem contrary to current views; but I must be given time to expound my own.

It should be seen from the foregoing that what makes the will general is less the number of voters than the common interest uniting them; for, under this system, each necessarily submits to the conditions he imposes on others: and this admirable agreement between interest and justice gives to the common deliberations an equitable character which at once vanishes when any particular question is discussed, in the absence of a common interest to unite and identify the ruling of the judge with that of the party.

From whatever side we approach our principle, we reach the same conclusion, that the social compact sets up among the citizens an equality of such a kind that they all bind themselves to observe the same conditions and should therefore all enjoy the same rights. Thus, from the very nature of the compact, every act of Sovereignty, i.e. every authentic act of the general will, binds or favors all the citizens equally; so that the Sovereign recognizes only the body of the nation, and draws no distinctions between those of whom it is made up. What, then, strictly speaking, is an act of Sovereignty? It is not a convention between a superior and an inferior, but a convention between the body and each of its members. It is legitimate, because based on the social contract, and equitable, because common to all; useful, because it can have no other object than the general good, and stable, because guaranteed by the public force and the supreme power. So long as the subjects have to submit only to conventions of this sort, they obey no one but their own will; and to ask how far the respective rights of the Sovereign and the citizens extend is to ask up to what point the latter can enter into undertakings with themselves, each with all, and all with each.

We can see from this that the sovereign power, absolute, sacred, and inviolable as it is, does not and cannot exceed the limits of general conventions, and that every man may dispose at will of such goods and liberty as these conventions leave him; so that the Sovereign never has a right to lay more charges on one subject than on another, because, in that case the question becomes particular, and ceases to be within its competency.

When these distinctions have once been admitted, it is seen to be so untrue that there is, in the social contract, any real renunciation on the part of the individuals, that the position in which they find themselves

as a result of the contract is really preferable to that in which they were before. Instead of a renunciation, they have made an advantageous exchange; instead of an uncertain and precarious way of living they have got one that is better and more secure; instead of natural independence they have got liberty, instead of the power to harm others security for themselves, and instead of their strength, which others might overcome, a right which social union makes invincible. Their very life, which they have devoted to the State, is by it constantly protected; and when they risk it in the State's defense, what more are they doing than giving back what they have received from it? What are they doing that they would not do more often and with greater danger in the state of nature, in which they would inevitably have to fight battles at the peril of their lives in defense of that which is the means of their preservation? All have indeed to fight when their country needs them; but then no one has ever to fight for himself. Do we not gain something by running, on behalf of what gives us our security, only some of the risks we should have to run for ourselves, as soon as we lost it? . . .

Chapter XI: The Various Systems of Legislation

If we ask in what precisely consists the greatest good of all, which should be the end of every system of legislation, we shall find it reduce itself to two main objects, liberty and equality — liberty, because all particular dependence means so much force taken from the body of the State, and equality, because liberty cannot exist without it.

I have already defined civil liberty. By equality, we should understand, not that the degrees of power and riches are to be absolutely identical for everybody, but that power shall never be great enough for violence, and shall always be exercised by virtue of rank and law; and that, in respect of riches, no citizen shall ever be wealthy enough to buy another, and none poor enough to be forced to sell himself;[3] which implies, on the part of the great, moderation in goods and position, and, on the side of the common sort, moderation in avarice and covetousness.

Such equality, we are told, is an unpractical ideal that cannot actually exist. But if its abuse is inevitable, does it follow that we should

---

[3] If the object is to give the State consistency, bring the two extremes as near to each other as possible; allow neither rich men nor beggars. These two estates, which are naturally inseparable, are equally fatal to the common good; from the one come the friends of tyranny, and from the other tyrants. It is always between them that public liberty is put up to auction; the one buys and the other sells.

not at least make regulations concerning it? It is precisely because the force of circumstances tends continually to destroy equality that the force of legislation should always tend to its maintenance.

But these general objects of every good legislative system need modifying in every country in accordance with the local situation and the temper of the inhabitants; and these circumstances should determine, in each case, the particular system of institutions which is best, not perhaps in itself, but for the State for which it is destined. If, for instance, the soil is barren and unproductive, or the land too crowded for its inhabitants, the people should turn to industry and the crafts, and exchange what they produce for the commodities they lack. If, on the other hand, a people dwells in rich plains and fertile slopes, or, in a good land, lacks inhabitants, it should give all its attention to agriculture, which causes men to multiply, and should drive out the crafts, which would only result in depopulation, by grouping in a few localities the few inhabitants there are. If a nation dwells on an extensive and convenient coastline, let it cover the sea with ships and foster commerce and navigation: it will have a life that will be short and glorious. If, on its coasts, the sea washes nothing but almost inaccessible rocks, let it remain barbarous and ichthyphagous:* it will have a quieter, perhaps a better, and certainly a happier life. In a word, besides the principles that are common to all, every nation has in itself something that gives them a particular application and makes its legislation peculiarly its own. Thus, among the Jews long ago and more recently among the Arabs, the chief object was religion, among the Athenians letters, at Carthage and Tyre commerce, at Rhodes shipping, at Sparta war, at Rome virtue. The author of *The Spirit of the Laws* [Montesquieu] has shown with many examples by what art the legislator directs the constitution toward each of these objects.

What makes the constitution of a State really solid and lasting is the due observance of what is proper, so that the natural relations are always in agreement with the laws on every point, and law serves only, so to speak, to assure, accompany and rectify them. But if the legislator mistakes his object and adopts a principle other than circumstances naturally direct, if his principle makes for servitude, while they make for liberty, or if it makes for riches, while they make for populousness, or if it makes for peace, while they make for conquest,

---

*fish-eating

the laws will insensibly lose their influence, the constitution will alter, and the State will have no rest from trouble till it is either destroyed or changed, and nature has resumed her invincible sway. . . .

BOOK III

Chapter VIII: That All Forms of Government Do Not Suit All Countries

Liberty, not being a fruit of all climates, is not within the reach of all peoples. The more this principle, laid down by Montesquieu, is considered, the more its truth is felt: the more it is combated, the more chance is given to confirm it by new proofs.

In all the governments that there are, the public person consumes without producing. Whence, then, does it get what it consumes? From the labor of its members. The necessities of the public are supplied out of the superfluities of individuals. It follows that the civil State can subsist only so long as men's labor brings them a return greater than their needs.

The amount of this excess is not the same in all countries. In some it is considerable, in others middling, in yet others nil, in some even negative. The relation of product to subsistence depends on the fertility of the climate, on the sort of labor the land demands, on the nature of its products, on the strength of its inhabitants, on the greater or less consumption they find necessary, and on several further considerations of which the whole relation is made up.

On the other side, all governments are not of the same nature: some are less voracious than others, and the differences between them are based on this second principle, that the further from their source the public contributions are removed, the more burdensome they become. The charge should be measured not by the amount of the impositions, but by the path they have to travel in order to get back to those from whom they came. When the circulation is prompt and well established, it does not matter whether much or little is paid; the people is always rich and, financially speaking, all is well. On the contrary, however little the people gives, if that little does not return to it, it is soon exhausted by giving continually: the State is then never rich, and the people is always a people of beggars.

It follows that the more the distance between people and government increases, the more burdensome tribute becomes: thus, in a democracy, the people bears the least charge; in an aristocracy, a greater charge;

and, in monarchy, the weight becomes heaviest. Monarchy therefore suits only wealthy nations; aristocracy, States of middling size and wealth; and democracy, States that are small and poor.

In fact, the more we reflect, the more we find the difference between free and monarchical States to be this: in the former, everything is used for the public advantage; in the latter, the public forces and those of individuals are affected by each other, and either increases as the other grows weak; finally, instead of governing subjects to make them happy, despotism makes them wretched in order to govern them.

We find then, in every climate, natural causes according to which the form of government which it requires can be assigned, and we can even say what sort of inhabitants it should have.

Unfriendly and barren lands, where the product does not repay the labor, should remain desert and uncultivated, or peopled only by savages; lands where men's labor brings in no more than the exact minimum necessary to subsistence should be inhabited by barbarous peoples: in such places all polity is impossible. Lands where the surplus of product over labor is only middling are suitable for free peoples; those in which the soil is abundant and fertile and gives a great product for a little labor call for monarchical government, in order that the surplus of superfluities among the subjects may be consumed by the luxury of the prince: for it is better for this excess to be absorbed by the government than dissipated among the individuals. I am aware that there are exceptions; but these exceptions themselves confirm the rule, in that sooner or later they produce revolutions which restore things to the natural order.

General laws should always be distinguished from individual causes that may modify their effects. If all the South were covered with republics and all the North with despotic States, it would be none the less true that, in point of climate, despotism is suitable to hot countries, barbarism to cold countries, and good polity to temperate regions. I see also that, the principle being granted, there may be disputes on its application; it may be said that there are cold countries that are very fertile, and tropical countries that are very unproductive. But this difficulty exists only for those who do not consider the question in all its aspects. We must, as I have already said, take labor, strength, consumption, etc., into account.

Take two tracts of equal extent, one of which brings in five and the other ten. If the inhabitants of the first consume four and those of the second nine, the surplus of the first product will be a fifth and that of the second a tenth. The ratio of these two surpluses will then be inverse to that of the products, and the tract which produces only five will give a surplus double that of the tract which produces ten.

But there is no question of a double product, and I think no one would put the fertility of cold countries, as a general rule, on an equality with that of hot ones. Let us, however, suppose this equality to exist: let us, if you will, regard England as on the same level as Sicily, and Poland as Egypt—farther south, we shall have Africa and the Indies: farther north, nothing at all. To get this equality of product, what a difference there must be in tillage: in Sicily, there is only need to scratch the ground; in England, how men must toil! but where more hands are needed to get the same product, the superfluity must necessarily be less. . . .

BOOK VI

Chapter II: Voting

It may be seen, from the last chapter, that the way in which general business is managed may give a clear enough indication of the actual state of morals and the health of the body politic. The more concert reigns in the assemblies, that is, the nearer opinion approaches unanimity, the greater is the dominance of the general will. On the other hand, long debates, dissensions, and tumult proclaim the ascendancy of particular interests and the decline of the State.

This seems less clear when two or more orders enter into the constitution, as patricians and plebeians did at Rome; for quarrels between these two orders often disturbed the comitia, even in the best days of the Republic. But the exception is rather apparent than real; for then, through the defect that is inherent in the body politic, there were, so to speak, two States in one, and what is not true of the two together is true of either separately. Indeed, even in the most stormy times, the *plebiscita** of the people, when the Senate did not interfere with them, always went through quietly and by large majorities. The citizens having but one interest, the people had but a single will.

At the other extremity of the circle, unanimity recurs; this is the case when the citizens, having fallen into servitude, have lost both liberty and will. Fear and flattery then change votes into acclamation; deliberation ceases, and only worship or malediction is left. Such was

*plebiscites or wishes

the vile manner in which the Senate expressed its views under the emperors. It did so sometimes with absurd precautions. Tacitus* observes that, under Otho, the senators, while they heaped curses on Vitellius, contrived at the same time to make a deafening noise, in order that, should he ever become their master, he might not know what each of them had said.

On these various considerations depend the rules by which the methods of counting votes and comparing opinions should be regulated, according as the general will is more or less easy to discover, and the State more or less in its decline.

There is but one law which, from its nature, needs unanimous consent. This is the social compact; for civil association is the most voluntary of all acts. Every man being born free and his own master, no one, under any pretext whatsoever, can make any man subject without his consent. To decide that the son of a slave is born a slave is to decide that he is not born a man.

If then there are opponents when the social compact is made, their opposition does not invalidate the contract, but merely prevents them from being included in it. They are foreigners among citizens. When the State is instituted, residence constitutes consent; to dwell within its territory is to submit to the Sovereign.

Apart from this primitive contract, the vote of the majority always binds all the rest. This follows from the contract itself. But it is asked how a man can be both free and forced to conform to wills that are not his own. How are the opponents at once free and subject to laws they have not agreed to?

I retort that the question is wrongly put. The citizen gives his consent to all the laws, including those which are passed in spite of his opposition, and even those which punish him when he dares to break any of them. The constant will of all the members of the State is the general will; by virtue of it they are citizens and free. When in the popular assembly a law is proposed, what the people is asked is not exactly whether it approves or rejects the proposal, but whether it is in conformity with the general will, which is their will. Each man, in giving his vote, states his opinion on that point; and the general will is found by counting votes. When therefore the opinion that is contrary to my own prevails, this proves neither more nor less than that I was mistaken, and that what I thought to be the general will was not so. If

*a Roman historian

my particular opinion had carried the day I should have achieved the opposite of what was my will; and it is in that case that I should not have been free. . . .

Chapter VIII: Civil Religion

. . . There is therefore a purely civil profession of faith of which the Sovereign should fix the articles, not exactly as religious dogmas, but as social sentiments without which a man cannot be a good citizen or a faithful subject. While it can compel no one to believe them, it can banish from the State whoever does not believe them—it can banish him, not for impiety, but as an antisocial being, incapable of truly loving the laws and justice, and of sacrificing, at need, his life to his duty. If anyone, after publicly recognizing these dogmas, behaves as if he does not believe them, let him be punished by death: he has committed the worst of all crimes, that of lying before the law.

The dogmas of civil religion ought to be few, simple, and exactly worded, without explanation or commentary. The existence of a mighty, intelligent, and beneficent Divinity, possessed of foresight and providence, the life to come, the happiness of the just, the punishment of the wicked, the sanctity of the social contract and the laws: these are its positive dogmas. Its negative dogmas I confine to one, intolerance, which is a part of the cults we have rejected.

Those who distinguish civil from theological intolerance are, to my mind, mistaken. The two forms are inseparable. It is impossible to live at peace with those we regard as damned; to love them would be to hate God who punishes them: we positively must either reclaim or torment them. Wherever theological intolerance is admitted, it must inevitably have some civil effect; and as soon as it has such an effect, the Sovereign is no longer Sovereign even in the temporal sphere: thenceforth priests are the real masters, and kings only their ministers.

Now that there is and can be no longer an exclusive national religion, tolerance should be given to all religions that tolerate others, so long as their dogmas contain nothing contrary to the duties of citizenship. But whoever dares to say, "Outside the Church is no salvation," ought to be driven from the State, unless the State is the Church, and the prince the pontiff. Such a dogma is good only in a theocratic government; in any other, it is fatal. The reason for which Henry IV is said to have embraced the Roman religion ought to make every honest man leave it, and still more any prince who knows how to reason.

8

IMMANUEL KANT

What Is Enlightenment?

1784

Immanuel Kant's (1724–1804) first love was Newtonian science. The progress that science and mathematics had made since the mid-seventeenth century fascinated him. He wanted to bring a comparable rigor, possibly even progress, to all branches of philosophy: ethics, epistemology, and especially metaphysics. At the heart of the "Copernican revolution" that Kant said he had begun in philosophy lay his belief that innate properties in the mind—the rules of selecting and combining sense data—govern the human construction of reality. In effect we think, but we also have the faculty of intuition, by which we grasp, for example, space and our position within it. Intuition of space and place relate to Kant's attempt to construct an enlightened ethical system. He believed that human beings must possess an interior moral sense that can be refined, a knowledge that can be translated into behavior. "Do I have, not merely a self-interested feeling, but also a disinterested feeling of concern for others? Yes," Kant said. How to achieve the moral balance between self-interest and benevolence occupied much of his writing and teaching life.

Kant lived out his sheltered days as a professor at Albertina University in Königsberg (now Kaliningrad). He became famous largely as a philosopher, and his formal philosophical writings are a mainstay of any university curriculum today. Kant should be seen as singularly important because of the range of his genius, his rigor in formal philosophy, and his search for the abstract and the universal. The selection that follows has been reprinted often. Its clarity and brevity recommend it, but many commentators have failed to notice that it is a distinctively conservative document. Think for yourself, Kant seems to be saying, but cause no trouble. Leave the state and its institutions alone; conform; think original thoughts after hours, in the privacy of your own home. The revolutionary Locke, the outrageous authors of Treatise of the Three Impostors, *Diderot, Rousseau, and perhaps even Lady Mary Wortley Montagu would*

---

*Immanuel Kant, "What Is Enlightenment?" trans. Peter Gay, *Introduction to Contemporary Civilization in the West* (New York: Columbia University Press, 1954), pp. 1071–76.

probably not have agreed with Kant's desire to alter the political status quo as little as possible.

Enlightenment is man's emergence from his self-imposed nonage. Nonage is the inability to use one's own understanding without another's guidance. This nonage is self-imposed if its cause lies not in lack of understanding but in indecision and lack of courage to use one's own mind without another's guidance. *Dare to know! (Sapere aude.)* "Have the courage to use your own understanding," is therefore the motto of the enlightenment.

Laziness and cowardice are the reasons why such a large part of mankind gladly remain minors all their lives, long after nature has freed them from external guidance. They are the reasons why it is so easy for others to set themselves up as guardians. It is so comfortable to be a minor. If I have a book that thinks for me, a pastor who acts as my conscience, a physician who prescribes my diet, and so on—then I have no need to exert myself. I have no need to think, if only I can pay; others will take care of that disagreeable business for me. Those guardians who have kindly taken supervision upon themselves see to it that the overwhelming majority of mankind—among them the entire fair sex—should consider the step to maturity not only as hard, but as extremely dangerous. First, these guardians make their domestic cattle stupid and carefully prevent the docile creatures from taking a single step without the leading-strings to which they have fastened them. Then they show them the danger that would threaten them if they should try to walk by themselves. Now, this danger is really not very great; after stumbling a few times they would, at last, learn to walk. However, examples of such failures intimidate and generally discourage all further attempts.

Thus it is very difficult for the individual to work himself out of the nonage which has become almost second nature to him. He has even grown to like it and is at first really incapable of using his own understanding, because he has never been permitted to try it. Dogmas and formulas, these mechanical tools designed for reasonable use—or rather abuse—of his natural gifts, are the fetters of an everlasting nonage. The man who casts them off would make an uncertain leap over the narrowest ditch, because he is not used to such free movement. That is why there are only a few men who walk firmly, and who have emerged from nonage by cultivating their own minds.

It is more nearly possible, however, for the public to enlighten itself; indeed, if it is only given freedom, enlightenment is almost inevitable. There will always be a few independent thinkers, even among the self-appointed guardians of the multitude. Once such men have thrown off the yoke of nonage, they will spread about them the spirit of a reasonable appreciation of man's value and of his duty to think for himself. It is especially to be noted that the public which was earlier brought under the yoke by these men afterward forces these very guardians to remain in submission, if it is so incited by some of its guardians who are themselves incapable of any enlightenment. That shows how pernicious it is to implant prejudices: they will eventually revenge themselves upon their authors or their authors' descendants. Therefore, a public can achieve enlightenment only slowly. A revolution may bring about the end of a personal despotism or of avaricious and tyrannical oppression, but never a true reform of modes of thought. New prejudices will serve, in place of the old, as guidelines for the unthinking multitude.

This enlightenment requires nothing but *freedom*—and the most innocent of all that may be called "freedom": freedom to make public use of one's reason in all matters. Now I hear the cry from all sides: "Do not argue!" The officer says: "Do not argue—drill!" The tax collector: "Do not argue—pay!" The pastor: "Do not argue—believe!" Only one ruler in the world says: "Argue as much as you please, and about what you please, but obey!" We find restrictions on freedom everywhere. But which restriction is harmful to enlightenment? Which restriction is innocent, and which advances enlightenment? I reply: the public use of one's reason must be free at all times, and this alone can bring enlightenment to mankind.

On the other hand, the private use of reason may frequently be narrowly restricted without especially hindering the progress of enlightenment. By "public use of one's reason" I mean that use which a man, as *scholar,* makes of it before the reading public. I call "private use" that use which a man makes of his reason in a civic post that has been entrusted to him. In some affairs affecting the interest of the community a certain [governmental] mechanism is necessary in which some members of the community remain passive. This creates an artificial unanimity which will serve the fulfillment of public objectives, or at least keep these objectives from being destroyed. Here arguing is not permitted: one must obey. Insofar as a part of this machine considers himself at the same time a member of a universal community—a world society of citizens—(let us say that he thinks of himself as a scholar rationally addressing his public through his writings) he may indeed argue, and the affairs with which he is associated in part as a

passive member will not suffer. Thus, it would be very unfortunate if an officer on duty and under orders from his superiors should want to criticize the appropriateness or utility of his orders. He must obey. But as a scholar he could not rightfully be prevented from taking notice of the mistakes in the military service and from submitting his views to his public for its judgment. The citizen cannot refuse to pay the taxes levied upon him; indeed, impertinent censure of such taxes could be punished as a scandal that might cause general disobedience. Nevertheless, this man does not violate the duties of a citizen if, as a scholar, he publicly expresses his objections to the impropriety or possible injustice of such levies. A pastor too is bound to preach to his congregation in accord with the doctrines of the church which he serves, for he was ordained on that condition. But as a scholar he has full freedom, indeed the obligation, to communicate to his public all his carefully examined and constructive thoughts concerning errors in that doctrine and his proposals concerning improvement of religious dogma and church institutions. This is nothing that could burden his conscience. For what he teaches in pursuance of his office as representative of the church, he represents as something which he is not free to teach as he sees it. He speaks as one who is employed to speak in the name and under the orders of another. He will say: "Our church teaches this or that; these are the proofs which it employs." Thus he will benefit his congregation as much as possible by presenting doctrines to which he may not subscribe with full conviction. He can commit himself to teach them because it is not completely impossible that they may contain hidden truth. In any event, he has found nothing in the doctrines that contradicts the heart of religion. For if he believed that such contradictions existed he would not be able to administer his office with a clear conscience. He would have to resign it. Therefore the use which a scholar makes of his reason before the congregation that employs him is only a private use, for, no matter how sizable, this is only a domestic audience. In view of this he, as preacher, is not free and ought not to be free, since he is carrying out the orders of others. On the other hand, as the scholar who speaks to his own public (the world) through his writings, the minister in the public use of his reason enjoys unlimited freedom to use his own reason and to speak for himself. That the spiritual guardians of the people should themselves be treated as minors is an absurdity which would result in perpetuating absurdities.

But should a society of ministers, say a Church Council, ... have the right to commit itself by oath to a certain unalterable doctrine, in order to secure perpetual guardianship over all its members and through them over the people? I say that this is quite impossible. Such a contract, concluded to keep all further enlightenment from humanity, is simply null and void even if it should be confirmed by the sovereign power, by parliaments, and by the most solemn treaties. An epoch cannot conclude a pact that will commit succeeding ages, prevent them from increasing their significant insights, purging themselves of errors, and generally progressing in enlightenment. That would be a crime against human nature, whose proper destiny lies precisely in such progress. Therefore, succeeding ages are fully entitled to repudiate such decisions as unauthorized and outrageous. The touchstone of all those decisions that may be made into law for a people lies in this question: Could a people impose such a law upon itself? Now, it might be possible to introduce a certain order for a definite short period of time in expectation of a better order. But while this provisional order continues, each citizen (above all, each pastor acting as a scholar) should be left free to publish his criticisms of the faults of existing institutions. This should continue until public understanding of these matters has gone so far that, by uniting the voices of many (although not necessarily all) scholars, reform proposals could be brought before the sovereign to protect those congregations which had decided according to their best lights upon an altered religious order, without, however, hindering those who want to remain true to the old institutions. But to agree to a perpetual religious constitution which is not to be publicly questioned by anyone would be, as it were, to annihilate a period of time in the progress of man's improvement. This must be absolutely forbidden.

A man may postpone his own enlightenment, but only for a limited period of time. And to give up enlightenment altogether, either for oneself or one's descendants, is to violate and to trample upon the sacred rights of man. What a people may not decide for itself may even less be decided for it by a monarch, for his reputation as a ruler consists precisely in the way in which he unites the will of the whole people within his own. If he only sees to it that all true or supposed [religious] improvement remains in step with the civic order, he can for the rest leave his subjects alone to do what they find necessary for the salvation of their souls. Salvation is none of his business; it *is* his business to prevent one man from forcibly keeping another from determining and promoting his salvation to the best of his ability. Indeed, it would be prejudicial to his majesty if he meddled in these matters and supervised the writings in which his subjects seek to bring their [religious] views into the open, even when he does this from his own highest insight, because then he exposes himself to the reproach: *Caesar non est supra grammaticos* [Caesar is not above grammarians]. It is worse when he debases his sovereign power so far as to support the spiritual despotism of a few tyrants in his state over the rest of his subjects.

When we ask, Are we now living in an enlightened age? the answer is, No, but we live in an age of enlightenment. As matters now stand it is still far from true that men are already capable of using their own reason in religious matters confidently and correctly without external guidance. Still, we have some obvious indications that the field of working toward the goal [of religious truth] is now being opened. What is more, the hindrances against general enlightenment or the emergence from self-imposed nonage are gradually diminishing. In this respect this is the age of the enlightenment and the century of Frederick [the Great].

A prince ought not to deem it beneath his dignity to state that he considers it his duty not to dictate anything to his subjects in religious matters, but to leave them complete freedom. If he repudiates the arrogant word *tolerant,* he is himself enlightened; he deserves to be praised by a grateful world and posterity as that man who was the first to liberate mankind from dependence, at least on the government, and let everybody use his own reason in matters of conscience. Under his reign, honorable pastors, acting as scholars and regardless of the duties of their office, can freely and openly publish their ideas to the world for inspection, although they deviate here and there from accepted doctrine. This is even more true of every other person not restrained by any oath of office. This spirit of freedom is spreading beyond the boundaries [of Prussia], even where it has to struggle against the external hindrances established by a government that fails to grasp its true interest. [Frederick's Prussia] is a shining example that freedom need not cause the least worry concerning public order or the unity of the community. When one does not deliberately attempt to keep men in barbarism, they will gradually work out of that condition by themselves.

I have emphasized the main point of the enlightenment—man's emergence from his self-imposed nonage—primarily in religious matters, because our rulers have no interest in playing the guardian to their subjects in the arts and sciences. Above all, nonage in religion is not only the most harmful but the most dishonorable. But the disposition of a sovereign ruler who favors freedom in the arts and sciences goes even further: he knows that there is no danger in permitting his subjects to make public use of their reason and to publish their ideas concerning a better constitution, as well as candid criticism of existing basic laws. We already have a striking example [of such freedom], and no monarch can match the one whom we venerate.

But only the man who is himself enlightened, who is not afraid of shadows, and who commands at the same time a well-disciplined and numerous army as guarantor of public peace—only he can say what [the sovereign of] a free state cannot dare to say: "Argue as much as you like, and about what you like, but obey!" Thus we observe here as elsewhere in human affairs, in which almost everything is paradoxical, a surprising and unexpected course of events: a large degree of civic freedom appears to be of advantage to the intellectual freedom of the people, yet at the same time it establishes insurmountable barriers. A lesser degree of civic freedom, however, creates room to let that free spirit expand to the limits of its capacity. Nature, then, has carefully cultivated the seed within the hard core—namely, the urge for and the vocation of free thought. And this free thought gradually reacts back on the modes of thought of the people, and men become more and more capable of acting in freedom. At last free thought acts even on the fundamentals of government, and the state finds it agreeable to treat man, who is now more than a machine, in accord with his dignity.

9

MOSES MENDELSSOHN

Jerusalem: Or on Religious Power and Judaism
1783

Born into a poor family in Dessau, Germany, Moses Mendelssohn (1729–1786) quickly exhibited his brilliance as a student of the Talmud. His fluency in both Hebrew and German gave him access to the secular world while he remained rooted in his religion—a believing Jew who

---

Moses Mendelssohn, *Jerusalem: Or on Religious Power and Judaism,* trans. Allan Arkush (Hanover, N.H.: University Press of New England, 1983), 33–45, 56–63, 94–98.

was also a freethinker, an advocate of toleration in a world where anti-Semitism flourished, especially among the enemies of the Enlightenment. Mendelssohn made a conscious effort not to dwell on the anti-Semitism of the established Christian churches. He also opposed the idea among Jewish reformers that if the Jews "modernized," the Prussian and Austrian states might treat them with more tolerance and grant them the rights they desired. Jews, like all peoples, have a natural right to freedom of religion and conscience and to the benevolence of the state, he said. If the state could not respect those rights, it must be changed. Mendelssohn also believed that Jews were exceptionally well suited to become model citizens. He based this belief on the fact that their religion was actually a body of law that prescribed actions and eschewed the doctrinal absolutism that led to persecution and dissension in the polity.

Mendelssohn's understanding of both Judaism and freedom of conscience can best be seen in Jerusalem: Or on Religious Power and Judaism, *which is the most imaginative eighteenth-century attempt to invent a religious enlightenment, once thought to be a contradiction in terms. In this selection, Mendelssohn advocates the creation of a state in which all religious minorities are full citizens and the government has no power over people's private beliefs.*

State and religion—civil and ecclesiastical constitution—secular and churchly authority—how to oppose these pillars of social life to one another so that they are in balance and do not, instead, become burdens on social life, or weigh down its foundations more than they help to uphold it—this is one of the most difficult tasks of politics. For centuries, men have strived to solve it, and here and there enjoyed perhaps greater success in settling it practically than in resolving it in theory. Some thought it proper to separate these different relations of societal man into moral entities, and to assign to each a separate province, specific rights, duties, powers, and properties. But the extent of these different provinces and the boundaries dividing them have not yet been accurately fixed. Sometimes one sees the church move the boundary stone deep into the territory of the state; sometimes the state permits itself encroachments which, according to accepted standards, seem equally violent. Immeasurable evils have hitherto arisen, and still threaten to arise, from the dissension between these moral entities. When they take the field against each other, mankind is the victim of their discord; when they are in agreement, the noblest treasure of human felicity is lost; for they seldom agree but for the purpose of banishing from their realms a third moral entity, *liberty of conscience,* which knows how to derive some advantage from their disunity.

Despotism has the advantage of being consistent. However burdensome its demands may be to common sense, they are, nevertheless, coherent and systematic. It has a definite answer to every question. You need not trouble yourself any more about limits; for he who has everything no longer asks, "how much?" The same holds true for ecclesiastical government, according to Roman Catholic principles. It deals fully with every circumstance, and is, as it were, all of a piece. Grant it all its demands; you will at least know where you stand. Your structure is completely built, and perfect calm reigns in all its parts. To be sure, only that dreadful calm which, as Montesquieu says, prevails during the evening in a fortress which is to be taken by storm during the night. Yet he who considers tranquillity in doctrine and life to be felicity will find it nowhere better secured to him than under a Roman Catholic despot; or rather, since even in this case power is still too much divided, under the despotic rule of the church itself.

But as soon as liberty dares to move anything in this systematic structure, ruin immediately threatens on all sides; and in the end, one no longer knows what will remain standing. Hence the extraordinary confusion, the civil as well as ecclesiastical disturbances, during the early years of the Reformation, and the striking embarrassment on the part of the teachers and reformers themselves whenever they had occasion to settle the question of "how far?" in matters of right. Not only was it difficult, in practice, to keep the great multitude within proper bounds, once it was released from its fetters, but even in theory, one finds the writings of those times full of vague and wavering ideas whenever the definition of ecclesiastical power is discussed. The despotism of the Roman church was abolished—but what other form was to be introduced in its place? Even now, in our more enlightened times, the textbooks of ecclesiastical law could not be rid of this vagueness. The clergy will not or cannot give up all claims to a *constitution,* yet no one really knows in what it should consist. One wishes to settle doctrinal differences, without recognizing a Supreme Judge. One still continues to refer to an independent church, without knowing where it is to be found. One advances a claim to power and rights, yet one cannot state who should exercise them.

Thomas Hobbes lived at a time when fanaticism, combined with a disorderly sense of liberty, no longer knew any bounds and was ready to bring royal authority under its foot and subvert the entire constitution of the realm (as it eventually did). Weary of civil strife and by nature inclined toward a quiet, speculative life, he regarded tranquillity and safety, no matter how they were obtained, as the greatest felicity; and these, he thought, were to be found only in the unity and indivisibility of the highest power in the state. He believed, therefore, that the public welfare would be best served if everything, even our judgment of right and wrong, were made subject to the supreme power of the civil authority. In order to do so more legitimately, he assumed that man is *entitled* by nature to everything it has endowed him with the *ability* to obtain. The state of nature is a state of tumult, a *war of all against all,* in which everyone *may* do what he *can* do; everything one has the power to do is right. This unfortunate condition lasted until men agreed to put an end to their misery, to renounce right and might, as far as public safety was concerned, and to place both in the hands of an established authority. Henceforth, whatever that authority ordered was right.

Hobbes either had no taste for civil liberty or wished to see it destroyed rather than have it thus abused. But in order to retain for himself the liberty of thought, of which he made more use than anyone else, he resorted to a subtle twist. According to his system, all *right* is grounded in *power,* and all *obligation* in *fear.* Since God is infinitely superior in power to any civil authority, the right of God is also infinitely superior to the right of the latter. Consequently, the fear of God obliges us to perform duties which must not yield to any fear of the civil authority. This, however, applies only to *inward religion,* which was the philosopher's sole concern. The outward [mode of] *worship* he subjected entirely to the dictates of the civil authority; every innovation in church matters without its sanction is not only high treason, but blasphemy as well. The collisions which are bound to ensue between inward and outward worship he sought to remove by means of the subtlest distinctions; and although many gaps still remain, making the weakness of the accord quite evident, one cannot help admiring the ingenuity with which he sought to render his system coherent.

There is, at bottom, a great deal of truth in all Hobbes's assertions. The absurd consequences to which they lead follow solely from the exaggeration with which he propounded them, whether out of a love of paradox or in compliance with the needs of his time. Moreover, in his day the concepts of natural law were, in part, still not sufficiently enlightened. In matters of moral philosophy Hobbes has the same merit as Spinoza has in metaphysics. His ingenious errors have occasioned inquiry. The ideas of *right* and *duty,* of *power* and *obligation,* have been better developed; one has learned to distinguish more correctly between physical and moral ability, between might and right. These distinctions have become so intimately fused with our language that, nowadays, the refutation of Hobbes's system seems to be a matter of common sense, and to be accomplished, as it were, by language itself. This is a distinctive feature of all moral truths. As soon as they are brought to light, they become so much a part of the spoken language and so connected with man's everyday notions that they become evident even to ordinary minds; and now we wonder how man could ever have stumbled on so level a road. But we fail to consider the pains it cost to clear this path through the wilderness.

Hobbes himself must have been aware, in more ways than one, of the inadmissible results which necessarily followed from his exaggerated propositions. If men are not bound by nature to any duty, they do not even have a duty to keep their contracts. If there is, in the state of nature, no binding obligation other than that based upon fear and powerlessness, contracts will remain valid only as long as they are supported by fear and powerlessness. Thus, men, by their contracts, will not have come any step closer to their security, and will still find themselves in the primitive state of universal warfare. But if contracts are to remain valid, man must by nature, without contracts and agreements, lack the moral ability to act against a compact into which he has voluntarily entered; that is, he must not be permitted to do so, even if he can; he must not have the *moral* faculty, even though he may have the *physical. Might* and *right* are, therefore, different things; and in the state of nature, too, they were heterogeneous ideas. Moreover, Hobbes prescribes to the highest authority in the state strict laws not to command anything which would be contrary to its subjects' welfare. For although that authority is not accountable to any man, it does owe an account to the Supreme Judge; and even though, according to his principles, it is not bound by the fear of any *human power,* it is still bound by the fear of the *Omnipotent,* who has made his will in this respect sufficiently known. Hobbes is very explicit on this point, and is, in fact, less indulgent to the gods of the earth than his system would lead one to expect. Yet this very fear of the Omnipotent, which should bind kings and princes to certain duties toward their subjects, can also become a source of obligation for every individual in the state of nature. And so we would once again have a *solemn* law of nature, even though Hobbes does not want to admit it. In this fashion, in our day, every student of natural law can gain a triumph over Thomas Hobbes, to whom, at bottom, he nevertheless owes this triumph.

Locke, who lived during the same period of deep confusion, sought to protect the liberty of conscience in another manner. In his letters *concerning toleration* he proceeds from the basic definition: *A state is a society of men who unite for the purpose of collectively promoting their temporal welfare.* From this it follows, quite naturally, that the state is not to concern itself at all with the citizens' convictions regarding their eternal felicity, but is to tolerate everyone who conducts himself well as a citizen, that is, who does not interfere with the temporal felicity of his fellow citizens. The state as such is not to take notice of differences of religion, for religion as such has no necessary influence on temporal matters, and is linked to them solely through the arbitrary measures of men.

Very well! If the dispute allowed itself to be settled by a verbal definition, I would know of none that is more convenient; and if by this means one could have talked the agitated minds of his time out of their intolerance, it would not have been necessary for the good Locke himself to go into exile as often as he did. But what prevents us, they ask, from seeing to promote collectively our eternal welfare as well? And indeed, what reason do we have to restrict the purpose of society solely to the *temporal?* If men *can* promote their eternal felicity by public measures, it should be their natural duty to *do* so, their rational obligation to join forces for this purpose and to enter into social relations. If, however, this be the case, and the state as such be preoccupied solely with the temporal, a question arises: To whom are we to entrust the care for the eternal? To the church? Now we are, once again, back at our starting point. State and church—concern for the temporal and concern for the eternal—civil and ecclesiastical authority. The former relates to the latter as the importance of the temporal does to that of the eternal. The state is, therefore, subordinate to religion, and must give way whenever a collision arises. . . .

I have sought, through the following considerations, to clarify for my own benefit the ideas of state and religion, of their limits and their influence on each other as well as upon [the state of] felicity in civil life. As soon as man recognizes that outside of society he can fulfill his duties toward himself and toward the author of his existence as poorly as he can fulfill his duties toward his neighbor, and, hence, can no longer remain in his solitary condition without a sense of wretchedness, he is obliged to leave that condition and to enter into society with those in a like situation in order to satisfy their needs through mutual aid and to promote their common good by common measures.

Their common good, however, includes the present as well as the future, the spiritual as well as the earthly. One is inseparable from the other. Unless we fulfill our obligations, we can expect felicity neither here nor there, neither on earth nor in heaven. Now, two things belong to the true fulfillment of our duties: *action* and *conviction.* Action accomplishes what duty demands, and conviction causes that action to proceed from the proper source, that is, from pure motives.

Hence actions and convictions belong to the perfection of man, and society should, as far as possible, take care of both by collective efforts, that is, it should direct the actions of its members toward the common good, and cause convictions which lead to these actions. The one is the *government,* the other the *education* of societal man. To both man is led by *reasons;* to actions by *reasons that motivate the will,* and to convictions by *reasons that persuade by their truth.* Society should therefore establish both through public institutions in such a way that they will be in accord with the common good.

The reasons which lead men to rational actions and convictions rest partly on the relations of men to each other, partly on the relations of men to their Creator and Keeper. The former are the province of the *state,* the latter that of *religion.* Insofar as men's actions and convictions can be made to serve the common weal through reasons arising from their relations to each other, they are a matter for the civil constitution; but insofar as the relations between man and God can be seen as their source, they belong to the *church,* the *synagogue,* or the *mosque.* In a good many textbooks of the so-called ecclesiastical law one reads serious inquiries as to whether Jews, heretics, and heterodox believers can also have a church. In view of the immeasurable privileges which the church so-called is in the habit of arrogating to itself, the question is not as absurd as it must appear to an unbiased reader. To me, however, as it can be easily imagined, the difference of nomenclature is of no consequence. Public institutions for the formation *[Bildung]* of man that concern his relations with God I call *church;* those that concern his relations with man I call *state.* By the formation of man I understand the effort to arrange both actions and convictions in such a way that they will be in accord with his felicity; that they will *educate* and *govern* men.

Blessed be the state which succeeds in governing the nation by education itself; that is, by infusing it with such morals and convictions as will of themselves tend to produce actions conducive to the common weal, and need not be constantly urged on by the spur of the law. In social life, man must renounce certain of his rights for the common good or as one may say, he must very often sacrifice his own advantage to benevolence. He will be happy if this sacrifice is made on his own prompting and when he realizes, in each instance, that he acted solely for the sake of benevolence. *Benevolence,* in reality, makes us happier than *selfishness;* but we must, while exercising it, be aware that it springs from ourselves and is the display of our powers. Not, as some sophists* interpret it, because everything in man proceeds from self-love; but because benevolence is no longer benevolence, and has neither value nor merit if it does not flow from the free impulse of the benevolent individual.

This will perhaps enable us to give a satisfactory answer to the well-known question: *Which form of government is the best?* This question has hitherto received contradictory answers, all of them having the same appearance of truth. It is, in reality, too vague a question, almost as vague as a similar one in medicine: *Which food is the most wholesome?* Every complexion, every climate, every age, sex, and mode of life, etc., requires a different answer. The same is true with regard to our politico-philosophical problem. For every people, at every level of culture at which it finds itself, a different form of government will be the best. Certain despotically ruled nations would be extremely miserable if they were left to govern themselves, as miserable as certain free-spirited republicans if they were subjected to the rule of a monarch. Indeed, many a nation will alter its form of government as often as changes take place in its culture, way of life, and convictions, and, in the course of centuries, will pass through the whole cycle of forms of government, in all their shades and combinations, from anarchy to despotism; yet it will always be found to have chosen the form of government which was best for it under existing circumstances.

Under all circumstances and conditions, however, I consider the infallible measure of the excellence of a form of government to lie in the degree to which it achieves its purposes by morals and convictions; in the degree, therefore, to which government is by education itself. In other words, in the degree to which the citizen is given the opportunity to understand vividly *(anschauend)* that he has to renounce some of his rights only for the common good; that he has to sacrifice some of his own advantage only for the sake of benevolence; and that he therefore gains as much, on the one hand, through a display of benevolence as he loses, on the other, by sacrifice. Indeed, that by means of sacrifice itself he greatly adds to his inner felicity, since it

*professional teachers of philosophy

enhances the merit and the worth of the benevolent act and therefore also the true perfection of the benevolent individual. It is, for example, not advisable for the state to assume all the duties of love for our fellow man down to the *distribution of alms,* and to transform them into public institutions. Man is conscious of his own worth when he performs charitable acts, when he vividly *(anschauend)* perceives how he alleviates the distress of his fellow man by his gift; when he gives because he *wants* to give. But if he gives because he *must,* he feels only his fetters.

Hence, one of the state's principal efforts must be to govern men through morals and convictions. Now, there is no other way of improving the convictions, and thereby the morals, of men than through *persuasion.* Laws do not alter convictions; arbitrary punishments and rewards produce no principles, refine no morals. Fear and hope are no criteria of truth. Knowledge, reasoning, and persuasion alone can bring forth principles which, with the help of *authority* and *example,* can pass into *morals.* And it is here that religion should come to the aid of the state, and the church should become a pillar of civil felicity. It is the business of the church to convince people, in the most emphatic manner, of the truth of noble principles and convictions; to show them that duties toward men are also duties toward God, the violation of which is in itself the greatest misery; that serving the state is true service of God; that charity is his most sacred will; and that true knowledge of the Creator cannot leave behind in the soul any hatred for men. To teach this is the business, duty, and vocation of religion; to preach it, the business and duty of its ministers. How, then, could it ever have occurred to men to permit religion to teach and its ministers to preach exactly the opposite?

But if the character of a nation, the level of culture to which it has ascended, the increase in population which has accompanied the nation's prosperity, the greater complexity of relations and connections, excessive luxury, and other causes make it impossible to govern the nation by convictions alone, the state will have to resort to public measures, coercive laws, punishments of crime, and rewards of merit. If a citizen is unwilling to defend the fatherland from an inner sense of duty, let him be tempted by rewards or compelled by force. If men no longer have any sense of the intrinsic value of justice, if they no longer realize that honesty in trade and traffic is true felicity, let injustice be chastised and fraud be punished. Admittedly, in this manner the state attains the ultimate aim of society only by half. External motivations do not make a man happy, even though they have an effect on him.

The man who avoids deception because he loves honesty is happier than one who is merely afraid of the arbitrary punishments the state linked with fraud. But to his fellow man it does not matter what motives cause the wrong to remain undone, or by what means his rights and property are safeguarded. The fatherland is defended, regardless of whether the citizens fight for it out of love or out of fear of positive punishment, even though the defenders themselves will be happy in the former and unhappy in the latter case. If the *inner felicity of society* cannot be entirely preserved, let at least *outward peace and security* be obtained, if need be, through *coercion.*

The state will therefore be content, if need be, with mechanical deeds, with works without spirit, with conformity of action without conformity in thought. Even the man who does not believe in laws must obey them, once they have received official sanction. The state may grant the individual citizen the right to pass judgment on the laws, but not the right to act in accordance with his judgment. This right he had to renounce as a member of society, for without this renunciation civil society is a chimera. Not so with religion! It knows no act without conviction, no work without spirit, no conformity in deed without conformity in the mind. Religious actions without religious thoughts are mere puppetry, not service of God. They themselves must therefore proceed from the spirit, and can neither be purchased by reward nor compelled by punishment. But religion withdraws its support also from civil actions, insofar as they are not produced by conviction, but by force. Nor can the state expect any further help from religion, once it can act only by means of rewards and punishments; for insofar as this is the case, man's duties toward God no longer enter into consideration, and the relations between man and his Creator are without effect. The only aid religion can render to the state consists in *teaching and consoling;* that is, in imparting to the citizens, through its divine doctrines, such convictions as are conducive to the public weal, and in uplifting with its otherworldly consolations the poor wretch who has been condemned to death as a sacrifice for the common good.

Here we already see an essential difference between state and religion. The state gives orders and coerces, religion teaches and persuades. The state prescribes *laws,* religion *commandments.* The state has *physical power* and uses it when necessary; the power of religion is *love* and *beneficence.* The one abandons the disobedient and expels him; the other receives him in its bosom and seeks to instruct, or at least to console him, even during the last moments of his earthly life, and not entirely in vain. In one word: civil society, viewed as a moral person, can have the *right of coercion,* and, in fact, has actually obtained this right through the social contract. Religious society lays no claim to the *right of coercion,* and cannot obtain it by any possible contract. The *state* possesses *perfect,* the *church* only *imperfect* rights. . . .

These are, in my opinion, the boundaries between state and church, insofar as they have an influence upon the actions of men. In respect to convictions, state and church come somewhat closer to each other; for here the state has no other means of acting effectively than the church has. Both must teach, instruct, encourage, motivate. But neither may reward or punish, compel or bribe; for the state, too, cannot have acquired by means of any contract the slightest compulsory right over our convictions. In general, men's convictions pay no heed to benevolence, and are not amenable to any coercion. I cannot renounce any of my convictions, as a conviction, out of love for my neighbor; nor can I cede and relinquish to him, out of benevolence, any part of my own power of judgment. I am likewise in no position to arrogate to myself or in any way acquire a right over my neighbor's convictions. The right to our own convictions is inalienable, and cannot pass from person to person; for it neither gives nor takes away any claim to property, goods and liberty.

Hence, the smallest privilege which you publicly grant to those who share your religion and convictions is to be called an *indirect bribe,* and the smallest liberty you withhold from dissidents an *indirect punishment.* They have, at bottom, the same effect as a direct reward for agreement, and a direct punishment for opposition. It is a paltry delusion when the distinction between *reward* and *privilege,* between *punishment* and *restriction,* is so much insisted upon in some text books of ecclesiastical law. To the linguist, such a notation may be useful, but to the poor wretch who must do without his rights as a man because he cannot say: *I believe,* when he does not believe, who will not be a Moslem with his lips and a Christian at heart, this distinction brings only a sorry consolation. And what are the limits of privilege, on the one hand, and of restriction, on the other? With a moderate gift for dialectics, one amplifies these concepts and goes on extending them until they become civil felicity, on the one hand, and oppression, exile, and misery on the other.

Fear and hope act upon men's *appetitive urge,* rational arguments on their *cognitive faculty.* You lay hold of the wrong means when you seek to induce men, through fear and hope, to accept or reject certain propositions. Indeed, even if this is not altogether your object, you still impede your better intentions if you do not try to keep fear and hope out of view as far as possible. You bribe and deceive your own heart, or your heart has deceived you, if you believe that examining the truth is feasible and that freedom of inquiry remains inviolate, when status and dignity await the inquirer if he arrives at one conclusion, and contempt and indigence if he arrives at another. Notions of good and evil are instruments for [directing] the *will,* those of truth and untruth for [directing] the *intellect.* Whoever wants to act upon the intellect must first of all lay aside the former instruments; otherwise he is in danger of proceeding contrary to his own intention. He may smooth over where he should cut right through, and fix where he should demolish.

What form of government is therefore advisable for the church? None! Who is to be the arbiter if disputes arise over religious matters? He to whom God has given the ability to convince others. For what can be the use of a government where there is nothing to govern? What use are authorities where no one is to be a subject? What good is a judiciary where there are no rights and claims to be adjudicated? Neither state nor church is authorized to judge in religious matters; for the members of society could not have granted that right to them by any contract whatsoever. The state, to be sure, is to see to it from afar that no doctrines are propagated which are inconsistent with the public welfare; doctrines which, like atheism and Epicureanism, undermine the foundation on which the felicity of social life is based. Let Plutarch and Bayle* inquire ever so much whether a state might not be better off with atheism than with superstition. Let them count and compare ever so much the afflictions which have hitherto befallen and still threaten to befall the human race from these sources of misery. At bottom, this is nothing else than inquiring whether a slow fever is more fatal than a sudden one. No one would wish either upon his friends. Hence, every civil society would do well to let neither of them, neither fanaticism nor atheism, take root and spread. The body politic becomes sick and miserable, whether it is worn down by cancer or consumed by fever.

---

*Plutarch, an ancient Greek historian; Pierre Bayle, a seventeenth-century French philosopher who supported religious tolerance

An Enlightenment Chronology (1685–1800)

1685 Louis XIV revokes the Edict of Nantes; more than 200,000 Protestants flee France.

James II ascends the English throne.

1687 Isaac Newton's *Principia* is published.

1688– James II is deposed in the Glorious Revolution; William and
1689 Mary ascend the throne.

1690 John Locke's *Two Treatises of Government* is published.

1690– War between England and France, led by William III of England
1697 and Louis XIV of France.

1691 In the Dutch republic, Balthasar Bekker's attack on the existence of witches, *World Bewitched,* is published.

1693 Locke's *Some Thoughts concerning Education* is published.

1695 Licensing Act is allowed to lapse in England; pre-publication censorship of books ends.

1696 John Toland's *Christianity not Mysterious* is published.

1697 In the Dutch republic, the Huguenot refugee Pierre Bayle publishes his *Dictionnaire,* the forerunner of Denis Diderot's *Encyclopédie.*

1701 French translation of Locke's second treatise is published.

1701– War of Spanish Succession ends with the Treaty of Utrecht.
1713

1704 Newton's *Opticks* is published.

1713 Anthony Collins's *Discourse of Freethinking* is published.

1717 Lady Mary Wortley Montagu arrives in Turkey and begins to write letters about her experience.

In London, four Masonic lodges form the Grand Lodge.

1719 *Treatise of the Three Impostors* is published.

1721 Montesquieu's *Persian Letters* is published.

1733–1734 Voltaire's *Letters concerning the English Nation* is published. French edition follows in 1734.

1738 Papal decree makes membership in a Masonic lodge grounds for excommunication from the Catholic Church.

1740–1748 War of Austrian Succession.

1743 *Le Philosophe* is published anonymously.

1747 Julien La Mettrie's *Man the Machine* is published in the Dutch republic.

France invades the Dutch republic.

1747–1748 Revolution in the Dutch republic.

1748 Montesquieu's *Spirit of the Laws* and the anonymous *Thérèse philosophe* are published.

1749 John Cleland's *Fanny Hill* is published.

1751 Masonic lodge for women meets in The Hague.

1751 First volume of Diderot's *Encyclopédie* appears in Paris; some contributors flee the country.

1762 Jean-Jacques Rousseau's *Social Contract* and *Émile* are published.

1772 Diderot's *Supplement to Bougainville's* Voyage begins to be circulated privately.

1774 Jean-Paul Marat's *The Chains of Slavery* is published in London.

1776 American Revolution begins; Diderot refers glowingly to "those brave Americans."

Thomas Paine's *Common Sense* is published.

1780s Illuminati spread throughout Germany.

1781 Immanuel Kant's *Critique of Pure Reason* is published.

Rousseau's *Confessions* appears three years after his death.

1783 One of the founders of Unitarianism, Joseph Priestley, publishes a defense of this sect in *Letters to Dr. Horsley.*

Moses Mendelssohn's *Jerusalem: Or on Religious Power and Judaism* is published.

1784 A Berlin newspaper asks, "What Is Enlightenment?" Kant replies.

1787 Revolution in the Dutch republic is stopped by a British-backed Prussian invasion.

1789 French Revolution begins in Paris in May; storming of the Bastille occurs on July 14.

1791 Priestley, seen to be a supporter of the French Revolution, has his home and laboratory destroyed by a mob in Birmingham, England; eventually, he flees to America.

1791–
1792 Paine's *Rights of Man* is published.

1792 Mary Wollstonecraft's *Vindication of the Rights of Woman,* the most important feminist tract of the age, is published.

English radicals go to Paris to praise and join the Jacobins.

1794 In hiding from the Terror, the last of the philosophes, the Marquis de Condorcet, writes *Sketch for a Historical Picture of the Progress of the Human Mind.*

Trials of radicals in England and Scotland begin.

1798 Sedition Act in Britain forces many radicals to leave for America.

1800 Repression and war bring the Enlightenment to a close.

Selected Bibliography

GENERAL WORKS

Assiter, Alison. *Enlightened Women: Modernist Feminism in a Postmodern Age.* New York: Routledge, 1996.

Carpanetto, Dino, and Giuseppe Ricuperati. *Italy in the Age of Reason 1685–1789.* New York: Longman, 1987.

Darnton, Robert. *The Literary Underground of the Old Regime.* Cambridge: Harvard University Press, 1982.

Dobbs, B. J. T., and Margaret C. Jacob. *Newton and the Culture of Newtonianism.* Amherst, N.Y.: Prometheus Books, 2000.

Jacob, Margaret C. *Living the Enlightenment: Freemasonry and Politics in Eighteenth-Century Europe.* New York: Oxford University Press, 1991.

Lund, Roger D., ed. *The Margins of Orthodoxy: Heterodox Writing and Cultural Response, 1660–1750.* Cambridge, England: Cambridge University Press, 1995.

Micale, Mark S., and Robert L. Dietle, eds., *Enlightenment, Passion, Modernity: Historical Essays in European Thought and Culture.* Stanford, Calif.: Stanford University Press, 2000.

Miller, Peter N., ed. *Joseph Priestley: Political Writings.* Cambridge, England: Cambridge University Press, 1993.

Munck, Thomas. *The Enlightenment: A Comparative Social History, 1721–1794.* London: Arnold, 2000.

Popkin, Richard H., ed. *The Columbia History of Western Philosophy.* New York: Columbia University Press, 1999.

Porter, Roy. *The Enlightenment.* Amherst, N.Y.: Prometheus Books, 1990.

Prickett, Stephen. *England and the French Revolution.* London: Macmillan, 1989.

Walters, Kerry S., ed. *The American Deists: Voices of Reason and Dissent in the Early Republic.* Lawrence: University Press of Kansas, 1992.

For works of science from the period, see <http://www.mala.bc.ca/~mcneil/s4.htm>.

LOCKE

Ashcraft, Richard, ed. *John Locke: Critical Assessments.* 4 vols. New York: Routledge, 1991.

Huyler, Jerome. *Locke in America: The Moral Philosophy of the Founding Era.* Lawrence: University Press of Kansas, 1995.

Spellman, W. M. *John Locke.* New York: St. Martin's Press, 1997.

Tully, James. *An Approach to Political Philosophy: Locke in Contexts.* Cambridge, England: Cambridge University Press, 1993.

Wolterstorff, Nicholas. *John Locke and the Ethics of Belief.* Cambridge, England: Cambridge University Press, 1996.

For many sources on Locke or texts by him, see <http://www.looksmart. com/eus1/eus317836/eus317911/eus53880/eus67423/eus535029/eus 534538/r?l&hl=4&ss=l&key=john+locke>.

TREATISE OF THE THREE IMPOSTORS

Anderson, Abraham. *The* Treatise of the Three Impostors *and the Problem of the Enlightenment.* New York: Rowman & Littlefield, 1997.

Berti, Silvia, Françoise Charles-Daubert, and Richard Popkin, eds. *Heterodoxy, Spinozism, and Free Thought in Early Eighteenth-Century Europe: Studies on the* Traité des trois imposteurs. Dordrecht: Kluwer, 1996.

Darnton, Robert. *The Corpus of Clandestine Literature in France 1769–1789.* New York: Norton, 1995.

Jacob, Margaret C. *The Radical Enlightenment: Pantheists, Freemasons and Republicans.* London: George Allen and Unwin, 1981.

For access to similar literary texts from the period, see <http://infidels. org/library/historical>/.

VOLTAIRE

Howells, R. J., and A. Mason, eds. *Voltaire and His World.* Oxford: Voltaire Foundation, 1985.

Mason, Haydn. *Voltaire.* Baltimore: Johns Hopkins University Press, 1981.

Spink, J. S. *French Free-Thought from Gassendi to Voltaire.* London: Athlone Press, 1960.

Wade, Ira. *Voltaire and Madame du Châtelet.* New York: Octagon Books, 1967.

For more information on Voltaire and texts by him, see <http://www. epistemelinks.com/Pers/VoltPers.htm>.

MONTAGU

Lowenthal, Cynthia. *Lady Mary Wortley Montagu and the Eighteenth Century.* Athens: University of Georgia Press, 1994.

Montagu, Lady Mary Wortley. *Selected Letters.* Edited by Isobel Grundy. New York: Penguin, 1997.

DIDEROT

Furbank, P. N. *Diderot.* New York: Knopf, 1992.
Wilson, Arthur M. *Diderot.* New York: Oxford University Press, 1972.
To see a copy of his great *Encyclopédie,* see <http://tuna.uchicago.edu/homes/mark/ENC_DEMO/>.

ROUSSEAU

Miller, James. *Rousseau: Dreamer of Democracy.* New Haven, Conn.: Yale University Press, 1984.
Rosenblatt, Helena. *Rousseau and Geneva: From the* First Discourse *to the* Social Contract, *1749–1762.* Cambridge, England: Cambridge University Press, 1997.
For an outline of Rousseau's life and the text of his *Confessions,* see <http://www.orst.edu/instruct/phl302/philosophers/rousseau.html>.

KANT

Covell, Charles. *Kant and the Law of Peace.* New York: St. Martin's Press, 1997.
Heath, Peter, and J. B. Schneewind, eds. *The Cambridge Edition of the Works of Immanuel Kant.* 3 vols. Cambridge, England: Cambridge University Press, 1997.
Zammito, John H. *The Genesis of Kant's Critique of Judgment.* Chicago: University of Chicago Press, 1992.
See also <http://www.arts.cuhk.edu.hk/Philosopy/Kant/cpr/>.

MENDELSSOHN

Sorkin, David. *Moses Mendelssohn and the Religious Enlightenment.* Berkeley: University of California Press, 1996.
For texts by Mendelssohn, see <http://acs6.acs.ucalgary.ca/~elsegal/363_Transp/MendelssohnJerusalem.html>.

Acknowledgments

Abraham Anderson, ed., *The Treatise of the Three Imposters and the Problem of Enlightenment. A New Translation of the Traite des trois imposteurs* (1777 edition). New York: Rowman and Littlefield, 1997, pp. 3–9, 23–25, 33, 39–40.

Voltaire, *Letters concerning the English Nation.* Reprinted with the permission of Simon & Schuster from *The Enlightenment* by Peter Gay. Copyright 1973 by Peter Gay.

Denis Diderot, *Encyclopedia.* Reprinted with permission of Stephen J. Gendzier from Denis Diderot, *The Encyclopedia: Selections,* edited and translated by Stephen J. Gendzier (1967), pp. 92–95, Harper & Row.

Denis Diderot, "Supplement to Bouganville's Voyage," from *Rameau's Nephew and Other Works,* translated by Jacques Barzun. Copyright 1965. Reprinted by permission of Prentice-Hall, Inc., Upper Saddle River, N.J., pp. 187–92, 194–207, 210–11, 213.

Jean-Jacques Rousseau, from *The Social Contract and Discourses and Other Essays,* by Jean-Jacques Rousseau, translated and with an introduction by G. D. H. Cole (1955). Everyman's Library edition, published by E.P. Dutton & Company, Inc., and J. M. Dent & Sons, Ltd. Copyright Everyman's Library.

Immanuel Kant, "What Is Enlightenment?" Translated by Peter Gay, Director, Center for Scholars and Writers, New York Public Library, in *Introduction to Contemporary Civilization in the West,* 2 vols., 2nd ed (New York: Columbia University Press, 1954), I, 1071–76.

Moses Mendelssohn, *Jerusalem: Or on Religious Power and Judaism,* translated by Allan Arkush, pp. 33–45, 56–63, 94–98 from *Jerusalem,* copyright 1983 by the Trustees of Brandeis University, reprinted by permission of University Press of New England.

Index